The 3-Dialogue Rule: One Hundred Muslim Marriages in One Thousand Days

Kamran A. Beg

2006/1427 AH: First Edition

First published 2006/1427 AH by Kamran A. Beg Events

Published by:
Kamran A. Beg Events
18 Milton Grove
Manchester
M16 0BP
UK
Tel: +44 7980 001426 or +44 7876 042660
E-mail: kamran@kamranabegevents.com
Web Site: www.kamranabegevents.com

ISBN-10 0-9554298-0-3
ISBN-13 978-0-9554298-0-4

Typesetting & Printing by:
Deluxe Printers Ltd,
245A, Acton Lane, Park Royal, London, NW10 7NR, UK.
Tel: +44 20 8965 1771.

Front Cover Page designed by:
MDUK Media Ltd,
65A, Grosvenor Road, London, W7 1HR, UK. Tel: +44 20 8799 4455.
MDUK Media Ltd also designed the Kamran A. Beg Events
web site: www.kamranabegevents.com

In the name of Allah
The Beneficent, The Merciful

"Verily, we have created all things with Qadar [Divine Preordainments of all things before their creation as written in the Book of Decrees – Al-Lauh al-Mahfooz]" (Quran 54:49).

"And among His signs is [the sign] that He created for you mates from among yourselves that you may dwell in peace and tranquillity with them and He put love and compassion between your hearts. Surely there are signs in this for those who reflect" (Quran 30:21).

This book has been written in total and absolute subservience to Allah (Subhana Wa'ta'la) and in deference to His Last Messenger, the Prophet Muhammad (Peace Be Upon Him), who was an impeccable embodiment of the noble Muslim value system gifted by Allah (Subhana Wa'ta'la) to the human family through him through the perfect religion of Islam.

This book is dedicated to my dearest and most beloved parents, Mirza Mohammed Anwar Beg and Javida Khanum Beg, who are the most exemplary Muslims and who have always inspired me, lead by example and are my greatest mentors and teachers, to my sister Tasveer and to my brother Osman both of whom are the most magnificent of siblings and the most virtuous of Muslims and to the outstanding global family of attendees, subscribers and members comprising the Kamran A. Beg Events family, each of whom is an excellent and prodigious ambassador for the Muslim community.

Table of Contents

Chapter 3

Glossary

Wherever a reference is made to Allah, that is Almighty God or The Lord Most High, it is absolutely incumbent to glorify, extol and celebrate His name and so Allah is always referred to as Allah (SWT) where SWT stands for Subhana Wa'ta'la which means 'Glory be to Allah on High. Far removed is He from any imperfection'.

The Prophet Muhammad (PBUH) is always referred to as the Prophet (PBUH) where PBUH stands for Peace Be Upon Him, which is mentioned every time the Prophet's name is stated in deference to him.

Alhamdulillah means 'All praise is for Allah (SWT)'.

Insha'Allah means 'If Allah (SWT) wills'.

About the Author

The author, Kamran A. Beg

Kamran A. Beg is the chairman of **Kamran A. Beg Events** (see www.kamranabegevents.com), which is a global leader in providing leading edge matrimonial services to Muslim professionals worldwide and has built up an outstanding global track record since its inception on July 11, 2003, achieving 100 marriages so far, subject to the Divine will, Alhamdulillah. **Kamran A. Beg Professional Muslim Singles Evening Events**, **Kamran A. Beg Professional Muslim Online Matrimonials** and **Kamran A. Beg Professional Muslim Marriage Bureau Matrimonials** are run by **Kamran A. Beg Events**.

Kamran was previously the Head of UK Strategy and Business Development at WorldCom, a global telecommunications enterprise.

Prior to his role with WorldCom, Kamran was a management consultant providing consulting expertise, predominantly to blue chip organisations, in a number of areas, including corporate strategy, leadership, knowledge management, change management, innovation, financial modelling, customer futures, customer relationship management (CRM), mergers and acquisitions (M&A), management buy-outs (MBOs) and risk management.

Kamran currently also runs his own management consulting practice, which is based in the UK, providing consulting advice to the boards of various enterprises. His consulting expertise has been applied to over 30 industry sectors and he has consulted for organisations globally.

Kamran's academic qualifications include an MBA (with Distinction), which he achieved in 1995, from Manchester Business School (MBS), The University of Manchester, UK. MBS kindly granted Kamran a scholarship, which covered the duration of the MBA course. In 2001, Kamran was kindly nominated by WorldCom to undertake executive development at the Graduate School of Business Administration, Harvard University, USA, where he completed the Leading Change and Organizational Renewal Executive Programme, and the MIT Sloan School of Management (MIT Sloan), Massachusetts Institute of Technology (MIT), USA, where he completed the Corporate Strategy Executive Programme.

In relation to board responsibilities, Kamran has previously held the position of Non-Executive Chairman at two companies and has also held the joint positions of Vice Chairman and President at two other companies.

Acknowledgements

It has been an absolute pleasure, privilege and honour to scribe this book, *The 3-Dialogue Rule: One Hundred Muslim Marriages in One Thousand Days*, which is dedicated to providing Muslims worldwide with a comprehensive understanding of and working appreciation for the 3-Dialogue Rule, which is a robust halal marriage-inspired dialogue framework founded by Kamran A. Beg Events that hitherto has inspired the crystallisation of 100 Muslim marriages worldwide, subject to the Divine will, through introductions effected courtesy of Kamran A. Beg Events. This book would not have been possible had it not been for the will of Allah (SWT) being exercised in favour of equipping the humble writer with the licence to undertake this work. As Allah (SWT) so poignantly and enlighteningly remarks: "Say: 'Nothing will befall us except what Allah has decreed for us; He is our Protector.' Let the believers, then, put all their trust in Allah" (Quran 9:51). And so it is to Allah (SWT) that the humble writer wishes to express first and foremost his humblest and most profound gratitude for empowering him with the humility, conviction and honour to write this book: "And you cannot will unless [it be] that Allah wills, the Lord of Creation" (Quran 81:29).

It should be noted, however, that wherever the Quran has been quoted in this work the source, unless otherwise stated, is Abul A'ala Maudoodi's monumental treatise, *Towards Understanding The Qur'an*, which was published by The Islamic Foundation in 2006. Maudoodi provides highly detailed narrative of the Qur'an thereby helping to furnish the reader with an in-depth understanding of the Qur'an.

Maudoodi's elaboration on developing an understanding of the Qu'ran bears testimony to his exceptional Islamic scholarship.

As any author would understandably profess writing a book itself can prove a very rejuvenating and humbling experience and the comforting and loving part played by one's family as one puts pen to paper simply cannot be overemphasised. During my writing travels in the course of producing this book I would like to acknowledge wholeheartedly and respectfully the impeccable support that my dear mother, Javida Khanum Beg, and my dear father, Mirza Mohammed Anwar Beg, have so very kindly shown. Their encouragement throughout cannot be underscored enough. Their love kept me going as indeed did their youthful enthusiasm. As my role models, teachers and mentors they never cease to amaze me. I am indeed a most blessed mortal to have been endowed with the most perfect parents. I would also like to thank Tasveer, my younger sister, and Osman, my younger brother, for the prodigious support they have shown throughout the writing of this book. Tasveer and Osman are the most impeccable siblings anyone could wish to have and their boundless keenness to see this humble mortal scribe this work was the most refreshing tonic I could have hoped for.

I would also like to salute, praise and celebrate the outstanding esprit de corps that the attendees, subscribers and members comprising the Kamran A. Beg Events global family have built up since our humble enterprise came into being on July 11, 2003. This exemplary, inspiring and model family has since the time of the organisation's inauguration generated a formidable 100 marriages worldwide. In the course of our existence as an enterprise serving the matrimonial needs of Muslim professionals globally this remarkable family comprised of individuals who are the most resplendent ambassadors for the Muslim *Ummah* or community has gone from strength to strength giving hope to many other Muslims around the world in search of their life partner. As an organisation Kamran A. Beg Events is totally indebted to this most harmonious and wonderful global family. It is a distinguished honour to serve and cultivate the growth of such a unique family whose appetite for marriage based on observing total deference to the beautiful values that so encompass the Muslim value system merits every plaudit. I would like to thank our global family of attendees, subscribers and members for kindly allowing Kamran A. Beg Events to embark on a progressive, high-trust based working relationship with them and their families. Their vital contribution and that of their families to the research underpinning this study is deeply appreciated and will define and permeate the pages that follow. Their adherence to the 3-Dialogue Rule, which forms the quintessential kernel of this book, deserves the very highest recognition and commendation.

In particular I would like to extend my deepest gratitude to two couples generated through Kamran A. Beg Events, namely Umer Majid and Aisha Janjua and Dr Ashraful Mirza and Andleeb Anwar, whose experiences of the 3-Dialogue Rule are discussed at length in chapter 4 and will provide the reader with compelling reading and great inspiration. They are, without doubt, star exponents of the 3-Dialogue Rule! Their experiences have acted as a beacon of light for many other Muslim professionals seeking marriage. I am indebted to all four for the great time and commitment they showed towards the research that was undertaken with a view to documenting their experiences of the 3-Dialogue

Rule, which will provide a model blueprint for many generations of Muslims to come. A profound thank you then to Umer, Aisha, Ashraful and Andleeb.

I am also very grateful to Surrya Jabeen, Abid Hussain and Dr Waqaar Shah, three outstanding attendees who define the very pulse of the Kamran A. Beg Events global family. Their deeply telling insights form a crucial part of chapter 4 and again I am humbly indebted to each for giving up so much of their precious time in allowing me to research their specific perspectives, which I promise the reader will find positively illuminating. Surrya, Abid and Waqaar are very highly revered members of our global family and carry the highest regard within the Muslim community. Each is renowned for their untold altruism and their informed insights in relation to the 3-Dialogue Rule and how to sustain a focused, halal marriage-inspired dialogue are indeed truly enriching.

Furthermore I would like to thank each of the 7,000 wonderful attendees, subscribers and members who currently at the time of this book being published comprise our noble, virtuous and honourable global membership. Each has made a highly palpable contribution to our research endeavours as an organisation. Each has lent very amiably, significantly and constructively to our global research effort. Each is an exemplar par excellence, a great advocate, of the 3-Dialogue Rule. One would need a book in its own right to list their names. In particular I would like to single out the following Muslim professionals for contributing their time and energy to the many animated, lively, thought-provoking, erudite, memorable and deeply insightful discussions we as an organisation have enjoyed the privilege of having with them regarding the 3-Dialogue Rule and gauging the formalities and challenges associated with finding a Muslim life partner:

17

Sarah Bano Khan, Shameem Akhtar, Nadia Arshad, Sufar Khan, Nadia Abouayub, Jamal Minhas, Shahbaz Shafi, Heanah Hussain, Nadim Batt, Dr Zobia Khan, Sobia Majid, Sonia Ahmed, Dr Nabila Minhas, Imran Ahmed, Naheed Chaudhry, Sohail Syed, Ambreen Khan, Fatema Jan, Raheela Zakir, Shakir Sufian, Saiqa Waheed, Tehmina Yakoob, Syeed Ali, Dr Mohammad Qureshi, Jasim Malik, Uzma Asghar, Mahvash Bukhari, Tariq Rashid, Azeemah Kaleem, Rehan Aslam, Sudeshini Veerabangsa, Dr Mohammad Naeem, Afshan Iqbal, Mohammed Fadi, Shameem Nawab, Rehan Khan, Rabia Alvi, Faisal Rashid, Shazia Chaudhry, Alia Ali, Mohammed Sadiq, Sajjad Hussain, Shazia Malik, Nadeem Batt, Zainab Rauf, Farzana Khan and Haleema Kausar. Each of the aforementioned persons embodies a sterling role model for the Muslim community and each has contributed greatly to the sense of fraternity and noble virtue epitomising the Kamran A. Beg Events global family.

I would also like to say a special thank you to the many other Muslim professionals based worldwide and not (presently) subscribed to Kamran A. Beg Events for the invaluable part they have played in our research to date. Their contributions are deeply welcomed!

I would also like to pay special homage to Sannah Muhammad, Saira Zitek, Farrah Malik, Rheam Mansour, Asia Fazal, Rabia Khan, Farah Gaffar and Aamena Khan who, in addition to myself, have chaired matrimonial events for Muslim professionals convened by Kamran A. Beg Events right across the world. Each has chaired events in the most exemplary and commendable manner and has communicated the 3-Dialogue Rule with untiring zest, dedication and energy. As I have often pointed out each of these remarkable and altruistic ladies personifies the most benevolent and dignified form of leadership.

Introduction

As the humble chairman of Kamran A. Beg Events, which is a global leader in providing leading edge matrimonial services to *Muslim professionals* worldwide, I have had the great honour, privilege and distinction of working in partnership with and serving Muslim professionals and their families alike as they (the Muslim professionals) honourably seek their life partner. By Muslim professionals we mean Muslims who are typically university educated and are either employed by an employer or self-employed. See chapter 2 for a more detailed insight. No single decision can possibly be more challenging, more taxing, more tantalisingly frustrating, more exacting, not to mention at times more unfathomable than the one pivotal and life-transforming decision that requires an individual to identify their other half with a view to marriage. As we shall learn in this book marriage occupies a very special, unique and sacred place within the bounds of the Muslim community since as the Prophet (PBUH) made abundantly evident it allows a Muslim to complete half of their faith thereby representing an enormous religious undertaking, which should never be taken lightly and must always be assigned the very highest priority. Every effort must therefore be made to help expedite the wish of Muslim professionals, who constitute the section of the Muslim community that Kamran A. Beg Events specifically deals with, and Muslims generally to progress their matrimonial deliberations with a view to proceeding to the wedding altar, subject of course to the Divine will.

Kamran A. Beg Events has built up an outstanding global track record since its inception on July 11, 2003, achieving 100 marriages so far, subject to the Divine will. These marriages have been predicated on the Muslim male and Muslim female dialogue incumbents adopting the **3-Dialogue Rule**, a robust halal marriage-inspired dialogue framework created and developed by Kamran A. Beg Events that forms the very kernel of this book and which as we shall discover in the course of our discussions is equally applicable to both family-based and non-family based introductions between a Muslim male and a Muslim female seeking marriage. Furthermore with the 100th marriage occurring within one thousand days of Kamran A. Beg Events being conceived the book has been aptly titled *The 3-Dialogue Rule: One Hundred Muslim Marriages in One Thousand Days*.

Kamran A. Beg Professional Muslim Singles Evening Events where *attendees* are introduced to one another through a matrimonial event they attend in person, **Kamran A. Beg Professional Muslim Online Matrimonials** where introduction between two Muslim professional *subscribers* is conducted via an online service and **Kamran A. Beg Professional Muslim Marriage Bureau Matrimonials** where *members* are provided with unlimited personalised matching, unlimited online subscription and allowed to attend up to three matrimonial events are run by **Kamran A. Beg Events**. For more detail see chapter 3. These three services therefore cover three non-family based introductions platforms through which Muslim professionals are respectfully introduced to each other: *matrimonial events*, *the online service* and *personalised matching*.

Hitherto Kamran A. Beg Events has respectfully accommodated and served 7,000 Muslim professional attendees, subscribers and members worldwide, indeed a distinguished global family that continues to grow from strength to strength having thus far spawned 100 marriages, subject to the Divine will. The whole organisational impetus is allied to inspiring as many marriages as possible among Muslim professionals, subject to the Divine will, in keeping with the enterprise vision expressly spelt out on the homepage of our web site (see www.kamranabegevents.com), which we now repeat here for the reader's immediate reference: *Kamran A. Beg Events aims to serve professionals by helping you to meet and converse with like-minded, potentially, matrimonial candidates drawn from the same faith.*

Provided below is a flavour of some of the key milestones that Kamran A. Beg Events has accomplished since being founded on July 11, 2003.

1. Kamran A. Beg Events has achieved 100 Muslim marriages to date in keeping with the spirit of the 3-Dialogue Rule.

2. Kamran A. Beg Events has thus far respectfully built up a global family of 7,000 Muslim professional attendees, subscribers and members.

3. Kamran A. Beg Events is the only Muslim organisation worldwide to have run matrimonial events for vetted Muslim professionals in America, Asia, Europe and Australia, that is across four continents! More specifically we have run events in the UK, Australia, Canada, USA and UAE. All of our

Muslim matrimonial events are run through a service called Kamran A. Beg Professional Muslim Singles Evening Events as stated above and cater only to vetted attendees. See chapter 3 for more discussion of our vetting-based approach.

4. We have Muslim professional female chapter chairs for Australia, Canada, USA and UAE. Each chair is an outstanding ambassador for the Muslim community and chairs events in person. Each female exhibits exemplary leadership and lends exceptionally well to the enterprise vision! It is our honourable belief at Kamran A. Beg Events that the Muslim community is graced with outstanding young Muslim professional females who should be encouraged to exercise and empowered with leadership positions within the Muslim community, which Kamran A. Beg Events has already clearly demonstrated through assigning chapter chair responsibilities to Muslim females as per the above.

5. We have at the time of going to press run 94 events worldwide for the Muslim professional community, accommodating over 6,200 attendees, with the first event convened in Manchester on July 11, 2003.

6. Kamran A. Beg Events became the first Muslim organisation worldwide to reach the 50 matrimonial events landmark for vetted, Muslim professionals on April 23, 2005, in Glasgow (UK).

7. On the weekend of March 19/March 20, 2005, Kamran A. Beg Events became the first organisation

worldwide to run Muslim matrimonial events in New York (March 19) and Sydney (March 20), that is in the USA and Australia, over the course of the same weekend.

8. On January 8, 2005, Kamran A. Beg Events became the first Muslim organisation worldwide to run an Over-40s event for the Muslim professional community. We have run six such events so far and have experienced marriages already from this event series. It should be noted, however, that all of our other events, with the exception of the Over-40s event, are open to all age groups.

9. 65 US-based Muslim professionals and 17 Canadian-based Muslim professionals have attended our UK matrimonial event programme so far.

10. Kamran A. Beg Events was the first organisation worldwide to introduce an online matrimonials service specifically designed for servicing the life partner needs of vetted Muslim professionals, where subscription is conditional on clearing rigorous vetting based on a vetting formula. At the time of writing we have accepted 454 subscribers (239 females, 214 males) and rejected 2,243 online applications. This online service as noted earlier is called Kamran A. Beg Professional Muslim Online Matrimonials.

11. As previously stated Kamran A. Beg Events also offers a marriage bureau matrimonials service called Kamran A. Beg Professional Muslim Marriage Bureau Matrimonials, which is designed to optimise

your chances of meeting a life partner by deploying an **integrated framework** comprising the personalised matching service and the events and online channels run by Kamran A. Beg Events. As we stated above members are provided with unlimited personalised matching, unlimited online subscription and allowed to attend up to three matrimonial events. This groundbreaking integrated approach, which originates for the member's needs, has been designed to give members maximum exposure in terms of meeting compatible life partner prospects. The reader is furnished with more detail about this innovative service in chapter 3.

12. In line with our pluralistic vision, Kamran A. Beg Events has recently rolled out the matrimonial events concept with a view to serving other faith-traditions, namely the Christian, Hindu and Sikh faiths. This initiative has generated a very positive response so far. Separate-faith events are conducted for professionals drawn from each of these faiths respectively. Kamran A. Beg Events looks forward to humbly serving these faiths, as it does the Muslim faith, by assisting professionals drawn from the Christian, Hindu and Sikh faiths with their life partner search in order to help them to proceed to marriage with a fellow professional on a same-faith basis! In keeping with the plurality and universal appeal intrinsic to Islam and in line with our organisation vision, we look forward to applying our Muslim matrimonial model to assisting Christian, Hindu and Sikh professionals in their search for a spouse drawn from their own respective faith.

As we have noted the 100 Muslim marriages that we have witnessed since our inception have been hinged on the ability of the Muslim male and Muslim female exploring marriage to follow the 3-Dialogue Rule. This robust halal marriage-inspired dialogue framework has been derived by Kamran A. Beg Events on the basis of extensive global research, which is discussed at length in chapter 3 where an in-depth discussion regarding the 3-Dialogue Rule is provided. The 3-Dialogue Rule is predicated on the definitive tenets of **balance** and **moderation**, which permeate every aspect of the Islamic faith.

As Muslim professionals embark on that greatest of journeys with a view to finding their much yearned for soulmate with a view to completing half of their faith the 3-Dialogue Rule is absolutely committed to ensuring that the chastity – be it physical, mental, religious, intuitive, emotional or otherwise – of the Muslim male and Muslim female ensconced in the soul-searching process of marriage-inspired dialogue is in no way compromised. This unmitigated and unfaltering commitment to ensuring that the chastity of the two Muslims in dialogue is not invaded or undermined is imperative especially in light of the dating culture that has sadly afflicted the Muslim professional community in particular, a theme we examine in detail in chapter 2 on the basis of groundbreaking global research conducted by Kamran A. Beg Events. Dating tragically prevails within the Muslim community. Dating, however, is not halal or Islamically permissible and the 3-Dialogue Rule recognising the vile tempest that dating is from an Islamic perspective provides a modus operandi for marriage-inspired dialogue between a Muslim male and a Muslim female that crucially safeguards them against the heinous perils of dating. The prevalence of an infectious dating culture in the Muslim professional community should not be underestimated as our research in chapter 2 highlights. By recognising that dating is a very serious problem that needs to be addressed clinically the 3-Dialogue Rule automatically subsumes within its remit safeguards that protect the two Muslim dialogue incumbents against the very real possibility of falling prey to it. Under no circumstances should the very noble values that define the very soul of Islam be surrendered as a Muslim male and a Muslim female explore each other's life partner potential. The 3-Dialogue Rule ensures that the basic Muslim value system is upheld since the framework itself has been configured in deference to preserving those very values that define the essence of the Muslim social imperative.

The book is divided into four chapters, which we briefly elaborate on now.

Chapter 1 expounds on the sacred importance of marriage in Islam providing the reader with a primer on the basic religious principles underpinning this most sacred union, which allows husband and wife to negotiate half of their faith. It is essential for any Muslim embarking on this most challenging and testing of journeys to find their other half to develop a solid appreciation of the religious foundations that inform marriage in the Muslim faith. Chapter 1 equips the reader with that appreciation and in particular shows how one's choice of life partner has already been preordained subject to the will of Allah (SWT). Only by fully relating to the overarching need to complete half of your faith through seeking marriage can one engender and sustain the unfailing sense of urgency needed to complete an odyssey that will eventually expose you to a life partner who had been predestined for you in accordance with the will of Allah

(SWT). Strive you must in order to discover your other half in accordance with His will.

Chapter 2 discusses in detail the nine basic attributes that should comprise a robust halal marriage-inspired dialogue framework. This discussion follows a comprehensive perspective and overview on just how profoundly the ugly menace of dating has impacted the Muslim professional community, with this assertion substantiated against the backdrop of global research conducted by Kamran A. Beg Events geared towards unearthing its adverse influence. In saying this in no way are we commenting on the practices, values, mores and norms of non-Muslim communities, which regard dating as socially acceptable. As Allah (SWT) reminds Muslims: "There is no compulsion in religion" (Quran 2:256). However, from an Islamic perspective dating is strictly prohibited, yet it clearly continues to rear its ugly head within the fold of the Muslim community. We then elaborate comprehensively on the nine key features integral to a robust halal marriage-inspired dialogue framework suitable for Muslim professionals (and for Muslim consumption in general) and conclude the chapter by way of acknowledging that the 3-Dialogue Rule comfortably satisfies each of the nine attributes identified. The 3-Dialogue Rule is strongly recommended as the robust halal marriage-inspired dialogue framework for Muslim professionals to deploy when engaged in matrimonial dialogue and, equally, is suitable on a broader scale for general Muslim consumption.

Chapter 3 elaborates on the 3-Dialogue Rule itself, which is the specific robust halal marriage-inspired dialogue framework developed by Kamran A. Beg Events that has guided many of the 100 Muslim professional couples who

28

have achieved marriage through Kamran A. Beg Events so far, subject of course to the Divine will, since the organisation came into being on July 11, 2003. Chapter 3 provides a detailed elaboration of what the 3-Dialogue Rule encompasses. The 3-Dialogue Rule is equally applicable to both family based and non-family based introductions. We strongly recommend that the Muslim male and Muslim female party to a marriage-inspired dialogue conform to the spirit and essence of the 3-Dialogue Rule. In particular, adherence to the 3-Dialogue Rule safeguards the Muslim female and her family. It also safeguards the male and female in question against dating and having a relationship, both of which are Islamically prohibited and non-permissible! Throughout the dialogue process the two individuals supported by their respective families must continue to remain steadfast in addressing the definitive question informing the marriage-inspired dialogue: *"Will the person with whom I am exploring a marriage-based dialogue allow me to complete half of my faith?"* In chapter 3 we examine why this should be the definitive question at the heart of any marriage-inspired dialogue between a Muslim male and a Muslim female exploring marriage. Indeed only then can the feasibility of a particular marriage prospect be properly assessed!

Chapter 4 shows that the 3-Dialogue Rule works very well in practice and we corroborate this through specific examples and case studies, which the reader will find very instructive and illuminating. In particular we relate to the experiences of two exemplary couples – namely Umer Majid and Aisha Junjua and Dr Ashraful Mirza and Andleeb Anwar – who were introduced courtesy of Kamran A. Beg Events and who applied the 3-Dialogue Rule. Through their experiences we derive an excellent insight into how the 3-Dialogue Rule should be articulated in practice. We also show how the 3-Dialogue Rule has helped to vanquish that most debilitating malaise, dating, and touch on various pitfalls that a Muslim male and a Muslim female should endeavour to avoid and show how the 3-Dialogue Rule vitally assists in these specific regards. We conclude the chapter and therefore the book by reminding ourselves that as Muslims we need to strive vigorously in order to find our life partner in order to complete half of our faith and therefore in the process totalise our faith but that our choice of life partner is predestined subject to the Divine will, that is the supreme will of Allah (SWT). In the final analysis there is only one matchmaker and He is The Lord Most High, Allah (SWT)!

Let us now embark on the momentous and revealing odyssey that will expose us to the formalities, principles, workings and dynamics of the 3-Dialogue Rule and in the process nourish us with a sound, in-depth and pragmatic understanding of the art and science of robust halal marriage-inspired dialogue between a Muslim male and a Muslim female.

Finally as a humble servant to the Muslim *Ummah* or fraternity I would like to take this opportunity to wish you, the avid, conscientious and honourable reader, every success in your search for a life partner, Insha'Allah.

Allah Hafiz.

Humbly always

Kamran
Manchester (UK)
August 27 2006

Kamran A. Beg
Chairman
Kamran A. Beg Events
18 Milton Grove
Manchester
M16 0BP
UK
Tel: +44 7980 001426 or +44 7876 042660
E-mail: kamran@kamranabegevents.com
Web Site: www.kamranabegevents.com

1. The Sacred Importance of Marriage in Islam

In the untiring quest for peace and happiness that each of us is relentlessly embarked on no one challenge quite stands out in the way that finding one's life partner does. In more or less every Muslim household that I know of the one burning question that never appears to be detached from the scene for too long is that which refers to how well one's search for the lady of one's dreams in the case of a male or for one's knight in shining armour in the case of a female is proceeding. Since founding Kamran A. Beg Events on July 11, 2003, a humble enterprise that assists Muslim professionals worldwide in their search for that elusive though markworthy to note predestined soulmate and which at the time of going to press has achieved 100 marriages among professionals drawn from the Muslim community I have received telephone calls at all times of the day from fellow Muslim brethren across the world who as accomplished as they undoubtedly are in their respective professional arenas have told of their otherwise untold anguish in not being able to find that vital 'other half'. Their search as incessant as it has been seems not to be yielding the one special person they so tightly yearn for in order to step up into that unparalleled world of matrimonial bliss. Such professionals have kindly requested that Kamran A. Beg Events assist them in seeking to discover that much sought after life partner.

It is only through examining the sacred importance assigned to marriage in Islam that we can truly begin to come to terms with the profound and pivotal position that this most sacred institution occupies in the Muslim community. As the

Prophet Muhammad (PBUH), hereafter referred to as the Prophet (PBUH), so enlighteningly pointed out: "Marriage is tantamount to completing half one of one's faith." Marriage therefore enables a Muslim to complete their faith in totality and if marriage is so sacred as to be placed on par with the other half of every Muslim's faith, which is to be totally worshipful of and subservient to Allah (SWT), then surely the wisdom conveyed by the Prophet (PBUH) signals why finding a life partner, subject to the pre-ordained will of Allah (SWT), is so challenging and so necessary.

Completing Half of Your Faith Through Marriage

To understand the eminently sacred stature ascribed by Islam to marriage we need to visit the basic foundations of our faith and in particular understand the two dimensions of faith – vertical and horizontal – comprising faith itself and how marriage seminally relates to both. After all as the Prophet (PBUH) so eloquently reinforced "marriage is tantamount to completing half of one's faith" and clearly for a Muslim to be able to reconcile with the centrality of marriage within the ambit of the Muslim social imperative a basic appreciation of faith itself is warranted. This is a point that I have been keen to express to Muslim professionals worldwide, not to mention their dear parents of course, whenever broached on the overarching theme of marriage. An erudite discussion on faith dissected along these parameters is provided by Imam Feisal Abdul Rauf in chapter 1 of his gripping monograph, *What's Right With Islam: A New Vision for Muslims and the West.*

The vertical dimension of faith is that which enamours a Muslim to love and worship Allah (SWT) with the entirety of their heart, mind, body and soul while the horizontal dimension of faith is that which makes it incumbent on a Muslim to love others as you love yourself, with these two fundamental commandments enjoined upon the human family by Allah (SWT) Himself (Rauf, 2004: p.18). Note the golden standard Allah (SWT) applies to humankind is one which makes it necessary for you to love everybody else in the same way as you love yourself, not one which insists that you love others like a brother or a sister for if that were the case Cain would not have killed his own brother Abel. And so it is the Prophet (PBUH) reminded us: "None of you is a believer (mu'min) until he loves for his brother what he loves for himself" (Rauf, 2004: p.24).

"And among His signs is [the sign] that He created for you mates from among yourselves that you may dwell in peace and tranquillity with them and He put love and compassion between your hearts. Surely there are signs in this for those who reflect" (Quran 30:21). Through this revelation Allah (SWT) makes it abundantly clear that your choice of life partner has been legislated according to a Divine will, which has already been exercised, and that compatibility between the Muslim male and Muslim female seeking marriage is necessary to sustain the marriage tie that Allah (SWT) had pre-ordained and that such compatibility cannot exist without love and compassion fuelling the bond of marriage between husband and wife. A marriage bereft of love and compassion simply has no soul and ceases to be a marriage in the true spiritual sense! Furthermore it is vitally important to note and can be inferred from this verse that if you seek to sustain a marriage you should be compatible with your spouse to the point that you can love them at least as much as you love yourself thereby enabling you to master the horizontal dimension of faith in one key regard, in this case through the sacred institution of marriage. We can only truly begin to master the vertical dimension of faith once we have sought to master the horizontal dimension of faith through the way we transact with our fellow human beings, with marriage providing one such prime example. As members of the human fraternity we cannot even begin to claim that our love for Allah (SWT) is complete and that we love Him with the totality of our heart, mind, body and soul in the way that the vertical dimension of faith exhorts us to do so unless we evidence through our deeds that we truly love our fellow human beings in the same way that we love ourselves since one of Allah's two key commandments is mastering the horizontal dimension of faith and unless that is negotiated accordingly fathoming the vertical dimension of faith in totality is not possible. Since marriage is clearly one pivotal institution through which to exhibit the horizontal dimension of faith this is all the more reason to assign it the utmost importance as one's ability to discharge marriage harmoniously will clearly exercise a significant bearing on the degree to which the horizontal dimension of faith overall is mastered by you, which in turn will affect your potential as a Muslim to show total deference to Allah (SWT) through the vertical dimension of faith. Granted there are other innumerable other forms of human interaction that affect our ability to engage horizontally in a faith sense, such as, inter alia, the humility with which we treat our family and friends, the honesty we show in our undertakings with people generally, the degree of compassion we show to those in need but marriage clearly wields a huge influence in this regard since the family itself defines the very focal point of the Muslim community and the only *halal* or Islamically legitimate manner in which to foster the creation of a family within Islam is through embracing the sacred covenant of marriage first.

Sexual intercourse between a man and woman therefore is only permitted subsequent to contracting marriage, with *zina* or extramarital intercourse between a man and woman deemed to be *haram* or strictly forbidden in the Islamic faith. In fact Allah (SWT) deems not just zina to be haram but warns against straying into situations that could encourage zina to be committed and classifies such situations as being haram also: "And do not even approach zina for it is ever an outrageous act, and an evil way" (Quran 17:32). Suffice it to say that dating and having a pre-marital relationship are expressly forbidden by Islam and are therefore deemed as haram. The whole notion of courtship is refuted in totality by Islam and has no place in the Muslim faith.

Islam fully recognises that sexual intimacy and relations between a man and a woman constitute basic emotional and physical needs that need to be fulfilled but such needs can only be pursued legitimately through the sacred route of marriage and so marriage clearly represents a lawful manner in which to satiate such needs and to engage in procreation and so create families. Dating and engaging in pre-marital relationships do not represent a halal association between a Muslim man and a Muslim woman and are entirely abhorred. These are themes we shall revisit subsequently in the remaining chapters of this book. With the family representing the very cornerstone of Muslim society it is all the more essential to nurture harmonious marriages that provide a stable and loving backdrop in which to raise children. Allah (SWT) commands the family to remain true to their faith as this is an essential pre-requisite to facilitating a harmonious marriage and cultivating a loving family: "Henceforth if there comes to you a guidance from Me, then whosoever follows My guidance shall neither go astray nor suffer misery" (Quran 20:123). Maintaining true faith coupled with discharging righteous deeds are pivotal to the intrinsic happiness that should form the bedrock of any marriage and the backbone of any family spawned by that marriage. The two go hand in hand and are rewarded handsomely by Allah (SWT) in both this life and the Hereafter: "Whosever acts righteously – whether a man or a woman – and embraces belief, We will surely grant him a good life; and will surely grant such persons their reward according to the best of their deeds" (Quran 16:97).

Marriage clearly allows a Muslim to excel in terms of making significant strides towards realising the horizontal dimension of faith. It pertinently safeguards an individual from falling foul of various social ills and temptations that would otherwise compromise their ability to remain chaste and therefore allows a Muslim as the Prophet (PBUH) maintained to complete half of their faith: "When a servant [i.e. individual] marries, he has completed half of his religion, so let him fear Allah concerning the other half" (Bayhaqi). Recourse to marriage provides a Muslim with a legitimate channel through which to satisfy their emotional and physical needs whilst at the same time remaining chaste since these needs are addressed within a framework of companionship, namely marriage, that is halal or Islamically legitimate. Furthermore, marriage incorporates within its ambit a component of *Ibadah* or being worshipful and subservient to Allah (SWT) since Muslims are exhorted to pursue marriage by Allah (SWT) Himself: "Marry those of you that are single" (Quran 24:32). Marriage therefore impacts directly your ability as a Muslim to master the vertical dimension of faith. By passing through the sacred gateway of marriage and embracing matrimonial life a Muslim notably exercises both the vertical and horizontal dimensions of faith concurrently, with marriage itself making a significant and palpable contribution to your earnest quest to master overall these two constituent dimensions of faith. As well as epitomising a social duty marriage clearly constitutes a fundamental religious priority and seminally fosters the family unit that represents the very hub of Muslim society and the definitive pulse of Muslim civilisation.

Marriage is Predestined Subject to the Will of Allah (SWT)

At this juncture in our deliberations it is essential to note that an understanding of *qadar* or predestination is vital if we are to put marriage into the appropriate Divine context. As we have already intimated marriage represents that most sacred covenant, which allows a Muslim to complete half of their faith and which actuates their ability to subscribe to the vertical and horizontal dimensions of faith simultaneously. Central to a Muslim's faith is their unmitigated and total belief in *qadar* or predestination, that is belief in the Divine destiny, which Allah (SWT) has enjoined upon His creation and therefore upon each of us, His slaves. Innumerable texts in the Quran support this assertion, without which a Muslim's faith in Allah (SWT) cannot be complete: "Verily, we have created all things with Qadar [Divine Preordainments of all things before their creation as written in the Book of Decrees – Al-Lauh al-Mahfooz]" (Quran 54:49).

A detailed and compelling study of the Divine will and predestination is provided by Umar S. al-Ashqar in his outstandingly well-researched book, *Divine will and predestination in the light of the Qur'an and Sunnah*, which the reader is strongly advised to consult. *Qadar* or predestination is a specific reference to "the prior knowledge of Allah and that which He created in accordance with that knowledge" (al-Ashqar, 2003: p.34). Allah (SWT) whose knowledge is all-encompassing, whose will is irresistible and whose power is perfect possessed knowledge of His creation before He exercised His will to create everything as it exists. "Verily, His Command, when He intends a thing, is only that He says to it, "Be!" – and it is!" (Quran 36:82 as quoted by al-Ashqar, 2003: p.46). In effect Allah (SWT) possessed knowledge of everything He in his infinite majesty created prior to creating it through exercising his irresistible and supreme will since knowledge precedes creation, which follows naturally from the premise that knowledge precedes will and will precedes creation.

Fifty thousand years prior to when Allah (SWT) created the heavens and the earth He created the Pen, which in fact constituted His very first creation. According to Tirmidhi, the Prophet (PBUH) then further elaborated that Allah (SWT) exhorted the Pen, His first creation, to write to which the Pen responded by enquiring of Allah (SWT) what it (the Pen) should scribe. The Prophet (PBUH) stated that Allah (SWT) then commanded the Pen to: "Write the decree (al-qadar) of what has happened and what is to happen, for all eternity" (al-Ashqar, 2003: p.44). The Pen in turn scribed the will of Allah (SWT) as manifested by "the decrees of His creation" (al-Ashqar, 2003: p.44), which resulted in Al-Lauh al-Mahfooz (the Preserved Tablet or the Book of Decrees), which therefore contains a record of everything that Allah (SWT) has decreed for His creation. In sum, Al-Lauh al-Mahfooz is a repository of the will that Allah (SWT) has exercised in relation to what we, each of His slaves, will execute during our lives and whatever Allah (SWT) has decreed for the whole of His creation. Al-Lauh al-Mahfooz is referred to by a whole gamut of names in the Quran including "Al-Kitaab, Al-Kitaab al-Mubeen, Al-Imam al-Mubeen, Umm al-Kitaab and Al-Kitaab Al-Mastoor" (al-Ashqar, 2003: p.44). "And verily, it [this Qur'an] is in the Mother of the Book [umm al-kitaab] [i.e. Al-Lauh al-Mahfooz] with Us, indeed exalted, full of wisdom" (Quran 43:4 as quoted by al-Ashqar, 2003: p.45).

As members of the human fraternity we strive to achieve those deeds, which Allah (SWT) has already willed for us to discharge and has had scribed by the Pen in Al-Lauh al-Mahfooz, which is only for Allah's reference and which charts in precise and graphic detail everything that we as His slaves will discharge throughout our lives. The ink has therefore dried and as the Prophet (PBUH) maintained: "Strive for each individual will be directed to do that for which he was created" (Muslim). Importantly, the deeds each person actually strives to discharge during the course of their lifetime stem from what Allah (SWT) has already decreed for that individual to carry out within the ambit of that lifetime courtesy of the Divine destiny already predestined upon that individual and recorded in Al-Lauh al-Mahfooz. "And everything they have done is noted in [their] Records [of deeds]" (Quran 54:52).

As an example to illustrate predestination, consider your professional aspirations. Before you embarked on the momentous and no doubt taxing journey that allowed you to fulfil your professional dreams you would have meticulously mapped out in your mind's eye an elaborate course of action or strategy that, if implemented effectively, would allow you to realise that dream. This typically for most professionals entails studying the relevant university degree course and negotiating a whole plethora of professional examinations particular to your specialist pursuit in parallel with acquiring the appropriate work experience. To make this dream a reality it goes without saying that the incumbent needs to be dedicated, prepared to burn the midnight oil and to strive tirelessly and with unending conviction inspired by the rejuvenating and buoyant vision that they will one day achieve that dream. To attain your professional objective and so create the professional reality you desire requires the application of your will to work towards achieving that goal while your will is driven by knowledge of what is needed to accomplish that professional aspiration and a belief that given a certain amount of hard work and consistency that professional objective is attainable. However, whether you actually attain the professional ambition you have set for yourself ultimately depends on whether the will of Allah (SWT) is conducive to that goal being met. In other words as the Prophet (PBUH) made abundantly clear you strive to attain that already known to and willed by Allah (SWT) since His will has already been exercised as laid out in Al-Lauh al-Mahfooz. "And you cannot will unless [it be] that Allah wills, the Lord of Creation" (Quran 81:29). In sum as Allah (SWT) acknowledges in the Quran the outcome is known to Allah (SWT) as His irresistible will has already been executed. That in no way detracts from your sense of longing and determination to achieve that professional landmark. This is why you strive in the hope that one day you will make that dream a reality. But whether it becomes reality is already known to Allah (SWT) as He has already legislated for the outcome through exercising His will as document in Al-Lauh al-Mahfooz. By extension then your life is a composite of deeds and outcomes that have already been decreed subject to the will of Allah (SWT). You strive

41

with a view to facilitating the realisation of these deeds and outcomes!

Predestination does not preclude you from striving nor should it discourage you from striving and being proactive. As we have already noted above you strive in accordance with the irresistible will of Allah (SWT) and discharge those deeds and experience those outcomes, which He has already predestined upon you as recorded in Al-Lauh al-Mahfooz. Thus Allah (SWT) reminds us: "He whom Allah guides, he alone is rightly guided; and he whom Allah lets go astray – it is they who are the losers" (Quran 7:178). Allah (SWT) in his infinite majesty therefore has already decreed who is blessed and destined for Paradise vis-à-vis who is doomed and destined for Hell. And therefore the Prophet (PBUH) said, as we have cited earlier: "Strive for each individual will be directed to do that for which he was created" (Muslim).

And so we return now to the focal point of our deliberations in this book, marriage, which as we have indicated is equivalent to completing half of your faith thereby representing a most profound sacred undertaking, which simply cannot be overemphasised. We again quote below two aayat or verses from the holy Quran that we have referred to previously in order to put marriage into the appropriate Divine context:

> "Verily, we have created all things with Qadar [Divine Preordainments of all things before their creation as written in the Book of Decrees – Al-Lauh al-Mahfooz]" (Quran 54:49).

> "And among His signs is [the sign] that He created for you mates from among yourselves that you may

dwell in peace and tranquillity with them and He put love and compassion between your hearts. Surely there are signs in this for those who reflect" (Quran 30:21).

These two Quranic verses make it abundantly conspicuous that without Allah's will marriage cannot happen and only with His will can it happen.

In particular, the second aayah or verse (Quran 30:21) quoted above shows that your choice of life partner has been expressly determined and legislated for by Allah (SWT), subject to a Divine will that has been predestined upon you and which we know is recorded in Al-Lauh al-Mahfooz (Quran 54:49). Temporally, in a life bounded by the dimensions of space and time, we strive to discover that which Allah (SWT) had already willed. This can only happen at the time He had willed it to happen. Hence, you will marry when He had willed you to marry and moreover with whom He had willed you to marry! However, since only Allah (SWT) knows who your life partner is, as He had predestined them to transpire as such in your life, your overriding duty as a God-fearing Muslim who values the prodigious sacred stature assigned by Allah (SWT) to the institution of marriage is to strive, to be proactive, to remain relentless in your life partner search until you discover during life's momentous and animated journey that soulmate or those soulmates whom He had willed for you to enter into matrimonial union with. When you discover the "one", it is importantly at that specific juncture in space and time that your temporal trajectory coincides with the will that Allah (SWT) had preordained upon you courtesy of qadar or predestination. Discovering your life partner is therefore essentially and critically a question of reposing total faith in

43

Allah's decree assigned to you on the matrimonial front. If, ultimately it is Allah's will that prevails, and indeed His will always prevails for He is "omnipotent, omnipresent and omniscient", then we have no excuse to despair as we indefatigably pursue our quest to find our other half. The key is that we continue to strive and strive tirelessly with unfailing patience, determination and resolve to discover the life partner that we all yearn for with a view to negotiating half of our faith, a life partner who has already been prescribed in the Divine scheme of things in accordance with the supreme will of Allah (SWT) as recorded in Al-Lauh al-Mahfooz. As Allah (SWT) enlightens the human family: "Verily, your Lord is the All-Knowing Creator" (Quran 15:86).

At Kamran A. Beg Events, as pointed out at the outset of this chapter, we are keen to remind the wonderful Muslim professionals who consult us for their life partner search that the quest for that all-imperative other half is one that inevitably allows you to complete half of your faith and is therefore one that must be assigned primacy in the overall scheme of things. Marriage as we have discussed allows a Muslim to exercise both the vertical and horizontal dimensions of faith concurrently and its profundity and life-transforming potential cannot be underscored enough. No amount of emphasis on the importance of marriage within the purview of the Muslim social imperative is sufficient enough emphasis. Marriage personifies the lifeline of any community and in particular the Muslim community. As we constantly remind the Muslim professionals who frequent Kamran A. Beg Events your choice of life partner has already been determined according to a Divine will documented in Al-Lauh al-Mahfooz and therefore in the Divine context that other half has already been selected and predestined upon you according to the irresistible, supreme and all-encompassing will of Allah (SWT). You strive with a view to discovering your predestined other half and since your spouse has already been earmarked in accordance with the will of Allah (SWT) in the Divine sense you have no choice in terms of that special person with whom you will eventually establish that all-sought after marriage tie.

Through remaining proactive and through persevering, persisting and constantly striving you expose yourself to a pool of marriage prospects. The key is to have uninterrupted access to a pool of marriage-worthy candidates who surface through halal channels that safeguard and celebrate the sanctity and sacred importance of marriage. As long as you are constantly being introduced to suitable marriage candidates your life partner search remains active and live and you afford yourself every opportunity to discover that soulmate you so keenly yearn for. Striving then will allow you to encounter that special person with whom Allah (SWT) has predestined you to enter into marriage with at a point in space and time predestined by Allah (SWT). Certainty, however, is the sole precinct of Allah (SWT). Whether you are ultimately destined to tie the knot is an outcome known only to Him. Through striving and exposing yourself to a continuum of marriage prospects you continue to journey in the direction of that outcome. Importantly without striving you would not be able to determine that outcome and so it is through striving and being inspired by the emphasis placed on striving stressed by the Prophet (PBUH) that you converge on an outcome – in this case in the matrimonial arena – already predestined according to the all-encompassing will of Allah (SWT) as elaborated precisely and eloquently in Al-Lauh al-Mahfooz.

Predestination therefore impresses on you the overriding need to remain active, to be proactive and to remain untiringly loyal to your life partner search in the hope that one day you will finally embrace your connubial destiny. Wedding vows cannot be embraced unless you vow to remain steadfast in your determination and tenacity to discover your other half as prescribed by the irresistible will of Allah (SWT). And however challenging this odyssey may prove you cannot afford to despair since ultimately the will of Allah (SWT) reigns supreme and has already pre-determined the outcome. After all what is at stake here is half of your faith. Marriage is incumbent for you to realise half of your faith and thus there is no room for despair and despondency. Despair and despondency, however, become unbearably acute and palpable when the striving stops. Therefore to temper the advent of such dejection you must continue to remain vigilant in your life partner search and not yield to that powerless feeling of demoralisation, which sadly as our research shows affects many Muslim professionals worldwide as they endeavour to find their other half.

The point to underscore is that finding your counterpart is analogous to running a marathon. When you run a marathon the finishing line only approaches you when you strive towards it. Predestination is the same: you converge on predestination – that Divine destiny - only through striving towards that Divine destiny. That is exactly the modus operandi your life partner search requires: constant striving until you approach the finishing line, which in this case is embodied by discovering that life companion who will allow you to glide towards the wedding altar and so complete half of your faith, a life partner who Allah (SWT) has already demarcated for you in the Divine scheme of things. Despair not because you have not yet found your life partner for that journey you can only complete when Allah (SWT) has predestined for you to do so. Ask rather what additional efforts you can apply and what further additional efforts you can overlay these efforts with in order to catalyse your search and reach that at times all-elusive but approachable finishing line. This is one race where the finishing line is certainly within your reach, subject of course to the pre-ordained will of Allah (SWT) articulated in Al-Lauh al-Mahfooz. This is one race you can finish provided you do not surrender to the debilitating malaise of not striving and that malady you can only circumvent by striving and further continuing to strive. If as a Muslim you genuinely seek marriage then Divine predestination should propel you to explore every available halal channel through which you can exact plausible marriage prospects and amalgamating these channels should then allow you to tap into a self-perpetuating continuum of prospects, which is indispensable if you are to exact and sustain the urgency needed to find your spouse and so realise half of your faith. Strive and embed your life partner search with unremitting zeal. Strive in the knowledge that as a Muslim you will wed that special person Allah (SWT) has already willed. Strive you must if you are to unravel your matrimonial destiny and be with the person of your dreams as enshrined by the will of Allah (SWT). And while you remain in search of your other half keep constant faith in Allah (SWT) for such faith is vital to navigate yourself to that finishing line. "Verily in the remembrance of Allah do hearts find rest!" (Quran 13:28).

The Two Objectives of Marriage According to the Islamic Marital Law

To put the sacred importance of marriage further into context it would be useful at this point to inform our discussions with a basic understanding of the Islamic Marital Law. A deeply erudite and insightful commentary on this aspect of the *Shariah* or Islamic Law is provided by Maulana Abul A'ala Maudoodi in his enlightening review, *The Laws of Marriage and Divorce in Islam*.

The Shariah is inspired by two specific sources: the first is the word of Allah (SWT) revealed in the Quran and the second is the Sunnah, that is the customs and practices embodying the life of the Prophet (PBUH).

The Islamic Marital Law is essentially based on observing two objectives, which form its very foundations. A fundamental appreciation of these two objectives is necessary in order to further gauge the sacred eminence associated with marriage. Since these two objectives are at the heart of the Islamic Marital Law as a corollary it therefore follows that they translate by extension into the two central objectives of marriage itself. In light of the fact that marriage equates to completing half of your faith it becomes all the more important to identify with these objectives especially if the Divine stature assigned to marriage is to be fathomed with even greater clarity.

The first objective underpinning the Islamic Marital Law is the preservation of morality and chastity, which represent Allah's limits insofar as safeguarding the sanctity of the marriage bond itself is concerned (Maudoodi, 2000). It is important to note that if these limits are in danger of being transgressed the limits must not be compromised in favour of sustaining the marriage tie. By all means the couple in question should seek to reconcile their differences but if they cannot the marriage tie should be surrendered at the behest of preserving Allah's limits, which must always reign supreme. Separation then becomes a viable remedy: *divorce*, technically according to the Shariah, is the right that the husband has to demand separation from the wife in the case of irreconcilable differences while *khula*, technically according to the Shariah, is the right the wife has to demand separation from the husband in the case of irreconcilable differences. Divorce or khula should only be resorted to as a final recourse after all possible avenues of reconciliation have been exhausted. However, divorce or khula become incumbent if Allah's limits are likely to be breached: in other words it is better to dissolve a marriage where Allah's limits of morality and chastity are likely to be violated than to sustain that marriage. Zina is haram and marriage is amongst other things a lawful response to accommodating your physical needs. The first objective of the Islamic Marital Law therefore translates into the first objective of marriage, which is the total preservation of morality and chastity in subservience to Allah's prescribed limits of morality and chastity, which define the very sanctity of the marriage bond itself (Maudoodi, 2000).

The second objective governing the Islamic Marital Law is that the marriage tie between man and woman should be predicated on love and compassion, which fuel compatibility between husband and wife (Maudoodi, 2000). This can be inferred directly when Allah (SWT) says: "And among His signs is [the sign] that He created for you mates from among yourselves that you may dwell in peace and tranquillity with them and He put love and compassion between your hearts.

49

Surely there are signs in this for those who reflect" (Quran 30:21). Love and compassion are intrinsic to sustaining a harmonious marriage, which in turn is necessary to foster a stable and peaceful family life. Without love and compassion a couple cannot be at peace with each other, which can be deduced directly from the Quranic verse just cited. Their ability then to provide their children with that loving family environment is irreparably impaired. The family symbolises the very hub of Muslim society. Love and compassion between husband and wife are therefore absolutely integral to sustaining the integrity of the family. The second objective of the Islamic Marital Law therefore translates into the second objective of marriage, which is that the sacred institution of marriage is built on the constructs of love and compassion, which define compatibility (Maudoodi, 2000). This message is emphatically stressed by Maudoodi (2000: p.10) when he poignantly remarks: "A marital bond which is devoid of love and compassion is a dead body, which if left unburied, is sure to putrefy and pollute its surroundings." Maudoodi (2000: pp. 9-10) stresses the vitality of love and compassion as the kernel of the marriage tie by quoting several supporting texts directly from the Quran, including the following verses, which drive home the point lucidly:

> "He it is Who created you from a single soul, and of the same kind He made his mate that he might find comfort in her" (Quran 7:189).

> "And treat them kindly" (Quran 4:19).

> "And in your mutual dealings, do not forget to be generous" (Quran 2:237).

Compatibility Between a Man and a Woman Seeking Marriage at the Individual and Family Levels

While the first objective of marriage takes precedence over the second objective of marriage since the first objective is based on maintaining subservience to Allah's limits of morality and chastity, which govern the very sanctity of marriage itself, the second objective that the marriage bond should be inspired by love and compassion as the basis for compatibility between husband and wife is central to sustaining the marriage tie itself and for fostering the peaceful, harmonious and progressive family enterprise, which is at the very heart of the Muslim community. Compatibility between two prospective life partners needs to be predicated on the pillars of love and compassion. Having said that compatibility needs to be dissected at two levels: at the level of the individual in terms of the extent to which the personalities of the man and woman exploring marriage overlap and complement each other and at the level of the family in terms of the extent to which the temperaments of the two families to which the man and woman belong are compatible in terms of their values, mores and norms. Family compatibility should not be ignored or de-emphasised as from an Islamic perspective marriage represents both a union of two individuals and a union of their respective families. That is why the Shariah strongly discourages marriage between two individuals where their families are highly incompatible as such a chasm between the two families in the way of their values, mores and norms is likely to exercise a detrimental impact on the marriage bond itself and the ability of the husband and wife to maintain the love and compassion needed to nourish the marriage itself.

A necessary condition for marriage is that the man and woman exploring the possibility of marriage acknowledge that their personalities overlap significantly in a complementary manner and therefore click otherwise the question of marriage should not be progressed at all. The two personalities ventured for marriage should bear the hallmarks of compatibility and both individuals should acknowledge of their own free will that their personalities click with each other significantly enough to warrant progressing the question of marriage. However, this is not a sufficient condition to ensure that the man and woman in question should in fact tie the knot. What is further needed is a detailed appraisal of the extent to which the values, mores and norms of the two families sit well with each other in order to determine the degree to which the temperaments of the two families are suited to each other as this will inevitably impact the love and compassion permeating the proposed marriage bond. This practice was strongly encouraged by the Prophet (PBUH). Such an appraisal, however, would not just stem directly from the two families transacting socially with each other through exchanging visits but also through broadening the spirit of enquiry by consulting people known to the family with whom marriage is being explored and factoring in their take on that family. If other parties known to the family with whom the question of marriage has been broached are contacted then given the sacred mantle associated with marriage being equivalent to completing half of your faith there is every onus on those parties to be transparent and truthful in their analysis, particularly if they are cognisant of any factors that could cast an unfavourable shadow on the plausibility of the proposed marriage. If such factors are revealed then the parties in question need to evidence their convictions as far as they can on the basis of hard facts or evidence. It is instructive to note that such an insight relayed by the additional parties consulted to the enquiring family is not regarded as backbiting, which Islam treats as a cardinal sin. On the contrary such feedback is Islamically permissible and *wajib* or obligatory on the parties approached for such consultation.

Furthermore as child ethology clearly illustrates 70-75% of an individual's personality is effectively defined in the first five years of infancy where the primary influence on the child's development is the family. This is all the more reason to assess family compatibility since a marriage prospect cannot be properly assessed in terms of suitability even at the individual level, not to mention at the family level, until the family of that individual is factored in.

As I have often reminded Muslim professionals being serviced by Kamran A. Beg Events you cannot judge the person with whom you are exploring marriage in an informed light until you have met and gauged their family with a view to ascertaining the degree of similarity between your respective families in terms of your basic values, mores and norms. This point cannot be stressed enough and will be discussed in more detail in chapter 2. Moreover, we shall reinforce the overriding need to assess family compatibility in chapters 3 and 4 also.

Meeting the family of the person that you are exploring marriage with not only allows you to see how congruous your families are but it also provides a mechanism for calibrating the true click you might feel with that person once you have legislated for their family values. "If a man and a woman belong to families that share close or partial similarities in their views on morality, religion, social behaviour and the day to day house-hold management, they are more likely to develop a bond of love and compassion. Their marriage tie can be expected to bring the two families closer together" (Maudoodi, 2000: pp.12-13).

As the Prophet (PBUH) warned a significant divergence between the temperaments of the two families is likely to exact a negative impact on the marriage tie so increasing the likelihood of divorce. That does not mean that divorce would necessarily follow in the case where the man and woman feel that they are suited to one another individually and the families are very dissimilar in their basic temperament. However, as the Prophet (PBUH) clarified the probability of divorce is increased where the families foster significant dissimilarity, a theme we shall revisit through empirical observation in chapter 2.

Marriage Should Be Intentioned by a Genuine Attitude of Permanence

The need to establish compatibility at both the individual and family levels in light of the love and compassion required to sustain, nourish, propel and strengthen the marriage bond is of unquantifiable importance. When a man and woman agree to marriage they need to appreciate that such a life-transforming agreement should be intentioned by a genuine attitude of permanence, that is both individuals should accept mentally that when entering into marriage with each other their intention is to commit themselves on a lifelong basis to that sacred union, which will allow them to complete half of their faith. Whatever the degree of compatibility between the man and woman and however similar their family values are both the man and woman must consent of their own free will to the marriage. Whatever the guardians to the two parties may feel as to the actual suitability of the man and woman to each other neither the man nor the woman who are exploring the prospect of marriage must be coerced into acceding to the proposed marriage. Islam strictly forbids coercion and insists that the man and woman agree to marriage as a direct consequence of their free will being exercised in favour of the proposed marriage and moreover that free will, if exercised in favour of the proposed marriage, should be predicated on the wholehearted intention to engage in a lifelong matrimonial commitment. Any intention, which does not correspond with this lifelong notion of permanence, is regarded as unacceptable and in such cases the marriage should not proceed.

Both the Man and Woman Should Agree to Marriage as a Consequence of Their Own Free Will and the Woman Must Not be Coerced into Marriage

While both the man and woman have the Islamic right to exercise their free will in view of whether they wish the proposed marriage to go ahead we note that Islam in particular makes it expressly clear that no woman should be coerced into agreeing to a marriage against her free will. No matter how suited the prospective husband is in the view of the woman's guardian the final say resides with the woman herself and her decision should reflect her (the woman's) own free will. A decision should not be foisted upon her by her family, which would be indicative of conduct most unbecoming from an Islamic viewpoint, would usurp the woman's basic fundamental human right to exercise her own free will in relation to the single most challenging question concerning her life (who to marry in order to complete half of her faith?) and is strictly forbidden.

The Prophet (PBUH) was adamant that the right of a woman to exercise her own free will in connection with whom she should marry should never be violated and made it clear that if a woman does not respond in the affirmative to a particular suitor then her decision should be respected and not frowned upon no matter how favourably her family may view the suitor in question. The Prophet (PBUH) in celebration of the most revered stature assigned to women in Islam thus kindly advised: "The widow and the previously married woman are not to be married until they have been properly consulted, and the virgin is not to be married until she has given her consent" (Bukhari). In all three cases, we note the Prophet's insistence on obtaining the free consent of the woman! The Prophet (PBUH) also specified what form this consent could take to further safeguard the basic right of the woman insofar as deciding on her choice of life partner: "The widow and the previously married woman must express their free will in favour of proceeding with a marriage through the provision of spoken consent, while the virgin when consulted may indicate her consent through remaining silent when asked whether she wishes to proceed with the marriage being proposed" (Muslim). We note then the widow and previously married woman must physically voice their consent while the virgin could express her consent through being silent when prompted whether she is amenable to the marriage being considered. That is not to say that a virgin cannot voice her consent when asked. What the Prophet (PBUH) was alluding to here was that in the case of the previously never married woman there is a veritable tendency on the part of the woman to articulate vocally her opinion against proceeding with a marriage when she is convinced that someone is not potentially suited for her hand in marriage, yet when the same woman is asked about someone whom she feels would make her a worthy husband there is an increasing tendency for her to initially animate her approval through a palpable and favourable silence!

Marriage Constitutes a Mithaaq or Solemn Covenant, which must be Documented in Writing as the Marriage Contract

Allah (SWT) explicitly enlightens the human family that marriage constitutes a *mithaaq* or solemn covenant between man and woman thereby making it absolutely necessary to itemise that sacred agreement as a written contract: "How can you take it away after each one has enjoyed the other, and they have taken a firm covenant from you" (Quran 4:21).

The 'firm covenant' that Allah (SWT) refers to here (Quran 4:21) is specifically the mithaaq or solemn covenant on which the marriage should be premised, which should assume the form of a written contract forming the very basis of the marriage bond itself. This mithaaq is binding on both spouses and as a consequence must be clearly understood by both parties before going through with the marriage ceremony, which is why the marriage contract is documented in writing so that there is no ambiguity regarding the rights and responsibilities administered to the two spouses. Documenting the mithaaq in writing also ensures that the man and woman have agreed to the marriage on the basis of acceding to a lifelong commitment and have therefore mentally embraced the lifelong notion of permanence on which the marriage should be intentioned in the first place.

The marriage contract is valid provided one party makes a proposal (*eejab*) and the other party accepts the proposal (*qubul*) such that the proposal and acceptance are made in the presence of two reliable (typically male) witnesses who must be physically present at the marriage ceremony itself and must bear witness to hearing the proposal offered by one party and its acceptance by the other party with both parties being physically present in the same place. The woman's guardian must be present also. The proposal may be put forward by the guardian of either the bride or the groom. In other words there is nothing wrong with the woman's guardian – typically her father - making the proposal! The mainstay of Islamic scholarly thought agrees that a woman must have a male *wali* or guardian in order to render the marriage contract valid and that the wali should be her nearest male kith and kin, which is normally her father.

The need for the woman to have a guardian so as to render the marriage valid is expressly supported by the Quran: "Likewise, do not give your women in marriage to men who associate others with Allah in His Divinity until they believe" (Quran 2:221). Furthermore as already mentioned two witnesses of recognised probity should also be present at the marriage in addition to the woman's guardian. The Prophet (PBUH) made the mandatory stipulation for the woman's wali to be present at the marriage ceremony abundantly clear in deference to the spirit of the Quran when he declared: "Any woman who has married without the consent of her guardian has entered into an invalid marriage" (Hakim). Again we remind ourselves that while a woman should consult her guardian on her choice of husband the final decision as to whom she should marry resides solely with her, is subject to her discretion and should be exercised in accordance with her own free will.

Once the proposal has been accepted the marriage contract comes into effect straight away since acceptance lawfully culminates in the conclusion of the marriage contract. The man and woman are now legally husband and wife and can lawfully exercise all the rights and responsibilities assigned to a couple and furthermore can according to the Shariah consummate the marriage without delay since their conjugal rights come into effect immediately once the proposal has been accepted. The Prophet (PBUH) in fact singled out consummation as the most profound effect resulting from conclusion of the marriage contract: "The most important conditions contained in the marriage contract that need to be fulfilled are those by which sexual intercourse has been made lawful" (Bukhari and Muslim). Seminally, the tendency in practice to defer consummation does not follow from the Shariah, which recognises the man and woman as husband and wife immediately upon conclusion of the marriage contract, but is a consequence of custom. Note the distinction between religion and custom, particularly in relation to consummation of the marriage.

Since this mithaaq is binding on both spouses it symbolises permanence and can only be dissolved in the case of death or divorce or khula or where one of the parties has been misled by the other party or where one of the parties did not declare a defect prior to the marriage contract being concluded since it (the defect) was unknown then but which only came to light after the marriage and which it has since transpired has significantly impaired the ability of the couple to enjoy normal marital relations. This set of outcomes, which allow the marriage contract to be dissolved, additionally ensures that the man and woman originally enter into marriage with the wholehearted intention of permanence that is absolutely necessary to safeguard not just the husband and wife but also their family in the way of warranting a stable framework within which the marriage itself can function and propagate. This bulwark of stability that lends vitality to the permanence represented by the marriage contract cannot be underscored enough in light of the mithaaq allowing the couple to complete half of their faith!

Whom a Muslim Man and a Muslim Woman may Enter into Marriage with

The mithaaq or solemn covenant epitomised by marriage allows a Muslim to complete half of their faith. This is no ordinary undertaking and represents as such a huge 'leap of faith' on the part of the individual. Deciding on your choice of spouse is quite easily the single most life-changing decision any Muslim can be expected to take. Your choice of life partner as we have gathered is predestined subject to the Divine will. Part of life's journey is geared to discovering that choice through striving with conviction to find your pre-ordained other half.

Allah (SWT) has laid down specific ground rules in the Quran in terms of whom a Muslim is permitted to marry and therefore what in the eyes of the Creator constitutes a lawful marriage for a Muslim. Allah (SWT) reveals these in meticulous detail providing impeccable guidance regarding a lawful choice of spouse. We now elaborate on whom Muslim men and Muslim women may or may not marry insofar as the faith-based background of the potential suitor is concerned.

Allah (SWT) states:

> "Marry not the women who associate others with Allah in His Divinity until they believe" (Quran 2:221).

> "And permitted to you are chaste women, be they from among the believers, or from among those who have received the Book before you" (Quran 5:5).

A Muslim man therefore cannot enter into marriage with an idolateress unless she reverts to Islam (Quran 2:221). A Muslim man can marry a woman provided she is a Muslim by faith or if the woman is non-Muslim she can either be Christian or Jewish but must be chaste (Quran 5:5), that is *muhsanat*. The marriage of a Muslim man to a woman who is not a Muslim or Christian or Jewish is not permissible and is considered to be unlawful.

Allah (SWT) further specifies:

"Likewise, do not give your women in marriage to men who associate others with Allah in His Divinity until they believe" (Quran 2:221).

"And when you have ascertained them to be believing women, do not send them back to the unbelievers. These women are no longer lawful to the unbelievers, nor are those unbelievers lawful to those [believing] women" (Quran 60:10).

A Muslim woman cannot enter into marriage with an idolater unless he reverts to Islam (Quran 2:221). A Muslim woman can only marry a man of Muslim faith (Quran 60:10). That is a Muslim woman must marry a Muslim man for the marriage to be deemed lawful from an Islamic perspective. The marriage of a Muslim woman to a man who does not subscribe to the Muslim faith is not permissible and is considered to be unlawful in the eyes of Allah (SWT) as the above verse (Quran 60:10) clearly testifies. "He makes His injunctions clear to people so that they may take heed" (Quran 2:221).

Muslim Reverts and the Unacceptable Indifference they Experience in the Mainstream Muslim Community when Seeking to Find a Life Partner

As we disclose in chapter 2 what is particularly worrying is the conspicuous indifference that Muslim reverts in particular experience when seeking to integrate themselves into mainstream Muslim community life and the heightened difficulties that they further experience in seeking to contract marriage with a Muslim born into Islam. We report on these issues in greater detail in chapter 2 based on highly telling research conducted by Kamran A. Beg Events.

In the eyes of Allah (SWT) there is no distinction between a Muslim born into Islam, that is an individual born into a Muslim family, and a Muslim revert, that is an individual who has reverted to Islam. All Muslims have an equal right to complete half of their faith through embracing the sacred beauty of marriage and the Muslim community needs to apply greater efforts in order to ensure that Muslim reverts are made to feel a more welcomed and wanted part and parcel of the community enterprise and are given ample opportunity to find a life partner from amongst their Muslim brethren and in particular are accommodated for marriage by those born into Islam.

After all Allah (SWT) reminds the Muslim community of the pivotal need to foster the notion of a Muslim brotherhood or *Ummah* that acts in concert, amity and cooperation when He says: "Surely the believers are none but brothers unto one another, so set things right between your brothers, and have fear of Allah that you may be shown mercy" (Quran 49:10). This Quranic verse shows that there is no distinction between Muslims born into Islam and those who have reverted to Islam! Muslims should view themselves in the light of an Ummah, which should define the cohesive sense of fraternity that should permeate every aspect of the Muslim community. This leaves absolutely no room for the 'them and us' mentality we sadly see in Muslim society demarcating between Muslims born into Islam and Muslim reverts, which effectively penalises Muslim reverts in their quest to feel an integral part of the broader Muslim community and to seek out marriage with a fellow Muslim born into Islam. Throughout his exemplary life the Prophet (PBUH) reinforced the concept of the Ummah for only an Ummah can harbour the esprit de corps needed for the Muslim community to progress in unison as a collective whole.

This spirit of brotherhood manifested by the notion of an Ummah was impeccably depicted during the life of the Prophet (PBUH) when the Prophet (PBUH) performed the *Hijrah* (Emigration) from Makkah to Madinah in 622 CE. The Prophet (PBUH) insisted that the *Ansar* who were the selfless Muslims already residing in Madinah treat and embrace the *Muhajirun* who were the courageous Muslim Emigrants from Makkah who accompanied the Prophet (PBUH) during the Hijrah as true brothers in Islam: "They [Ansar] love those who have migrated [Muhajirun] and do not covet what has been given them; they even prefer them above themselves though poverty be their own lot" (Quran 59:9). In promoting this exemplary sense of brotherhood between the Ansar and the Muhajirun the Prophet (PBUH) provided the Muslim community with the perfect example of how the selfless provider of hospitality (Ansar) can live in unison and harmony with the selfless recipient of hospitality (Muhajirun) and how through respecting the bond of brotherhood created between them the two (or more) stakeholders can cultivate the ambience indispensable for sustaining a seamless community enterprise, which assumes the form of an Ummah, and so develops as a collective whole. The Prophet (PBUH) inspired the creation of a cohesive community infrastructure where each Muhajirun could turn for help and advice to an Ansar since a bond of brotherhood had been established at the Prophet's disposal between that Muhajirun and that Ansar, which obliged the two to relate to each other as true brothers in Islam. It is precisely this sense of fraternity, which is the order of the day and is urgently needed to help construct bridges of communication and support between Muslim reverts and those Muslims born into Islam so that the Muslim community can move as a coherent and seamless one. This will then allow the 'them and us' mindset, which has tragically and unacceptably left many Muslim reverts out in the cold, to be dissolved and replaced instead by the workings of a social infrastructure that allows Muslim reverts to contribute more easily to the mainstream Muslim community and which facilitates and welcomes the marriage of Muslim reverts to Muslims born into Islam.

Allah (SWT) also places absolute stress on the requirement for Muslims to cooperate with fellow members of the Muslim community only when discharging good deeds: "Help one another in acts of righteousness and piety, and do not help one another in sin and transgression. Fear Allah: Surely Allah is severe in retribution" (Quran 5:2). Suffice it to say the noble deed of helping a member of the Muslim community to find a life partner carries enormous stature. To expedite their wish to proceed to the wedding altar there is a social and religious responsibility on the part of the wider Muslim community to provide as much support and assistance as possible to Muslim reverts and not to undermine their quest for marriage on the basis of the abhorrent 'them and us' mindset, which appears to have prevailed and runs totally contrary to the spirit of Islam. Muslim reverts should not be excluded by the mainstream community and one way to ensure that is to encourage more Muslims born into Islam to be joined in marriage with those of our Ummah who have reverted to Islam. Actions speak louder than words and the Muslim community needs to lead by example in this regard!

Honouring the Wife through the Mahr or Bridal Gift

For a Muslim marriage to be valid the groom must respectfully honour and grace his wife with a *mahr* or bridal gift, which also notably evidences the man's genuine intention to marry his prospective wife with that true intention of lifelong permanence, which should support the mithaaq heralded by the marriage in the first place: "Give women their bridal-due in good cheer [considering it a duty]: but if they willingly remit any part of it, consume it with good pleasure" (Quran 4:4). This bridal-due or mahr is usually agreed upon between the two parties before the marriage contract has been finalised. The mahr is the wife's exclusive property and she may do with as she and only she pleases. It is a marital right that cannot be denied to the wife and has been expressly conferred upon her by Allah (SWT) though she may remit a part or the whole of the mahr to her husband but only as a matter of her own free will as revealed in the second part of the above verse (Quran 4:4). The wife, however, surrenders the mahr to her husband either in full or in part if she petitions for khula.

The mahr can be material or non-material or a hybrid of the two. The mahr is obligatory and the man may either give the woman her mahr promptly after the marriage has been consummated or it may be deferred in part or in whole in tune with what was agreed between the two parties at the time the actual marriage contract was drawn up: "And give bridal-due of those whom you have enjoyed in wedlock as an obligation. But there is no blame on you if you mutually agree to alter the settlement after it has been made. Surely Allah is All-Knowing, All-Wise" (Quran 4:24). If the mahr is deferred it should be paid to the wife within the mutually agreed time limit endorsed by the two parties making it a truly deferred mahr or is either payable on divorce should the marriage tie be severed on account of her husband's wish to dissolve the marriage or on the death of her husband if in either of the two aforesaid cases the mahr had not been imparted to the wife beforehand (Maudoodi, 2000).

If the marriage ends in divorce before it has been consummated assuming the mahr had been agreed at the time of the marriage (which is usually the case but not necessarily always so) then the man would be required to give at least half the mahr to the woman as compensation though a more noble act in the eyes of Allah (SWT) would be to compensate the woman with the full mahr: "And if you divorce them before you touch them or settle bridal gift upon them, then [give them] half of what you have settled unless either the women act leniently and forgo their claim, or he in whose hand is the marriage tie acts leniently [and pays the full amount]. If you act leniently, it is closer to God-fearing. And forget not to act gracefully with one another, for indeed Allah sees all that you do" (Quran 2:237). If, however, the mahr had not been agreed at the time of marriage (which is not usually the case) and the man were to divorce the woman before the marriage is consummated he must still gift the woman with some compensation in line with what he can afford but at the same time this compensation should legislate for the distress caused to the woman on account of the divorce and her social standing: "There is no blame upon you if you divorce your wives before you have touched them or settled a bridal gift upon them. But even in this case you should make some provision for them: the affluent, according to his means; the straitened, according to his means – a provision in fair manner. That is a duty upon the good-doers" (Quran 2:236).

Before we proceed further, it is further instructive to clarify that the mahr is obligatory and cannot be nullified irrespective of whether the Muslim man marries a Muslim woman or a Christian or Jewish woman. In this regard Allah (SWT), the Mighty and Majestic, remarks: "And permitted to you are chaste women, be they from among the believers, or from among those who have received the Book before you, provided you become their protectors in wedlock after paying them their bridal-due, rather than going around committing fornication and taking them as secret-companions" (Quran 5:5).

Whilst no limits have been placed stipulating how large or small the mahr can be the Prophet (PBUH) stressed that given the sacred importance of marriage in allowing a Muslim to realise half of their faith what is of central importance here is that the marriage be progressed and actioned and therefore the mahr, which is obligatory on the man as a token of goodwill to his wife as enjoined by Allah (SWT), should be affordable and manageable as opposed to extravagant and beyond the groom's means. The Prophet (PBUH) clearly insisted on moderation in line with the

68

groom's means when deciding on an appropriate mahr as we can conclude directly when he stated: "The best mahr is the easiest (to give)" (Hakim). This is consistent with the Prophet's position on the ease with which a marriage should be facilitated. Thus the Prophet (PBUH) stated: "The best marriage is the easiest" (Abu Dawud). However, the mahr should not be so insignificant as to demean or denigrate the wife!

Allah (SWT) introduced the mahr as a marital right conferred upon the wife in order to honour her and to assure her that the man with whom she is entering into marriage with truly intends lifelong commitment. Such is the insistence in Islam on according the woman every respect and dignity and endeavouring to do away with anything that belittles or degrades her, such as the heinous practice sadly seen in some sections of the Muslim community where the man's family demand a *dowry* or payment from the woman's family in order to facilitate the marriage. That derogatory practice, which blatantly denigrates the virtuous posture of the woman, has no place in Islam! The woman's family have no such obligation for such a demand on the part of the man's family is ignoble and unacceptable and violates the very essence of Islam. The mahr is an obligatory bridal gift from the husband to his wife and is an important, constitutive and irrefutably integral part of the equality that women have been granted in Islam, an equality gifted to them courtesy of the Divine will exercised by Allah (SWT). And so it is that Allah (SWT) states: "Marry them, then, with the leave of their guardians, and give them their bridal-due in a fair manner that they may live in the protection of wedlock rather than be either mere objects of unfettered lust or given to secret love affairs" (Quran 4:25). Allah (SWT), the All-Compassionate, assigns a whole surah or chapter in the

Quran to the role of women and the equality they have been ordained by Him, specifically Surah 4 Al-Nisa [Women], which the reader is well-advised to consult in addition to the other Quranic references cited above.

Faith in Conjunction with Personal Preference Should Inspire your Choice of Spouse

We now explore the issue of compatibility in more detail. A very well written succinct primer on marriage in the Muslim faith is provided by Sheikh Nasir Al-Omar in his highly readable book, *The Ingredients for a Happy Marriage*. A part of this finely compiled study is dedicated to what should inspire the actual decision-making process itself when it comes to selecting one's life partner. This area is very important to grasp as marriage allows you to complete half of your faith and given the mithaaq or solemn covenant that the marriage contract signifies both man and woman should enter into this sacred undertaking with the noble intention of permanence as underscored above. As we have already highlighted assuming there is a significant measure of individual compatibility between the man and woman what is further recommended is a good degree of overlap between the families of the man and woman exploring marriage. As we have noted the Prophet (PBUH) advised against pursuing marriage if the family values, mores and norms of the two families are markedly different as then the likelihood of divorce is accentuated. The man and woman must of course agree to the marriage of their own free will and in no way be coerced into acceding to the proposed marriage.

Compatibility, as we have intimated, should be fuelled by mutual love and compassion. It is important that the man and woman exploring marriage relate to each other physically, mentally, religiously, intuitively and otherwise and foster a chemistry that allows them to be at peace with each other. Moreover, and most importantly, this chemistry should allow them to contemplate marriage as a vehicle through which to conclude half of their faith. Since marriage enables the marriage-seeker to complete half of their faith it stands to reason that faith should be assigned primary billing in one's choice of life partner. This applies equally from a male and female perspective as we can see on the basis of the Prophet's instructive advice, which singles faith out as the single most important criterion when selecting a spouse (Al-Omar, 1999).

When choosing a wife the Prophet (PBUH) stated: "A woman is married for one of four reasons: for her beauty, her wealth, her genealogy and her faith. So be successful with a woman of faith. May Allah bless you" (Al-Omar, 1999: p.12). As this hadith so eloquently reveals faith should constitute the primary parameter in selecting a wife since marriage allows both spouses to complete half of their faith and an understanding of faith fuels the appropriate ambience in which to cultivate the marriage and provide the stable environment needed to raise a family. The other three criteria whilst important are secondary parameters in choosing a wife and only come to the fore if the marriage prospect has the commensurate level of faith to start off with. In the spirit of the hadith the other three criteria should only enter the fray provided the woman with whom marriage is being considered has the right level of faith. Granted what may constitute the right level of faith for a man will inevitably vary from one man to another but faith all the same should be the primary factor guiding a man's decision in terms of whom to marry. Of course the man should also be physically, mentally, intuitively and otherwise attracted to his future wife but these secondary parameters in the overall scheme of things embody his personal preference and should only strike a chord if the man and woman see the right level of faith in each other in the first place.

Similarly when choosing a husband the primary parameter that should inspire the woman's selection of soulmate is his adherence to the faith and so the suitability of any man as a potential counterpart should be calibrated primarily in terms of the degree of religious piety he exercises. The centrality of faith to the choice of husband is lucidly spelt out in the following hadith when the Prophet (PBUH) beseeched the woman and her family to prioritise faith in terms of whom to marry: "When a man whose character and faith you like approaches you (for marriage), then marry him. If you do not then there will be great trials and widespread disruption on earth" (Al-Omar, 1999: p.12). Granted what may constitute the right level of faith for a woman will inevitably vary from one woman to another but faith all the same should be the primary factor guiding a woman's decision in terms of whom to marry. Of course the woman should also be physically, mentally, intuitively and otherwise attracted to her future husband but these secondary parameters in the overall scheme of things embody her personal preference and should only strike a chord if the woman and man see the right level of faith in each other in the first place. Insofar as the woman's choice of husband is concerned it is noteworthy that the potential spouse should also carry *kafa'ah* in her eyes or be perceived by her in an equal light. This additional secondary parameter, which also contributes to a woman's personal preference, cannot be disregarded as most women would openly admit that they are more likely to respect their husband if he is perceived by them to carry an equal status at least in some tangible regard. For example, the vast mainstay of university trained Muslim professional females that have accessed Kamran A. Beg Events have stated that they prefer a life partner who is a fellow professional with academic credentials acquired from a university. What they have lent expression to here is what in their eyes correlates with kafa'ah at least in terms of their educational and professional expectations about a future spouse.

We note then the distinction between the primary parameter guiding your choice of life partner, which is faith, and the secondary parameters informing your choice of life partner, which include the physical, mental, intuitive and other parameters of attraction that in composite embody your personal preference. As the Prophet's advice so sublimely stresses personal preference is important but should only come into the reckoning provided the right level of faith has been identified in the prospective spouse. Of course you should feel physically, mentally, intuitively and otherwise attracted to your prospective life partner but these terms of endearment only enter the equation if that person has the right degree of faith or religious piety in keeping with the counsel of the Prophet (PBUH). While faith takes precedence over personal preference in your choice of life partner, it is faith in conjunction with personal preference that should inspire your choice of spouse! As I have explained to all of the Muslim professionals who have kindly consulted Kamran A. Beg Events for advice on the life partner front since marriage essentially represents an undertaking that allows you to complete half of your faith, faith cannot be excluded from a life partner decision-making model especially in light of the primary status assigned to it by the Prophet (PBUH). Not legislating for the right level of faith in your prospective soulmate is tantamount to missing the point altogether! Personal preference only assumes stature and gathers momentum if the appropriate level of faith or a level of faith that you feel comfortable with is instilled in the prospective spouse to start off with. Personal preference is not being devalued here; it is absolutely essential that you connect physically, mentally, intuitively and otherwise with your potential counterpart but such chemistry only becomes workable if your prospective counterpart houses the right level of faith. The Prophet (PBUH) through his vitally judicious counsel on the matter therefore allows you to calibrate personal preference in the light of faith and therefore in the right light. Personal preference without faith does not augur well for a good marriage! Faith coupled with personal preference is the recipe for a good marriage! This is the Prophet's timeless advice: this is advice that every Muslim should take heed off when deliberating over the most important decision concerning their future well-being, which revolves around whom they should marry with a view to embracing half of their faith!

The Need for Physical Attraction

Personal preference as we have seen above is in part determined by whether the man and woman feel physically attracted to each other. The extent to which physical compatibility is weighted as a priority will vary from one person to another but what is undeniable is the fundamental desire that each of us harbours in that we wish to partake in a lifelong partnership of marriage with someone who is appealing to our eye. That is perfectly in keeping with human nature and not something one should be embarrassed to admit! The Prophet (PBUH) touched explicitly on the

74

need to feel physically attracted to one's future spouse. Beauty, for example, is earmarked as one of the three secondary parameters comprising the personal preference of a man when choosing a wife as we have already witnessed in the Prophet's advice above to men when selecting a wife. The Prophet (PBUH) further exhorted that if a man finds his prospective wife to be physically attractive it will help to nourish that bond of love and compassion, which underpins compatibility. Thus the Prophet (PBUH) remarked: "Look at her, for it is more likely to establish affection between you" (Ahmed, Abu Dawud, Tirmidhi, Nisai and Ibn Majah). The Prophet (PBUH) also acknowledged that physical chemistry greatly helps to sustain a marriage: "Look at her because that will be more conducive to a longer marriage" (Al-Omar, 1999: p.13). Physical compatibility is not inconsequential: it clearly has a vital role to play in safeguarding the longevity of a marriage. As the Prophet's observations show to discount the need for physical compatibility is to ignore it at your own peril! That is not to say the physical attraction a man feels for a woman is the only secondary parameter informing his life partner choice but none-the-less assuming the woman has the right level of faith, which is the primary parameter driving a man's life partner choice, the woman he marries should have the right blend of secondary parameters in unison with his personal preference with physical attraction for the woman clearly having an important role to play in that personal preference as the Prophet's timeless advice displays.

Equally the Prophet (PBUH) was keen to highlight the importance of a woman feeling physically attracted to her husband and how such attraction for her prospective life companion should form a key consideration in her personal preference. We can decipher this in particular through two oft-quoted landmark jurisprudential decisions the Prophet (PBUH) made during his momentous and exemplary life where in both cases the marriage was repudiated and therefore dissolved on account of the woman not feeling physically attracted to the husband (Maudoodi, 2000). In both cases the marriage tie was therefore severed on account of a khula or female-initiated separation. These two khulas featured Thabit bin Qais, an eminent Meccan noble who was renowned for his sense of faith or religious piety and respected for his upstanding character. Thabit's two wives, Jamilah and Habibah, separately petitioned the Prophet (PBUH) for a khula on the express grounds that they did not find Thabit to be physically attractive and as a result they could not sustain their marriage with him. The Prophet (PBUH) assessed their petitions on the basis of the first objective of the Islamic Marital Law, which is to preserve Allah's limits of morality and chastity, which define the very sanctity of the marriage bond itself. In both cases the Prophet (PBUH) concluded that a lack of physical attraction for Thabit could result in Allah's limits being transgressed by Jamilah and Habibah and in each case a khula was granted on the basis of incompatible physical chemistry (Maudoodi, 2000). The Prophet (PBUH) noted the very considerable degree of disgust Jamilah and Habibah harboured towards Thabit on the basis of not being physically attracted to him and in deference to Allah's limits of morality and chastity sanctioned these two khulas.

As we expounded before if there is any likelihood of Allah's limits of morality and chastity being violated despite an attempt to reconcile the couple over their differences in deference to these sacred limits the marriage should be dissolved. In much the same way it is important for a man to find his wife physically endearing the converse is equally true. A woman should find her prospective life partner to be physically attractive, as the Prophet's groundbreaking decisions bear resounding testimony to. That is not to say that physical attraction is the only secondary parameter that makes up a woman's personal preference. It may well be that a woman places more stress on the mental or intuitive connection she has with the man in question but even so what the Prophet's decisions in the cases of Jamilah and Habibah clearly highlight is that if a woman feels a lack of physical chemistry with her husband that is a sufficient enough condition on which to base the dissolution of the marriage tie especially if there is any danger of Allah's limits of morality and chastity being undermined. A corollary of these two legal decisions is that to feel physical attraction for a man is a perfectly acceptable and natural sentiment for a Muslim woman to harbour if she wishes to marry that Muslim man. Granted a woman should temper each of the secondary parameters, which make up her personal preference, so that the marriage prospect should ideally possess the right blend of qualities in keeping with that preference but the physical attraction she feels for the man should not be discounted or ignored as the two cases above signify. Also what we can gauge from the Jamilah and Habibah precedents is that while faith is the primary parameter guiding a woman's life partner choice, faith alone does not guarantee the sustainability of a marriage. Faith in conjunction with personal preference should inform a woman's life partner choice! Assuming the man has the right level of faith in keeping with the woman's wishes she should also feel physically, mentally, intuitively and otherwise connected with the man in deference to her personal preference. In their khula petitions Jamilah and Habibah never once doubted the moral integrity of Thabit and indeed both acknowledged that he was a true man of faith. But that

77

was not enough to sustain their marriages to him as he fell well below par in terms of the physical chemistry they yearned for in a husband and as a result he did not oblige with their personal preferences.

Since launching Kamran A. Beg Events it would be true to say that hardly a week goes by when a highly anxious Muslim professional female through no fault of her own does not respectfully contact our humble organisation to discuss how to break the news to her parents that she does not find the male suitor to whom she has been introduced sufficiently attractive in physical terms and predominantly as a result does not wish to pursue marriage with that individual. These are not isolated cases and certainly not the exception! Since marriage represents a mithaaq or solemn covenant that allows you to complete half of your faith you should only enter into marriage if your free will consents to it. Your free will is inevitably based on calibrating the suitability of the marriage prospect on the basis of how they relate to the set of faith-inspired and personal preference expectations you have of your life partner. In all such cases that I have personally addressed I have explained to the Muslim female in question that it is her Islamic prerogative that she feels physically attracted to her prospective husband and in no way should she feel embarrassed to enlighten her parents that she does not wish to proceed with a particular male suitor if she feels there is a worrying lack of physical compatibility. Such advice is always driven by the Prophet's impeccable counsel and his decisions regarding the Jamilah and Habibah scenarios as itemised above. No matter how suitable a particular marriage prospect may appear on paper until you have an opportunity to meet that person you cannot really begin to gauge the degree of compatibility. Since Islam celebrates compatibility between a husband and wife based on mutual love and compassion we should not pay scant regard to compatibility. To do so would be equivalent to undermining the very sanctity of the marriage bond itself.

In April 2006 I was contacted by a very distressed, and rightly so, Muslim female scientist based in London. She had been introduced a couple of months earlier to "the perfect match" in the words of her mother. The Muslim gentleman is a highly qualified medical doctor who holds a full repertoire of advanced academic and professional qualifications to his credit. He and his family also reside in London. The female scientist had concluded when he was introduced to her in the presence of his and her very keen parents that she did not find the doctor physically amenable to the eye, which had persuaded her to draw matters to a close with immediate effect. She had diplomatically and very politely communicated her disinclination to pursue the matter further to her parents who did not react too well and berated her for being "incredibly superficial and immature" in the words of her father. This had put the female at loggerheads with her parents and as a result the parent-child relationship became increasingly strained. Pressure was then applied on the female to encourage her to change her decision with the young lady's uncles and aunts jumping onto the matrimonial bandwagon at the behest of her disbelieving parents. Her mother had assured her that she could grow to love the man and even though he was not her physical match he could provide her with the security that all women strive for and that he was from a very highly respected family, which was an additional super-plus, not to mention the fact that he belongs to a very noble profession, medicine, and was conscious of his religious obligations. Her parents had further contended that it was un-Islamic for her to spurn the offer of marriage on the basis of looks and that she needed to

79

grow up. They had spoken to the man's parents regularly since the meeting and had assured them that all would be well and things were heading in the right direction.

Sadly, though understandably, the female scientist's health began to deteriorate and she became very ill and was put on the appropriate medication by her doctor. When she contacted me she was distraught and emotionally shattered. I assured her that her decision to refute a marriage request, in this case on the basis of physical incompatibility, was perfectly Islamic and her reasoning was consistent with the Prophet's advice. As we have already elaborated one should only consent to marrying someone as a matter of free will and marriage should not be forced upon one against the grain of that free will. Faith in conjunction with personal preference should govern your life partner choice. I then requested to speak the female's parents, which I did. Initially I received a very frosty reception but over the course of several exchanges convinced them that their daughter's fundamental right not to progress marriage with the doctor could not be denied to her and the fact that she found him physically incompatible and therefore wished to disengage from any further discussion on the matter was her basic Islamic right and wholly consistent with the Prophet's counsel! The reader will be relieved to learn that the female's wishes were eventually respected by her parents who were entirely ignorant of the true Islamic position until I had spoken to them and had clarified it to them over a number of discussions. The Prophet (PBUH) was the perfect embodiment of the Quran in practice and his prodigious decisions in the cases of Jamilah and Habibah make it crystal clear that physical attraction should not be discounted when choosing a husband. On hearing these precedents the female scientist's parents suddenly realised the error of their ways, became conspicuously contrite and eventually apologised to their daughter for their acute lack of understanding and complete insensitivity to her feelings. Additionally, the reader will be delighted to learn that the parent-child relationship has now been restored to normalcy, all credit being attributable to the female scientist's perseverance and the Prophet's Divinely-guided wisdom!

Individual-cum-family Compatibility Lends Favourably to the Sustainability and Longevity of a Marriage

In sum, whether you are a man searching for the lady of his dreams or a woman endeavouring to discover her knight in shining armour the aim should be to enter into marriage with that person with whom you feel a significant measure of compatibility. This compatibility should be premised on mutual love and compassion and as such should be inspired primarily by faith and secondarily by personal preference. It is a combination of faith and personal preference as embodied by the confluence of physical, mental, intuitive and any other germane secondary parameters that should inform your choice of spouse in line with the Prophet's sublime perspective. It is that unique blend of faith and personal preference, which defines this special chemistry you are in hot pursuit of in deference to completing half of your faith.

As indicated earlier compatibility needs to be understood at two levels: at the individual level between the man and woman and at the family level in terms of how congruous the basic temperaments of the two families are. Even if you feel a significant degree of individual compatibility with the person with whom you are exploring marriage that compatibility can only be put into perspective and as such calibrated through assessing the extent to which the values, mores and norms of your family and the marriage prospect's family converge. The Prophet (PBUH) advised against marriage if the values of the two families are significantly at variance with each other as then the probability of divorce is increased. The Prophet (PBUH) encouraged marriage in cases where the man and woman feel a significant degree of individual compatibility and where the values of their two families bear a significant degree of similarity. Individual-cum-family compatibility lends favourably to the sustainability and longevity of a marriage, which should only be entered into where the man and woman prior to agreeing to the marriage wholeheartedly intend to engage in lifelong companionship with each other so respecting the notion of permanence that should motivate their decision to marry each other in the first place and so fulfil half of their faith.

The Khitbah or Formally Making a Marriage Proposal

We now examine what the relevant Islamic formality relating to the *khitbah* is, that is formally making a marriage proposal.

The khitbah must be initiated by the man's party since by definition it encompasses a formal request for the woman's hand in marriage. The khitbah could be undertaken directly by the man himself but it is more usual for his guardian to make it on his behalf directly to the woman's guardian. Given the enormity of the marriage decision since it is associated with completing half of your faith the Prophet (PBUH) advised, as with any halal undertaking where there is an element of risk concerning its capacity to impart benefit to the incumbent, that *Istikhara* be offered as a supplication seeking Allah's counsel on the matter: "If you intend something that is halal pray two rakaahs other than the obligatory prayer and then recite Istikhara" (Bukhari).

As the Prophet (PBUH) explained through Istikhara Allah (SWT) should be directly consulted on the halal matter in question – in this case marriage. The Creator then signals His verdict on the matter either through the seamless ease with which He allows the marriage to happen or not, which could well be the case, since whether the marriage will or will not occur has already been predestined subject to the Divine will. Having performed Istikhara the key is to respect Allah's verdict on whether the marriage transpires or not and whatever the outcome turns out to be to respect that outcome wholeheartedly and with total faith since Allah (SWT) knows best! Allah (SWT), however, does not necessarily signal His verdict through the medium of a dream contrary to popular Muslim belief!

Ideally, Istikhara should be performed by the man before his guardian goes ahead with the khitbah. It may well be that on performing Istikhara the man experiences considerable agitation and discomfort more or less straight away and decides not to proceed with the khitbah. This state of unease could materialise in the form of an unfavourable dream or more likely manifest itself through a feeling of complete discord between his heart and mind. Then again he may not experience any palpable perturbation immediately and the answer to the Istikhara may well surface as a consequence, for example, of the favourable or unfavourable social interaction that subsequently plays out between the man and the woman and their respective families once the khitbah has been actioned.

Once the woman's party receive the khitbah the woman whose hand in marriage has been requested and her guardian may wish to perform Istikhara themselves with a view to seeing whether they wish to explore the possibility of marriage that has arisen. If they do perform Istikhara and decide to proceed with the marriage proposal in addition to further ascertaining the degree of individual compatibility between the man and woman the two families would seek to gauge further the degree to which the values, mores and norms of the two families correlate along the lines we described earlier in the chapter. Identifying the degree to which the two families are similar in terms of basic temperament as we noted would rely on not just direct social interaction between the families but also on each family speaking to parties known to the marriage prospect's family in order to develop a more informed perspective about that family. As the Prophet (PBUH) advised where the man and woman bear a high degree of individual compatibility and the families are also congruous in large measure marriage is advisable; whatever the degree of individual compatibility if the families are at significant variance in terms of basic values, mores and norms then marriage is not advised since the ability of the couple to retain and propagate the love and compassion intrinsic to the compatibility on which the marriage bond is based will be markedly impaired and the probability of divorce is heightened!

The Walimah or Wedding Party is Sunnah

Assuming the decision is to proceed to marriage then as we touched on earlier a marriage contract would be drawn up between the two parties and once concluded in the manner prescribed already the man and woman would lawfully be husband and wife. The marriage is usually celebrated through a wedding party or *walimah* for which the husband bears sole responsibility as a befitting Islamic courtesy to his wife and her family. We repeat the husband bears complete responsibility for the walimah and in no way should the husband or his family lean on the wife and her family in relation to discharging this courtesy.

While the walimah is not obligatory the Prophet (PBUH) very keenly favoured it as the preferred vehicle through which to make public news of the marriage. The walimah is therefore a very strongly recommended *Sunnah* and is an expression of good faith on the part of the husband and his family towards his wife and her family. It represents a means of honouring the wife! The walimah could be held at the time the marriage contract is concluded or at the time the marriage is consummated. The timing of the walimah tends very largely to be influenced by custom.

The Rights of the Wife, the Rights of the Husband and the Mutual Rights Shared by the Couple

We now discuss the rights administered separately to the husband and wife and those that the couple share mutually, all of which stem from the marriage contract being concluded. Al-Omar (1999) and Maudoodi (2000) both provide very rigorous commentaries on these three sets of rights, which are central to the husband and wife accommodating their marital responsibilities with conviction and passion. The purpose of this section is to furnish the reader with a basic overview of these rights while more detailed discussions can be found in either of these two references.

The wife's rights include:

1. Being entitled to a mahr or obligatory bridal gift, a theme we have already touched on thoroughly earlier in this chapter: "Give women their bridal-due in good cheer [considering it a duty]: but if they willingly

86

remit any part of it, consume it with good pleasure" (Quran 4:4).

2. Being provided with a residence and living expenses by her husband specifically in accordance with his means (Al-Omar, 1999): "Lodge them according to your means wherever you dwell" (Quran 65:6) and "Whoever has abundant means, let him spend according to his means; and he whose means are straitened, let him spend out of what Allah has given him. Allah does not burden any human being beyond the means that he has bestowed upon them. Possibly Allah will grant ease after hardship" (Quran 65:7). The residence should afford the wife an adequate degree of privacy and security and moreover should support an ambience, which makes her feel comfortable and at home. The maintenance of the wife is clearly borne by the husband in line with his means (Maudoodi, 2000). Even if the wife works and/or has assets at the time of marriage, the family residence and living expenses must be borne by her husband in keeping with his financial disposition. If, however, the wife wishes to contribute to the household, which she is under no Islamic obligation to do so, she may do so only with the consent of her husband but such contribution would be deemed surplus to the financial responsibilities that the husband would ordinarily be expected to discharge towards looking after his wife and family. The wife has every right to spend her work earnings and/or assets as she wishes, in much the same way as she holds total sovereignty over how her mahr is spent. The wife must not be coerced by her husband to help him shoulder the duty placed upon him by Allah (SWT) to provide a residence and living expenses for

his wife and family in line with his means. Any work earnings and/or assets she remits towards the family must be of her own volition provided she has consulted her husband and sought his prior approval. If a wife wishes to work and the husband has agreed to this then the husband has to honour this agreement and cannot go back on his word (Al-Omar, 1999). This follows from the judicious advice of the Prophet (PBUH) who exhorted: "Muslims are bound by their conditions (in contracts)" (Al-Omar, 1999: p.41). What contract can be more important than the marriage contract? If as a part of that covenant the husband has agreed to allow his wife to work then any decision regarding her future work status would reside entirely with her. It is then for the wife to decide whether she wishes to continue working and if so how long or if she wishes to leave work when she wishes to do so. By all means she may consult her husband should she wish before arriving on a decision but whatever decision she exercises she must do so of her own free will though it is always advisable that the decision made should not compromise the marriage tie and should place the well-being of the family first.

3. Being treated by her husband with the utmost civility, kindness, dignity and sincerity: "And treat them kindly" (Quran 4:19 as quoted by Maudoodi, 2000: p.10). Note this also applies in the case of divorce where the man has absolutely no excuse not to behave with kindness and civility towards the woman. Thus Allah (SWT) explicitly enjoins: "Divorce can be pronounced twice: then, either honourable retention or kind release should follow"

(Quran 2:229). Divorce is examined subsequently in a later part of this chapter.

4. Being allowed to grow Islamically in partnership with her husband and being encouraged by him to observe her religious duties. If previous to the marriage the wife has not been too committed to observing her devotional duties then the husband should provide her with the necessary impetus to develop this inclination at her own pace, including conveying whatever religious knowledge he has to her with humility, compassion and understanding. The husband should also be keen on visiting other channels within the community through which she may acquire the necessary religious instruction. On one occasion the Prophet (PBUH) allowed a marriage to go ahead where the man's economic circumstances were so severely straitened that at first glance it appeared he would not be in a position to afford his wife-to-be a mahr. The Prophet (PBUH) ruled that the religious knowledge, which the man could impart to his wife, would act as her mahr and so allowed the marriage to ensue on that basis (Bukhari). Such then is the importance of affording the wife an ambience that will allow her to develop Islamically and undertake her religious duties: "Whoever obeys Allah and His Messenger has achieved a great triumph" (Quran 33:71).

5. The husband protecting her person and ensuring that her dignity, respect and integrity are in no way compromised (Al-Omar, 1999).

6. Being treated equitably by her husband if she is part of a polygamous marriage where the man has more than one wife (Maudoodi, 2000). *Polygamy*, which allows a Muslim man to have at maximum four

wives concurrently, is discussed briefly later in this chapter.

The husband's rights include:

1. Being regarded by the wife as the leader of the household as Allah (SWT) has assigned the husband the role of the wife's *qawwam* or maintainer: "Men are the protectors and maintainers of women because Allah has made one of them excel over the other, and because they spend out of their possessions [to support them]" (Quran 4:34). A *qawwam* role effectively renders the husband the wife's supervisor and in turn the supervisor of the family should they have children and notably is a position of leadership and authority designated to the husband by Allah's command. It is a position of leadership that the husband should discharge respectfully, kindly, courteously and politely in relation to his wife and family.

2. Being obeyed by the wife in light of the fact that Allah (SWT) has assigned the husband the role of the leader of the household or the *qawwam*: "Thus righteous women are obedient and guard the rights of men in their absence under Allah's protection" (Quran 4:34). However, such obedience should only be exercised by the wife if the husband makes requests of her that are halal in nature otherwise the wife should flatly refuse without reservation to accede to the request since a husband cannot compel his wife to discharge requests that represent a violation of Allah's commandments (Maudoodi, 2000). Furthermore the husband when making requests of his wife should do so with sensitivity,

politeness, civility and kindness and not with arrogance and in a disrespectful manner: "And treat them kindly" (Quran 4:19 as quoted by Maudoodi, 2000: p.10). Moreover, a wife cannot engage in the act of voluntary fasting unless she seeks leave from her husband first though obviously this condition does not apply to the period of compulsory fasting observed during Ramadan. Thus it is in relation to voluntary fasting that the Prophet (PBUH) said: "No woman should fast while her husband is present except without his leave" (Al-Omar, 1999: pp.18-19). Similarly the wife should seek leave from her husband in terms of ascertaining who is allowed to enter the house when she is not sure whether her husband would be receptive to that person or those persons entering their house. In this regard the Prophet (PBUH) stated: "No woman should allow anyone in his house while he is present except with his leave" (Al-Omar, 1999: p.19).

3. Expecting his wife to manage the household in line with custom and to serve his needs provided those needs are halal. The husband should seek to cooperate with his wife as much as possible in contributing to managing the household as this helps to foster a spirit of progressive partnership and mutual goodwill between the two spouses but the overall responsibility for the management of the household still resides with the wife: she has executive jurisdiction over this domain! Any cooperation proffered by the husband in this regard should be coordinated through the wife with her approval. Any help offered with managing the household should be appreciated by the wife, which male readers should note is invariably the case!

4. Expecting his wife to be fiercely vigilant in his absence in relation to safeguarding his honour, property, wealth and children and the moral climate of the household, which are reposed by the husband in his wife as a trust for her to protect (Al-Omar, 1999; Maudoodi, 2000): "Thus righteous women are obedient and guard the rights of men in their absence under Allah's protection" (Quran 4:34).

5. Being allowed to discipline his wife in accordance with the Shariah should she be fiercely disobedient and show sustained unreasonable defiance in allowing the husband to exercise his legitimate Islamic rights as her spouse (Al-Omar, 1999; Maudoodi, 2000): "As for women of whom you fear rebellion, admonish them, and remain apart from them in beds, and chastise them. Then if they obey you, do not seek ways to harm them" (Quran 4:34). The right to discipline his wife does not give the husband the right to violate his wife by meting out vile treatment. It does not give the husband a licence to subjugate his wife to unbridled harm, which is conduct unbecoming and plainly inhumane; should such misdemeanours on the part of the husband be committed these would rightly give the aggrieved wife every right to obtain a khula (Maudoodi, 2000). The disciplinary measure applied by the husband should according to the Shariah reflect the degree of unreasonable defiance shown by the wife and should only be applied if the husband genuinely believes it can help to salvage the marriage tie but should not fall outside the limits prescribed by the Shariah, which crucially demarcates between discipline and oppression, the latter being totally unacceptable. Ideally, the husband should seek to respectfully

counsel his wife through benevolent reasoning and gentle persuasion, which is the option that the Prophet (PBUH) strongly encouraged.

We now touch on the mutual rights shared by the husband and wife, which include:

1. Keeping a very strict vigil on maintaining each other's confidentiality, advising each other constructively, consulting with one another regarding household and family matters and treating each other with the utmost love, dignity, kindness and fairness (Al-Omar, 1999). These mutual behaviours clearly lend favourably to building the trust between the husband and wife that is essential for fostering a harmonious marriage. For example, if we look at just the first of these mutual behaviours, it goes without saying that breaching your spouse's confidentiality will inevitably breed mistrust between husband and wife, which can undermine the whole trust basis on which a marriage is pillared in the first place. Allah (SWT) reminds a couple of their duty to guard each other's secrets and confidentiality strictly when He comments: "The Prophet confided something to one of his wives [Hafsah] and then she disclosed it [to another i.e. Aisha]; so after Allah revealed to the Prophet [that Hafsah had disclosed that secret], he made a part of it known to her and passed over a part of it. And when he told her about this [i.e., that she had disclosed the secret entrusted to her], she asked: 'Who informed you of this?' He said: 'I was told of it by He Who is All-Knowing, All-Aware'" (Quran 66:3). Negligence in guarding your other half's confidentiality is frowned upon by Allah (SWT)!

93

This can also be inferred from the Prophet (PBUH) when he said: "The man who will be the most wretched in status, in the Eyes of Allah on the Day of Judgment, will be the husband who confides in his wife and she in him, and then he goes and reveals her secret" (Al-Omar, 1999: p.25).

2. Engaging in sexual relations with each other though sexual intercourse is expressly forbidden by Allah (SWT) when the wife is experiencing menstruation: "They ask you about menstruation. Say: 'It is a state of impurity; so keep away from women in the state of menstruation, and do not approach them until they are cleansed. And when they are cleansed then come to them as Allah has commanded you.' Truly, Allah loves those who abstain from evil and keep themselves pure" (Quran 2:222).

3. Parenthood of children conceived through the marriage (Al-Omar, 1999; Maudoodi, 2000). The family is at the very heart of Muslim society. The Prophet (PBUH) encouraged couples to procreate in order to help perpetuate the Muslim community and moreover will derive enormous pride from "the number of followers he will have on the Day of Judgement" (Al-Omar, 1999: p.32). Whether in fact children are spawned by the marriage is entirely down to Allah's will (Al-Omar, 1999). This can be concluded when Allah (SWT) remarks: "The dominion of the heavens and the earth belongs to Allah. He creates whatever He pleases. He grants females to whomever He pleases and males to whomever He pleases, or grants them a mix of males and females, and causes whomever He pleases to be barren. He is All-Knowing, All-Powerful" (Quran 42:49-50). Divine predestination determines whether

a couple are blessed with any children or not and if they do have children how many and in what gender-mix.

4. Endeavouring to raise children in the right moral climate and endowing them with an understanding of Islam and the need to be God-fearing and righteous: "Your wives are your tilth; go, then, into your tilth as you wish but take heed of your ultimate future and avoid incurring the wrath of Allah. Know well that one Day you shall face Him. Announce good tidings to the believers" (Quran 2:223). Moral excellence should form the very foundation stone of the family: "And those who are prone to pray: 'Our Lord! Grant us that our spouses and our offspring be a joy to our eyes, and do make us the leaders of the God-fearing' " (Quran 25:74). Furthermore Allah (SWT) has promised enormous rewards in the Hereafter to couples who remain steadfast in terms of exercising their faith obligations and invoking this sense of faith in their children: "They and their spouses shall be reclining on their couches in shady groves" (Quran 36:56). Breeding the family with such piety attracts the boundless joys of Paradise: "Our Lord, admit them and those of their fathers and spouses and progeny that were righteous. Surely you alone are Most Mighty, Most Wise" (Quran 40:8).

5. Expressing endearing words of love towards each other and not shying away from doing so (Al-Omar, 1999). Such warmth can only help to draw the couple towards each other! A husband and wife should not be embarrassed to intimate through venturing warm and sensitive words that they love each other. The Prophet (PBUH) encouraged this practice as it clearly allows the two spouses to feel more comfortable and

relaxed in each other's presence and allows them to celebrate their life partner companionship with greater sensitivity and due care and consideration. Such expression can only help to fortify the love and compassion, which premise the compatibility that feeds the marriage bond. Marriages where the husband and wife become inarticulate to express warm words of mutual love and appreciation are essentially lifeless and conspicuously so! The Prophet (PBUH) encouraged the husband and wife to further enamour the marriage bond through greeting each other with a smile and kind words. Smiles after all are a manifestation of kindness and nothing is more reassuring than being greeted politely and with a sanguine countenance, both of which are examples of charity or *sadaqah* according to the Prophet (PBUH). Additionally giving gifts to each other also allows a husband and wife to endear the marriage bond further. It puts spice into the marriage! Gifts do not necessarily have to be given just on special occasions. The occasional gift at any other time can act as a real tonic for the marriage and whatever the occasion the gift should be selected with great care and sensitivity so that it is valued by your spouse and registers an eternal smile on their face. This is a practice that was also recommended by the Prophet (PBUH) since endowing your life partner with a gift requires you to legislate for their specific tastes and requires you to relate to them with the humblest and most loving of *Salaams* (Greetings) when handing over the gift. Salaams always lend favourably to strengthening the harmony intrinsic to a marriage. Thus it is that the Prophet (PBUH) elegantly remarked: "Offer gifts to one another and you will increase love for one another" (Al-Omar, 1999: p.44).

6. Honouring the marriage bond by acting kindly and gracefully towards each other and the husband in particular not being remiss of his wife enjoying similar rights in kindness: "Women have the same rights against their men as men have against them" (Quran 2:228). For example, if the husband expects his wife to look beautiful in terms of her appearance he should reciprocate his wife's wish for him to look presentable to her (Al-Omar, 1999)! Appearance without a doubt helps to strengthen the marriage bond and so both spouses should respect the other spouse's wish to look amenable to the eye. Kindness towards your spouse inevitably begets kindness in return and helps to maintain that lasting congeniality between husband and wife, which is absolutely vital for a healthy marriage: "Can the reward of goodness be any other than goodness?" (Quran 55:60).

7. Ensuring that they both continue to respect their own parents and act as a solid bridge to each other's family. It is absolutely essential in keeping with the spirit of the Quran that both the husband and wife make every effort to honour their own parents and their in-laws. In Islam marriage as we have already stated is not just a union of two individuals; it also serves as a bridge through which to connect two families thereby lending to the esprit de corps vital to sustaining the whole notion of the Ummah that should define the very pulse of the Muslim community. Parents should not be excluded from the modus operandi of a couple, which sadly in some cases they are. Whether the wife lives with her in-laws or not there is an onus on her to be kind and

97

endearing towards her in-laws as there is an obligation on the part of her husband to assign the utmost respect and sensitivity to his in-laws. Both husband and wife need to strike a sensible balance between their parents' rights and those of their spouse and family. The parents' rights must not be belittled as Allah (SWT) makes it expressly clear that in terms of companionship parents carry more rights over an individual than any one else: "Your Lord has decreed: (i) Do not worship any but Him; (ii) Be good to your parents; and should both or any one of them attain old age with you, do not say to them even 'fie' neither chide them, but speak to them with respect, and be humble and tender to them and say: 'Lord show mercy to them as they nurtured me when I was small' " (Quran 17:23-24). This, however, does not open the floodgates for interfering in-laws seeking to undermine the sovereignty of a marriage as a couple should seek to resolve their personal differences in line with the advice offered by the Shariah. Ideally the couple should not take their problems outside the home and should work in concert with each other to resolve them (Al-Omar, 1999). If, however, a serious rift is likely to occur between them where third party mediation may be conducive to addressing the problem then it is advisable for the couple to appoint a mediator from each of their respective families in an effort to iron out any differences and allow reconciliation to occur: "If you fear a breach between the two, appoint an arbitrator from his people and an arbitrator from her people. If they both want to set things right, Allah will bring about reconciliation between them. Allah is All-Knowing, All-Aware" (Quran 4:35). Such

98

arbitration, however, is mostly tenable in cases where the dispute between husband and wife does not revolve around exacting and complex legal issues and if anything shows the allowance the Shariah makes for resolving problems without having to resort to the courts, which in any event should only be visited as a last port of call (Maudoodi, 2000). The couple should not forget that the Prophet (PBUH) clarified that in terms of companionship a mother should be treated with the highest respect followed by the father. In fact when asked who should be assigned the highest respect the Prophet (PBUH) specifically said your mother, then your mother, then your mother and then your father (Bukhari and Muslim). A mother is assigned three times more respect than the father as she carried the child in her womb, experienced the pain of giving birth to that child and for the untold dedication she showed during the years of weaning the child. Thus in striking a balance between the rights of the spouse and the parents' rights neither husband nor wife should lose sight of the need to respect their own parents and should make every effort to assist their other half in making sure that this respect is not compromised otherwise as Allah (SWT) warns: "They shall suffer chastisement in the life of the world, and surely the chastisement of the Hereafter is even more grievous. None has the power to shield them from [the chastisement of] Allah" (Quran 13:34). Assigning reverence to your life partner's parents and family and observing respect for your own parents can only help to strengthen the marriage bond between husband and wife!

8. Respecting that there prevails a *mahram* relationship meaning someone that you cannot marry between the husband and his wife's mother, grandmothers, daughters and granddaughters and between the wife and her husband's father, grandfathers, sons and grandsons. Allah (SWT) makes clear to men: "Forbidden to you are your mothers, your daughters, your sisters, your father's sisters and your mother's sisters, your brother's daughters and your sister's daughters, your milk-mothers, your milk-sisters, the mothers of your wives, and the stepdaughters – who are your foster-children, born of your wives with whom you have consummated the marriage; but if you have not consummated the marriage with them, there will be no blame upon you [if you marry their daughters]. It is also forbidden for you to take the wives of the sons who have sprung from your loins and to take two sisters together in marriage, although what is past is past. Surely Allah is All-Forgiving, All-Compassionate" (Quran 4:23). There is no mahram relationship between the husband and his wife's sisters, aunts and nieces. Equally there is no mahram relationship between the wife and her husband's brothers, uncles and nephews. It is also instructive to note that in the case of polygamy a man cannot be married to two sisters at the same time. A man could, however, marry his wife's sister should his wife expire or should he divorce his wife first, that is the sister of the woman he wishes to marry.

9. Inheritance from the deceased spouse in accordance with distribution guidelines specified by Allah (SWT) in the Quran: "And to you belongs half of whatever has been left behind by your wives if they die childless; but if they have any children then to

you belongs a fourth of what they have left behind, after payment of the bequest they might have made or any debts outstanding against them. And to them belongs a fourth of what you leave behind, if you die childless; and if you have any child then to them belongs one eight of what you have left behind, after the payment of the bequest you might have made or any debts outstanding against you" (Quran 4:12). As we can see from this aayah, if the wife dies before the husband, the husband will receive an inheritance amounting to half of the wife's bequest if they have no children or one-quarter of the wife's bequest if the couple had children though the bequest can only be given to the husband once any debts owed by the deceased wife have been settled. If the husband dies before the wife, the wife will receive an inheritance amounting to one-quarter of the husband's bequest if they have no children or one-eight of the husband's bequest if the couple had children though the bequest can only be given to the wife once any debts owed by the deceased husband have been settled. Exactly the same shares would apply in the case of a deceased husband if he was part of a polygamous marriage in which case the wives would receive a total combined inheritance amounting to one-quarter of the husband's bequest if there are no children or one-eight of the husband's bequest if there are children though the bequest can only be shared equally among the wives once any debts owed by the deceased husband have been settled.

Polygamy

As we commented earlier in this chapter Islam permits a man to exercise polygamy, that is have more than one wife concurrently, but limits the number of wives a man can have legally at any one time to a maximum of four. The legal status ascribed to polygamy is majestically clarified by Allah (SWT) when He reveals: "If you fear that you might not treat the orphans justly, then marry the women that seem good to you: two, or three, or four. If you fear that you will not be able to treat them justly, then marry [only] one, or marry from among those whom your right hands possess. This will make it more likely that you will avoid injustice" (Quran 4:3). It is therefore clear that in exercising their right to polygamy Allah (SWT) strongly encourages men to marry orphans, that is women who are either orphans or widows with children, as a fundamental expression of noble humanitarianism on the part of men towards orphans provided that they (the orphans) are treated justly. If, however, a man cannot treat orphans justly then he may marry a widow who has no children or a divorcee or a spinster. The legal restriction placed by Allah (SWT) on the number of wives that a man may command at the same time is clearly four. Furthermore, as this Quranic verse insightfully reveals, it is important to grasp that Allah (SWT) only permits polygamy if the husband can treat each of his wives equitably otherwise polygamy is discouraged and a monogamous arrangement is recommended where the man has just the one wife. Treating wives with justice is central to a man being able to exercise polygamy. Men should not use polygamy as a convenient vehicle through which to justify their carnal desires! Even in the specific cases where the first wife may be infertile or chronically ill or mentally impaired she would still need to give her husband her consent of her own free will before he could practise polygamy!

While the Quran accepts that a man may not be able to show equality towards each wife emotionally it is, however, incumbent on that man to be able to show equality to each wife on the basis of "living expenses, social contact and sexual relations" (Maudoodi, 2000: p.22): "You will not be able to treat your wives with [absolute] justice not even if you keenly desire to do so. [It suffices in order to follow the Law of Allah that] you do not wholly incline to one, leaving the other in suspense. If you act rightly and remain God-fearing, surely Allah is All-Forgiving, All-Compassionate" (Quran 4:129). If such equality is not delivered then the man would be deemed not to be treating his wives equitably. Justice then would not be upheld equitably in relation to each of his wives as stipulated by Allah (SWT). In such cases a man should be compelled to practise monogamy in light of his failure to comply with Allah's insistence on treating each of his wives equitably! Therefore men engaged in polygamy need to take heed that Allah (SWT) is very exacting in that He commands men to behave equitably towards their wives otherwise monogamy is exhorted!

The Prophet (PBUH) had 12 wives in total, namely, Khadija, Sawdah, Aisha, Hafsah, Zaynab bint Khuzayamah, Umm Salamah, Juwayriyah, Zaynab bint Jahsh, Umm Habibah, Safiyyah, Maymunah and Maryam Qibityah, and practised polygamy after the death of his first wife, Khadija, to whom he remained married for twenty five years. In discharging polygamy the Prophet (PBUH) showed meticulous justice to each of his wives treating them with impeccable equality and therefore equitably. Of his 12 wives, one was a divorcee (Zaynab bint Jahsh), two were previously never married and

103

therefore virgin wives (Aisha and Maryam Qibityah) while nine of his wives had been widowed. The Prophet (PBUH) was the perfect embodiment of how a husband should treat his wives equitably in the case of polygamy!

In sum polygamy is a right granted to Muslim men by Allah (SWT), which can only be practised subject to a man being able to treat each of his wives equitably. If this condition cannot be obliged then polygamy is discouraged and the man should practise monogamy only. Given the typically polygamous psychological disposition associated with the male gender vis-à-vis the invariably monogamous psychology inherent to the female gender Allah (SWT) strikes a perfect balance between these two conflicting gender psyches by allowing the man to exercise polygamy under specific circumstances subject to his ability to treat each wife equitably otherwise monogamy is the preferred option!

Widows Seeking Remarriage

We now clarify the waiting period following the death of her husband or *iddah* that has to be observed by a widow before she can contemplate remarriage. During this period remarriage for a widow is prohibited. A widow may remarry as soon as she has observed the *iddah*. Islam encourages widows to remarry and every effort should be made by the Muslim community to assist widows to find a way forward on this front. Remarriage should not be frowned upon, as it sadly is in some quarters. Widows have as much a right to seek a life partner and embrace marriage as do divorcees or women who have never been married. At Kamran A. Beg Events we have been honoured enough to see a number of

Muslim professional females who had been widowed find their other half and so complete half of their faith. To discourage a widow from remarriage is scandalous; sadly we still have a section of the Muslim community, which discourages both widows and divorcees from revisiting matrimonial bliss and seeks to alienate them from the notion of remarriage as if to suggest that remarriage is shameful, which it is absolutely not. Islam celebrates the rights of widows (and divorcees) to remarry and every effort should be made by the Muslim community to expedite and facilitate remarriage! All women, whatever their marital status, are entitled to the physical, emotional and economic stability afforded by the sacred institution of marriage and above all have a right to secure half of their faith through this solemn covenant or mithaaq.

The waiting period or iddah in the case of a non-pregnant widow, that is a widow who was not pregnant at the time her husband expired, is four months and ten days as commanded by Allah (SWT) irrespective of whether the marriage had been consummated or not: "The wives of men who have died must observe a waiting period of four months and ten days; when they have reached the end of the waiting term, there is no blame upon you regarding what they may do with themselves in a fair manner. Allah is well aware of what you do" (Quran 2:234). The iddah has been fixed at this length of time so as to allow the grieving widow enough time to bereave the death of her husband before she can contemplate remarriage in a clear and objective light and take a more informed decision regarding whom to marry rather than making a hasty decision, which she might rue later.

The iddah for a pregnant widow ends as soon she gives birth and is not capped at four months and ten days as in the case

105

of a pregnant widow. As Ibn Majah narrates on one occasion a woman visited the Prophet (PBUH) seeking to clarify the iddah for a pregnant widow. She was not sure when it would be halal for her to contemplate remarriage so quickly as she had given birth to the child twenty five days following her husband's demise. The woman was under the impression that she would still need to observe the iddah applying to a non-pregnant widow. The Prophet (PBUH) explained that the iddah for a pregnant widow is different to that observed by a non-pregnant widow and that in the case of the former remarriage can be contemplated as soon as the child has been born even if the interval of time that has elapsed between the husband's death and the child's birth is less than four months and ten days. The Prophet (PBUH) recommended that widows consider remarriage as quickly as possible once they have seen through their respective iddah.

Allah (SWT) further clarifies that while it is acceptable for a prospective suitor to hint marriage to a widow during her iddah what is not halal is for the suitor to forward a khitbah or formal marriage proposal for her hand-in-marriage during the iddah or to venture a promise that he will marry her while she is still mourning the death of her husband during her iddah: "There is no blame upon you whether you hint at a marriage proposal to such women or keep the proposal hidden in your hearts. Allah knows that you will think of them in that connection. But do not make any secret engagement with them and speak openly in an honourable manner. Do not resolve on the marriage tie until the ordained term has come to its end. Know well that Allah knows even what is in your hearts. So, have fear of Him and know well that Allah is All-Forgiving, All-Forbearing" (Quran 2:235).

Divorce or Khula to be Deployed as Legal Remedies in the Last Resort

As we discussed before *divorce*, technically according to the Shariah, is the right that the husband has to demand separation from the wife in the case of irreconcilable differences while *khula*, technically according to the Shariah, is the right the wife has to demand separation from the husband in the case of irreconcilable differences. Divorce or khula should only be resorted to as a final recourse after all possible avenues of reconciliation have been exhausted. If the husband and wife have truly exhausted all possible ways in which to resuscitate and rescue the marriage bond then divorce or khula is the legal remedy but only as a last resort. Divorce or khula should not be deployed as a convenience through which to pursue an insatiable sexual lust but only as a lawful remedy where the husband and wife have made every effort to save the marriage bond but cannot revive it despite their genuine resolve to preserve it.

The Prophet (PBUH) was emphatic that divorce and khula should not be treated casually and stated: "Allah does not like sex-hungry men and sex-hungry women. Allah's curse falls on the sex-hungry man who is prone to divorce women. A woman who obtains a separation from her husband without any misbehaviour on his part, stands cursed by Allah, by the angels and by humanity. Women who make khula a play thing are hypocrites" (Maudoodi, 2000: p.34). Moving from one marriage partner to the next solely to appease one's libido is absolutely abhorred and viewed as a moral outrage. Thus it is that Allah (SWT) says: "Live with your wives gracefully. If you dislike them in any manner, it may be that you dislike something in which Allah has placed much good for you" (Quran 4:19). To reiterate: the marriage tie should only be dissolved after every genuine attempt has been made to resurrect the marriage and not because one houses an uncontrollable libido prone to causing one to change spouses like we change our socks!

The Formalities of Divorce and Subsequently Seeking Remarriage

When a man divorces his wife he cannot claim back the mahr that was given to her whereas when a woman petitions for a khula she is required to surrender the mahr to her husband either in whole or in some part thereof depending on what she and her husband have agreed to: "[While dissolving the marriage tie] it is unlawful for you to take back anything of what you have given to your wives unless both fear that they may not be able to keep within the bounds set by Allah. Then, if they fear that they might not be able to keep within the bounds set by Allah, there is no blame upon them for what the wife might give away of her property to become released from the marriage tie" (Quran 2:229).

The waiting period or iddah for a woman who has been divorced is measured from the time the divorce is first pronounced and is three months in duration, which is the time attributed to three menstrual discharges: "Divorced women shall keep themselves in waiting for three menstrual courses and it is unlawful for them, if they believe in Allah and the Last Day, to hide whatever Allah might have created in their wombs. Should their husbands desire reconciliation during this time they are entitled to take them back into wedlock" (Quran 2:228). The iddah allows sufficient time for reconciliation between the two spouses, which is why the woman should not be sent away from the family home during the waiting period as Allah (SWT) clearly advises: "O Prophet, when you divorce women, divorce them for their waiting period, and compute the waiting period accurately, and hold, Allah, your Lord, in awe. Do not turn them out of their homes [during the waiting period] - nor should they go away [from their homes] – unless they have committed a manifestly evil deed. Such are the bounds set by Allah; and he who transgresses the bounds set by Allah commits a wrong against himself. You do not know: maybe Allah will cause something to happen to pave the way [for reconciliation]" (Quran 65:1).

Moreover divorce should not be pronounced more than twice if it is to be revocable so that remarriage is permissible should the husband and wife opt to remarry once the iddah has expired: "Divorce can be pronounced twice: then, either honourable retention or kind release should follow" (Quran 2:229). In any event with the waiting period being three months each divorce should be punctuated by one period of menstrual discharge though the first divorce must be pronounced when the wife is in a state of purity and not during the course of her menstrual period (Maudoodi, 2000). If the husband and wife have not reconciled their differences by the end of the first period of menstrual discharge the second divorce could be pronounced at the beginning of the second period of menstrual discharge. Then it is judicious in keeping with Allah's advice (Quran 2:229) to allow the third period of menstrual discharge to elapse without pronouncing the third divorce since this gives leeway to the possibility of revoking the divorce. The iddah affords the couple adequate time to pave the path for reconciliation otherwise if the couple still cannot pull on the marriage tie should be dissolved and the man and woman should part company on

109

amicable terms eligible to partake in marriage with someone else.

If divorce is pronounced three times then the marriage bond becomes permanently dissolved and the man cannot remarry that woman again, not until she has married another man with a view to entering into a permanent marriage with her new husband, that marriage has been consummated and then ends in divorce as a consequence of her new husband insisting on divorce for genuine reasons (Maudoodi, 2000). A divorce is revocable provided it is pronounced at maximum two times. The point to underscore is that if divorce is pronounced three times then that divorce becomes irrevocable and remarriage with the same woman would only be permissible subject to the condition described: "Then, if he divorces her [for the third time, after having pronounced the divorce twice] she shall not be lawful to him unless she first takes another man for a husband, and he divorces her. There is no blame upon them if both of them return to one another thereafter, provided they think that they will be able to keep within the bounds set by Allah. These are the bounds of Allah which He makes clear to a people who have knowledge [of the consequences of violating those bounds]" (Quran 2:230). To circumvent this condition some men seek to usurp Allah's condition for entering into remarriage with the same woman after she has been irrevocably divorced by pursuing the unlawful practice of *tahleel* where the husband arranges for the woman he has divorced irrevocably to enter into a sham marriage with another man who is paid a fee for agreeing to divorce the woman in question without consummating the marriage and therefore engaging in conjugal relations with her. Tahleel, which is a form of temporary marriage since permanence is not intended between the woman and her new husband, is unlawful, vile and totally repudiated by Islam.

The concurrent pronouncement of three divorces, which still sadly afflicts parts of the Muslim community, is irrefutably a cardinal sin! This was explained by the Prophet (PBUH) who described it as an unlawful practice as it flagrantly violates Allah's limits as highlighted above (Quran 65:1) showing absolutely no deference to the Divinely-ordained waiting period that allows for the possibility of reconciliation (Maudoodi, 2000). Pronouncing three divorces in one fell swoop shows complete disregard for the sacred eminence of marriage, completely ignores the need for an iddah to be observed and eliminates any and every possibility for reconciliation! Such pronouncement has no lawful foundation in Islam and is tantamount to a transgression of Allah's Law.

Allah (SWT) in His infinite majesty commands: "And so, when you divorce women and they reach the end of their waiting term, then either retain them in a fair manner or let them go in a fair manner" (Quran 2:231). In other words if reconciliation between the two spouses is untenable at the end of the waiting period the marriage bond should be dissolved and the man and woman should part company amicably. Furthermore the divorced woman should be given every encouragement to remarry should she wish to revisit half of her faith again through entertaining marriage with another man: "When you divorce women and they have completed their waiting term do not hinder them from marrying other men if they have agreed to this in a fair manner. That is an admonition to everyone of you who believes in Allah and the Last Day; that is a cleaner and purer way for you. For Allah knows whereas you do not know" (Quran 2:232).

Also, when the iddah expires it is essential for the couple to invite two individuals of upstanding character to bear witness to the divorce, that is the dissolving of the marriage bond, or to the revocation of the divorce should reconciliation between husband and wife prevail: "And when they reach the end of their term [of waiting], then either honourably retain them [in the bond of wedlock] or honourably part with them, and call two persons of known probity as witnesses from among yourselves, and [let these witnesses] give upright testimony for the sake of Allah" (Quran 65:2). If two witnesses do not bear testimony to the divorce or its revocation this would clearly symbolise a violation of this instruction but even so the divorce or its revocation would still stand as all Islamic jurists agree.

Allah (SWT) warns men against retaining the marriage bond when they clearly harbour no intention to pull on with the wife and do justice to her and the marriage and do not dissolve the marital tie only to cause her torment, misery, injury and oppression (Maudoodi, 2000). Such behaviours are expressly forbidden and despised by Allah (SWT): "And do not retain them to their hurt or by way of transgression; whosoever will do that will indeed wrong himself. Do not take the Signs of Allah in jest and remember Allah's favour upon you" (Quran 2:231). For example, some – though a very small minority of - men have an inveterate disposition for restoring the marital tie after two pronouncements of divorce with no real intention of accommodating harmonious marital relations with their wife but merely retain the marriage bond to oppress that wife and dehumanise her further through the manifestation of various unpalatable and inhuman behaviours. Such pronouncements followed by restoring the marriage tie are repeated on an ongoing basis in order to torture the woman and to prevent her from contracting marriage with another man. This is why Allah (SWT) clearly commands the marriage tie to be dissolved if the man after pronouncing two revocable divorces has no sincere intention to foster a harmonious marriage with his wife (Quran 2:229 and Quran 2:231).

If the husband abstains from sexual relations with his wife there is an absolute onus on him to restore conjugal relations with her within a four-month time limit if the marriage bond is to remain intact: "For those who vow abstinence from their wives there is a respite of four months. Then, if they go back on their vow they will find that Allah is All-Forgiving, All-Compassionate" (Quran 2:226). If, however, sexual relations are not revived within this time limit the marriage must end in divorce, which applies to all scenarios where sexual relations are withheld intentionally including the one where the husband deliberately sets out to torture his wife by way of withholding conjugal relations: "And if they resolve on divorce, surely Allah is All-Hearing, All-Knowing" (Quran 2:227).

The Formalities of Khula and Subsequently Seeking Remarriage

Khula is the right the wife has to sever the marriage tie in the case of irreconcilable differences with her husband. We provided two specific examples of khula earlier in this chapter regarding Jamilah and Habibah and how they both obtained a khula from Thabit bin Qais. If the husband has the right to dissolve the marriage tie through divorcing his wife

113

this right has to be counterpoised by the wife's right to dissolve the marriage bond through seeking a khula. Such is the discernible nature of the equality conferred upon both spouses by Islam! A woman's right to obtain a khula can be inferred directly when Allah (SWT) remarks: "[While dissolving the marriage tie] it is unlawful for you to take back anything of what you have given to your wives unless both fear that they may not be able to keep within the bounds set by Allah. Then, if they fear that they might not be able to keep within the bounds set by Allah, there is no blame upon them for what the wife might give away of her property to become released from the marriage tie" (Quran 2:229). The key always is to preserve Allah's limits or "bounds" of morality and chastity, which must never be compromised. Therefore a woman has as much a right to dissolve the marriage bond through khula as a man does through divorce in deference to safeguarding these limits and making sure that they are not transgressed. However, when a woman seeks khula she is required to return the mahr her husband had gifted to her in full or part, subject to what she and her husband agree to. The Prophet (PBUH) recognising that the Quran does not place a cap on the compensation that a woman is required to give her husband in the case of khula advised that this compensation should not exceed the mahr gifted to her by the husband and said: "The man granting khula should not take from the woman more than what he gave her" (Maudoodi, 2000: p.41).

But how does a woman exercising her right to khula know that she has obtained a legally sound khula from her husband? Giving the man compensation, which they have agreed on, is part of the requirement integral to seeking a khula; the other part is that the man must accommodate her request for separation by actually divorcing her. A khula can only be obtained by the woman when the man has both accepted compensation from her and proceeded to divorce her. Only then is the woman who has obtained a khula free to contract marriage with another man. Recourse to the courts is only necessary if the man refuses to accede to the woman's request for ending the marriage and in such cases a court decree can be obtained sanctioning the khula.

The Prophet (PBUH) stressed that khula translates into the equivalent of an irrevocable divorce (Maudoodi, 2000). This effectively means that if the woman should ever wish to remarry the man she has obtained a khula from she must first marry another man with the intention of permanence inspiring their marriage, have conjugal relations with him and he (the new husband) must divorce her for genuine reasons, and only then would she be free to contract marriage with the man she had originally obtained a khula from. Khula, like divorce, should not be treated lightly, and should always be pursued as a last resort after all possible means of reconciliation between the couple have been explored and exhausted!

The Dissolution of Marriage in the Light of Apostasy

It is imperative to note that if either the husband or wife becomes an apostate or *murtadd*, that is leaves the fold of Islam, then that marriage is automatically dissolved and becomes null and void as a Muslim cannot remain married to a spouse who has succumbed to apostasy. Furthermore neither a Muslim man nor a Muslim woman may marry an apostate! This can be deduced directly when Allah (SWT) warns: "You shall not find a people who believe in Allah and the Last Day befriending those who oppose Allah and His

115

Messenger" (Quran 58:22). To reiterate: a Muslim in subservience to the Law of Allah (SWT) may not contract marriage with an apostate.

In May 2006, Kamran A. Beg Events was contacted by a 35 year-old Muslim female lawyer based in London who wished to contract marriage with a 37 year-old male journalist from New York who had committed apostasy and left the pale of Islam. The lawyer wished to justify the proposed marriage. We explained that the marriage could not go ahead on two grounds. Firstly, the man was a non-Muslim and a Muslim woman may not marry a non-Muslim. Secondly, a Muslim woman (like a Muslim man) cannot marry an apostate. The lawyer claimed to be ignorant of the actual Islamic position regarding her scenario and immediately clarified to the journalist that she would not be able to pursue marriage with him in deference to the Divine requirements placed on her by the Muslim faith, which the reader will be pleased to learn she has fully respected since we counselled her on the issue.

The Igloo Test and the Stress it Places on the Need to Ensure that the Family Values of the Couple are Compatible

As we shall see in chapter 2, 81% of the divorcee Muslim professionals who have accessed services provided by Kamran A. Beg Events have confirmed that the primary motivation behind their divorce stemmed from their family values and those of their then spouse being markedly at variance. This is precisely what the Prophet (PBUH) warned against when he underscored the need for family compatibility and not just individual compatibility in order to assess the viability of a marriage and to mitigate the

116

probability of divorce. This leads to another very interesting observation that we at Kamran A. Beg Events have made based on extensive research. We now elaborate on The Igloo Test, an analogy that the humble writer has developed in order to comprehend better whether there is any significant correlation between a couple living with the man's parents in the same residence, that is the wife living with her in-laws, and the likelihood of divorce. It is important that we cross this bridge at this juncture as I know from having dealt with many Muslim female enquirers worldwide that often for them a worrying feature is whether they may be expected to live with their in-laws and their concern that the portend of interfering in-laws may well jeopardise the ability of the proposed marriage to survive.

There is no correlation between a wife living with her in-laws and divorce. There is however a significant correlation between the spouses being the products of two different family value systems and divorce since as we have already noted an individual in large measure is a personification of their family value system. Assume we have a Muslim man and Muslim woman who have tied the knot and in doing so have along with their families ignored the need to assess whether their family temperaments are indeed congruous in large measure. Based on the Prophet's exhortation we immediately note that the alarm bells will start ringing if the couple have two essentially different sets of family values as represented by their actual families. Let us assume we isolate the couple and they live away from their in-laws in a separate residence. In order to eliminate the worry that the wife may be harbouring regarding the frightening prospect of the interfering in-law assume we isolate the couple totally and place them in an igloo composed of the world's most fortified ice and situated somewhere in the North Pole. We now have a situation where neither the husband nor wife could plead that their in-laws have put their marriage into peril by seeking to undermine the sovereignty of either spouse. We naturally suppose that the in-laws have not suddenly decided to migrate to the North Pole and set up shop in either the same igloo or a neighbouring igloo!

If the husband and wife stem from two families with very different family values The Igloo Test shows that no matter how hard they try to pull on the couple may find it increasingly different to reconcile their differences as the values they execute as individuals are largely reflective of their respective family values, which they in significant measure personify. This chasm between their family temperaments will eventually surface in their individual personalities and begin to adversely impact their marriage bond. It will place strains on the marriage. Note neither the man nor woman can use the convenient excuse that their in-laws are responsible for the fractures that start to surface in their marriage. You cannot be any more isolated from your wonderful in-laws than being a resident of a beautiful igloo situated in the breathtaking and humbling expanse of the North Pole! The igloo in which the couple had set up home will invariably melt, at least figuratively speaking, under the unfathomable tension of the differences that flow between the two personalities being at variance with each other in terms of the values, mores and norms they can relate to, which are influenced mainly by the families in which they were nurtured. And remember this was no ordinary igloo. On the contrary the igloo that housed the couple was made of the world's most fortified ice, a modern acropolis that could not take the heat of the friction resulting between the husband and wife as their temperaments could not meld with each other on account of their basic values being significantly divergent. The Igloo Test categorically shows that it is not the presence of a woman's in-laws in the same home that should be her main concern. The primary variable that can make or break a marriage is the degree to which the family values of the two spouses converge or diverge. This follows logically from the Prophet's advice, which so brilliantly signalled that no matter how compatible the man and woman may appear on the surface if their family values are markedly at variance it is advisable for the proposed marriage not to succeed. Therefore there is an onus on the man and woman seeking marriage with each other and their respective families to wrestle with how congruous their family values are before deciding on the merits of that marriage. As we stated earlier, in Islam marriage, which is that most sacred covenant that allows you to complete half of your faith, is a marriage not just of two individuals but also of two families!

The Igloo Test certainly provides a thought-provoking analogy. In sum, The Igloo Test states that it is the not the wife's in-laws as such and their living with the couple that put intractable strains on the marriage and increase the likelihood of that marriage bond being severed bur rather it is a marked variance between the family values of the husband and wife, which inhibits the ability of their marriage to succeed and increases the likelihood of the marriage bond being dissolved. The Igloo Test is consistent with the Prophet's wise advice.

We note that of the 100 marriages Kamran A. Beg Events has been responsible for initiating so far in the case of 70 of these marriages the Muslim professional females who proceeded to marriage are currently living under the same roof as their in-laws and in no way has their marital harmony with their husband been impaired as a consequence since in each of these cases both the man and woman and their families were careful to identify significant convergence between their respective family values before the marriage was sanctioned. This is not to say that it is not right not to live with the in-laws. What The Igloo Test shows is that it is family values that make the individual that determine the likelihood that the marriage may succeed or not depending on the degree of overlap between the two families in terms of their basic values and not whether the husband insists on his parents residing with the couple. In fact the feedback from the females above has been very favourable in terms of how accommodating their in-laws have been to them and how welcomed they have been made to feel by their in-laws. So remember it is not in-laws who are the primary cause of matrimonial discord: it is the degree to which the family values of the two spouses overlap and resonate, which exercises a first order effect on the ability of that marriage to survive or not. Furthermore the fear of living with her in-laws should not cause the wife undue anguish; the fear of the family values of the wife and her husband not being similar in large enough degree should be the primary source of concern as this can make or break a marriage as we have seen on the basis of the sentiments expressed by 81% of the divorcees who have sought services from Kamran A. Beg Events. Next time you ask for an extra ice cube when consuming that ultimate mango milkshake spare a thought for The Igloo Test!

The Need for a Robust Halal Marriage-inspired Dialogue Framework Tempered with Balance and Moderation

In this chapter we have elaborated on the sacred importance of marriage in Islam providing the reader with a primer on the basic religious principles underpinning this most sacred union, which allows husband and wife to negotiate half of their faith. It is essential for any Muslim embarking on this most challenging and testing of journeys to find their other half to develop a solid appreciation of the religious foundations that inform marriage in the Muslim faith. Only by fully relating to the overarching need to complete half of your faith through seeking marriage can one engender and sustain the unfailing sense of urgency needed to complete an odyssey that will eventually expose you to a life partner who had been predestined for you in accordance with the will of Allah (SWT).

An untiring desire to find this seemingly all-elusive soulmate encompasses a voyage of self-discovery since discovering your other half allows you to complete half of your faith and therefore by extension enables you to totalise your faith. In sum without fathoming with resolute conviction the spiritual parameters, which circumscribe the vitality of marriage in the Muslim community, that voyage of self-discovery simply cannot be put into the germane context. Ultimately finding your life partner amounts to a test of faith in Allah (SWT) and part of that test involves maintaining an unswerving resolve to discover your other half through reposing complete faith in Him. Being tested by Allah (SWT) is after all central to remaining subservient to His will and accepting His outcomes: "Do people think that they will be let go merely by saying: 'We believe', and that they will not be tested, and for We indeed tested those who went before them. Allah will most certainly ascertain those who spoke the truth and those who lied" (Quran 29:2-3).

Having expounded on the sacred importance of marriage in Islam in chapter 1 we now turn our attention to proposing a robust halal marriage-inspired dialogue framework that should be adopted by a Muslim male and Muslim female when exploring the life-changing and faith-completing question of marriage. The framework we propose is called the **3-Dialogue Rule**, which we note is predicated on the definitive tenets of **balance** and **moderation** that permeate every aspect of the Islamic faith. The 3-Dialogue Rule can be applied equally to family based and non-family based introductions.

While chapter 2 engages the reader in the nine basic attributes that should comprise a robust halal marriage-inspired dialogue framework chapter 3 elaborates on the **3-Dialogue Rule** itself, which is the specific robust halal marriage-inspired dialogue framework developed by Kamran A. Beg Events that has guided many of the 100 Muslim professional couples who have achieved marriage through Kamran A. Beg Events so far, subject of course to the Divine will, since the organisation came into being on July 11, 2003. We strongly recommend that the Muslim male and Muslim female party to a marriage-inspired dialogue conform to the spirit and essence of the **3-Dialogue Rule**, which has built up an outstanding track record worldwide as we shall see. Chapter 4 shows that the 3-Dialogue Rule works very well in practice and we substantiate this through specific examples.

2. The Essential Features Integral to a Robust Halal Marriage-inspired Dialogue Framework

Since founding Kamran A. Beg Events on July 11, 2003, I have been contacted by several thousand Muslim professionals worldwide and their parents enquiring what halal dialogue framework should be adopted with another Muslim for the express purpose of marriage-inspired dialogue, such that the basic Muslim value system is upheld and in no way compromised, but which at the same time provides the male and female locked in dialogue with ample opportunity and leverage to establish whether there prevails a sufficient degree of mileage between the two individuals to facilitate their parent(s)/guardian(s) becoming directly engaged in the dialogue process. Muslim females who have contacted me have voiced in particular their grave and understandable concerns regarding their profound fear that they could be exposed to the perdition emanating from falling victim to a "self-perpetuating dating culture", which appears to have penetrated the very heart of the Muslim professional community, while honourable and upstanding Muslim males who have been in contact with Kamran A. Beg Events have also stressed their seminal concern not to undermine the integrity and dignity of a Muslim female when exploring marriage with her as each and every female is a "much respected and highly valued daughter of the Muslim community".

The Ugly Menace of Dating in the Muslim Professional Community Exposed Through Research Conducted by Kamran A. Beg Events

Dating sadly and undeniably exists in the Muslim community! That is a fact and not heresay as our research demonstrates though admittedly all of the research undertaken by Kamran A. Beg Events specifically concerns Muslim professionals as we service this group directly through our matrimonial services.

As we spelt out in the introduction to this book by 'Muslim professional' we mean a Muslim who is typically university educated and is either employed by an employer or self-employed. This is the definition of 'Muslim professional' that underpins the various research studies conducted by Kamran A. Beg Events and profiled in this book. 98% of the Muslim professional attendees, subscribers and members accommodated by Kamran A. Beg Events hold at least one university degree. Professionals are represented from a diverse spectrum of fields, including, amongst others, medicine, dentistry, nursing, law, accounting, journalism, the media sector, consultancy, IT, marketing, engineering, science, and banking, not to mention individuals running their own enterprises and businesses.

It is deeply saddening and perturbing that Muslim professionals are dating and are involved in pre-marital relationships with each other and with brethren drawn from other faith traditions. As we have stressed in chapter 1, dating and having a relationship out of wedlock are both Islamically prohibited and not halal: put plainly they are not Islamically tenable modes of conduct and are therefore classified as haram. Those Muslim professionals who have fallen victim to the heinous consequences of dating and having a pre-marital relationship have discovered, as our research clearly evidences, that these behaviours do not expedite the journey of the incumbent to the wedding altar but rather seriously impair one's desire to experience matrimony within the fold of the Muslim community. Furthermore, while some Muslim professionals may have jumped onto the dating bandwagon feeling that it is "fashionable" to date, I wish to make it perfectly clear that I and my humble organisation stand tooth and nail against the whole concept of Muslims dating and having a relationship before marriage, practices which have no place in the Muslim faith, are alien to Islam and which will never be accepted by the Muslim community enterprise in deference to the very halal sanctity that Islam requires Muslims to calibrate male-female interaction with. This is a message that we have tirelessly communicated to all of our Muslim attendees, subscribers and members worldwide. Whilst we as professionals would like to sit comfortably at the interface between the traditional values so germane to the very pulse of Islam and the values of modernity consistent with the basic principles of Islam, that, however, does not give Muslim professionals carte blanche or a licence to undermine the basic tenets of our faith, which is driven by the forces of balance and moderation. Islamically, dating and having a pre-marital relationship are absolutely prohibited and there are no two ways about that!

In making this observation the writer wishes to stress that he is referring specifically to the Muslim community and to the irrefutable fact that the notion of dating and the concept of having a pre-marital relationship are abhorred by Islam and have no legitimate place whatsoever within Muslim society. To clarify as we did in the introduction to this book in no way is any comment being made on the practices, values, mores and norms of non-Muslim communities, which view dating and partaking in pre-marital relationships as socially palatable. As Allah (SWT) impresses upon Muslims: "There is no compulsion in religion" (Quran 2:256). Thus as Muslims we fully accept that our values cannot be disseminated to others by compulsion nor must they ever be forced upon others. However, from an Islamic perspective dating and surrendering to pre-marital relationships are strictly prohibited and considered to be haram!

In developing a suitable marriage-inspired framework for dialogue between a Muslim man and a Muslim woman it is absolutely indispensable therefore that the framework seeks to eliminate the possibility of the dialoguing parties falling victim to the ugly menace of dating. This is even more important especially in light of recent research conducted by Kamran A. Beg Events, which we presently discuss.

During the period March 2005 to March 2006, 500 Muslim professional singles were interviewed worldwide as part of a research project designed to establish the extent to which dating had impacted the Muslim professional community. The definition of 'Muslim professional' is as above and this definition has been consistently applied across any research conducted by Kamran A. Beg Events and therefore discussed within the scope of this book. *Being 'single' for the purposes of this research project and indeed any other research conducted by Kamran A. Beg Events and reported in this book can be construed as meaning 'never married' or 'divorced' or 'legally separated' or 'widowed'.* The sample comprised 250 females and 250 males with participants drawn from the UK, Ireland, France, Germany, Australia, the USA and Canada. These singles had been introduced to matrimonial dialogue prospects through both the conventional family channel and also through non-family conduits.

80% of all Muslim professional males interviewed confirmed that they had dated by age 30 and furthermore 70% acknowledged that they had engaged in some form of physical relationship with a female drawn from the Muslim faith by the same age. Moreover, 65% of the males interviewed indicated that they had dated and/or experienced a physical relationship with females drawn from other faiths. As for the female contingent interviewed the research is equally revealing. 78% of all Muslim professional females interviewed confirmed that they had dated by age 30 and furthermore 68% acknowledged that they had engaged in some form of physical relationship with a male drawn from the Muslim faith by the same age. Moreover, 50% of the females interviewed indicated that they had dated and/or experienced a physical relationship with males drawn from other faiths even though a Muslim female may only marry a member of the Muslim faith as we have discussed in chapter 1. What this groundbreaking research demonstrates is the very painful reality that dating and/or experiencing a pre-marital relationship are not as uncommon amongst Muslim professionals as conventional wisdom may once have suggested. In addition, dating and/or experiencing a pre-marital relationship are not gender-specific meaning confined to Muslim professional males only; in fact, they are gender neutral and more or less equally preponderant amongst both Muslim professional males and Muslim professional females, certainly in terms of the participants who bravely featured in the research undertaken.

A parallel research project was progressed over the same time frame (March 2005 to March 2006) as the above project whereupon Kamran A. Beg Events interviewed 100 Muslim professional singles who had been introduced to one another through the traditional family channel and had been left to their own devices by their parents to develop an apparently halal understanding to see whether they wished to proceed to marriage. These are individuals who had subsequently not proceeded to marriage with the family-led introduction. 50 males and 50 females constituted the research sample with the interviewees all UK-based. The participants had been allowed to communicate with family-inspired marriage dialogue prospects. The research clearly showed the complete absence of a marriage-inspired framework for dialogue where essential safeguards had been put into place to protect the halal sanctity of the dialogue and to preserve the emotional integrity of the incumbents integral to the dialogue. As one female doctor aged 32 and living in London at the time of the research commented: "I was introduced to a 35 year old management consultant by my parents. The families initially met at our home. We then afforded him and his family a visit. After taking some time out, we agreed that it was too early too say whether he and I were suited in terms of being each other's life partner. So our parents left it to us to get to know each other over the next few months. After all we are both educated and intelligent. Our parents said they had complete trust in us. The reality is we parted company after dating and having a physical relationship." At this juncture, I think it only appropriate to remind the keen reader that the case alluded to here does not represent an isolated exception; it appears to be the rule insofar as our research sample is concerned.

Muslim parents keen to see their children tie the knot increasingly recognise that unless there is some spark or connection between the individuals in dialogue there is no merit in progressing a particular matrimonial proposal. The whole idea then is to give the male and female in question sufficient time to ascertain whether their chemistries are compatible. However, in empowering the male and female in question the parents have naturally assumed that any conduct between the two parties in dialogue would be conceived along halal lines. After all, they would have absolutely no idea to think otherwise. How could their bright and diligent child, an ambassador for the family and the community, a role model to many other aspiring Muslims, possibly err on the wrong side of caution? Well, I have a very simple and conspicuous message for parents and their children alike. Such an assumption on the part of the parent or guardian, whilst most laudable in that it assigns empowerment to the Muslim singles in dialogue based on that most cherished attribute, namely trust, is blatantly over-presumptuous! Bearing in mind none of the 100 singles who made up the research sample ended up marrying the individual they had been introduced to through the endearing and time-honoured safety and security of the family channel, 75% of the sample acknowledged that in retrospect they fully accepted they had "dated" the other party and 71% admitted that they had engaged in some measure of "physical intimacy" with the person they had been in dialogue with. After being allowed by their unsuspecting parents to "get to know each other" they had decided not to progress to marriage with the person in question. Once again this specific piece of research featuring Muslim professional singles not only highlights the damaging presence of dating and the increasing penchant for pre-marital relationships in the Muslim (professional) community, both of which are strictly alien to Islam and irrefutably and incontrovertibly prohibited by the Muslim faith, but moreover stresses, and emphatically so, the absence of a halal marriage-inspired dialogue methodology that could preserve the integrity of the individuals in dialogue and the abundantly visible oversight on the part of Muslim parents to equip their child with a framework for dialogue that allows a decision to be made sooner rather than later regarding whether "marriage is truly on the cards".

In reporting on the above research, it is in no way the intention of the writer to undermine the integrity of the Muslim professionals who selflessly volunteered their bold contributions to the research. Quite simply we as a community owe them a debt of gratitude in allowing the Muslim Ummah to come to terms with the seriousness and complexity of the problems that encumber us. The interviewees displayed enormous courage and resolve in discussing their experiences graphically and transparently with Kamran A. Beg Events. It is precisely such honesty that is required if the Muslim community is to face up to and identify accurately the problems, which currently hamper it and stifle progress! Only then can we engineer solutions, which are sustainable, serve the community effectively and in no way compromise the basic tenets of Islam that crucially define the personality of a Muslim! Nor is anyone in a position to judge the courageous interviewees who gave up so much of their time and energy so that we could fathom the painful reality that stares us in the face at a community-level. Only Allah (SWT) is in position to judge the character of a person for that is a sovereign office exercised by Him and Him alone!

Each of the interviewees is a consummate professional. Their capabilities as practitioners drawn from a whole spectrum of professional backgrounds are laudable, each excelling in their chosen profession and each having studied at university. What their tortuous experiences in seeking a life partner emphasise is the overriding need need to put a halal marriage-inspired dialogue framework into place, which safeguards both the Muslim male and Muslim female exploring marriage, allows them to establish sooner rather than later whether there is any real mileage in terms of progressing a marriage, and which above all does not compromise or in any way undermine or usurp the honourable values intrinsic to the Islamic faith!

So many of the professionals interviewed reported that they had been left emotionally shattered when they had parted company with the other party. An emotional bond had developed between them and the dialoguing party and when one or both parties felt there was no future in terms of a marriage the damage had already been done. As a 29-year-old male actuary based in New York remarked: "I had dated a young lady I had met through a friend. We went out with each other for two years. I had wanted to end the relationship much sooner since we were getting nowhere. I did not know how to tell her and when I did she fell apart. I have to live with the knowledge that I emotionally scarred her and pray that God will forgive me. I have done wrong. We were both wrong. I just wish I had had the courage to get out sooner." A very highly articulate 25-year-old teacher based in Sydney made the poignant observation: "As a community, we are not skilled at the process of matrimonial dialogue. This is a very grey area and we have been left to ourselves to discover if we like the other person enough to want to marry them. As Muslims intent on completing half of our faith never have we needed to be guided more!"

The Nine Features Comprising a Proposed Robust Halal Marriage-inspired Dialogue Framework

The Prophet Muhammad (PBUH) so eloquently and gracefully reminded the Ummah during his illuminating, benevolent, exemplary and Divinely enlightened life that: "Actions shall be judged by their intention". This *hadith* or saying of the Prophet (PBUH), which quintessentially forms the central bedrock of all legal systems – Islamic or otherwise - the world over and is the veritable cornerstone of any accountable, responsible and God-fearing community that prioritises social justice, applies to every sphere of a human being's life. Its sagacity cannot be overemphasised enough. It is equally applicable to an individual embarked on that very time consuming, challenging, at times frustrating and despondent, odyssey of seeking a life partner with a view to "completing half of one's faith". Speak to your friends who have been blessed with finding their other half. This journey, as we have noted in chapter 1, ultimately boils down to a question of unswerving faith in the one God, Allah (SWT), who has already predestined you with your actual choice of life partner in accordance with a Divine will that He has already exercised and which is captured in Al-Lauh al-Mahfooz (the Preserved Tablet or the Book of Decrees). As we highlighted in chapter 1 this can be inferred directly from the following two Quranic verses:

> "Verily, we have created all things with Qadar [Divine Preordainments of all things before their creation as written in the Book of Decrees – Al-Lauh al-Mahfooz]" (Quran 54:49).

> "And among His signs is [the sign] that He created for you mates from among yourselves that you may

dwell in peace and tranquillity with them and He put love and compassion between your hearts. Surely there are signs in this for those who reflect" (Quran 30:21).

Divine predestination – discussed in extensive detail in the previous chapter - should encourage you to strive tirelessly with a view to discovering the soulmate that Allah (SWT) has preordained for you so that you may complete half of your faith and in the process totalise your faith.

In venturing a robust halal marriage-inspired dialogue framework that will allow a Muslim male and a Muslim female to engage in dialogue specifically with a view to exploring the possibility of marriage, it is vital to ensure that the dialogue visited by both parties is halal and kept halal. Consequently, it is important that we underpin the proposed framework with the overarching tenets of 'balance' and 'moderation' for it is precisely these definitive attributes that so explicitly characterise the essence of the Quran, which drive Islam as a perfect code of life and that were so eloquently and majestically articulated and manifested by the Prophet (PBUH) during his momentous life and so pervade the sublime essence of the Sunnah.

In pursuit of adhering to such balance and moderation, it is recommended on the basis of global research undertaken by Kamran A. Beg Events that we incorporate the following nine features into a proposed robust halal marriage-inspired dialogue framework suitable for both family based and non-family based introductions and satiate each of them respectfully in deference to the Muslim value system impeccably portrayed by Allah (SWT) in the Quran and discharged to perfection by the Prophet (PBUH):

(i)   Making sure that the dialogue is inspired by marriage

(ii) Informing the parent(s)/guardian(s) about the dialogue and keeping them abreast of how it is developing

(iii) Circumscribing within reason the time over which individual compatibility is gauged

(iv) Eliminating the scourge of dating

(v)   Navigating dialogue closure with the utmost sensitivity

(vi) Engendering a progressive, high-trust based working relationship between the dialogue incumbent and their parent(s)/guardian(s)

(vii) Not penalising and showing indifference towards divorcees or widows or widowers

(viii) Not penalising and showing indifference towards Muslim reverts

(ix) Applying cultural, ethnic, sectarian and racial tolerance when considering Muslim life partner choices

Detailed Discussion of the Nine Features Comprising a Proposed Robust Halal Marriage-Inspired Dialogue Framework

A detailed discussion of each of the nine features comprising a robust halal marriage- inspired dialogue framework featuring a Muslim male and Muslim female exploring marriage and which have been itemised above now follows. Such a framework would be equally applicable to both family based and non-family based introductions.

(i)   **Making sure that the dialogue is inspired by marriage:** Since "actions are judged by their intention" the Muslim male and Muslim female in question should only agree to a matrimonial dialogue if genuinely they wish to explore the question of marriage with each other and that too in a halal manner, which prohibits any penchant to date or have a pre-marital relationship. It is incumbent on both individuals therefore to exercise clinical honesty in this regard before acceding to an introduction conceived along matrimonial lines either through the family channel or for that matter through any other halal means.

A female management consultant wrote to me recently from Toronto recounting an unpleasant episode she had experienced in 2005. She had evidently attended a professional Muslim networking gathering in North America. The whole idea was to have a forum that would allow Muslim professionals to network and build bridges with fellow Muslim professionals in other parts of North America. At the event she met a whole gamut of professionals and was awestruck by the number of professionals present reflecting the excellence the Muslim community has achieved in North America. It was during her deliberations with a group of investment bankers that she came across one particular gentleman. As she went on to say: "I felt an instant attraction to him and I could see a mental chemistry developing. My heart started palpitating. Now that's never happened before. We exchanged business cards and met up that evening for coffee. He had to return to New York the following day and suggested we keep in touch. A couple of weeks later I was in New York on business and we met up a couple of times. Over the next 9 months we would speak regularly on the phone, communicate via the e-mail and visit each other. I told my parents everything is under control and we are spending time getting to know each other and in due course his mother would call. My parents were fine about it, my mother exclaiming that she was pleased someone had finally registered on my matrimonial radar. One weekend we went rollerblading. It was so heavenly. I had found my Mr Right! He was perfect. And then my whole world came tumbling down. I pressed him a few times on when his mother would call mine so that the families could meet. We had been getting to know each other for 6 months by then. He said soon. Soon then became later and later got delayed more and more. And then one week, frustrated and feeling low, I went to New York and asked him directly about when the families could meet to discuss marriage. He was momentarily speechless and retorted by saying: 'I thought we were friends and I see you as a friend and no more. I do not regard you as someone I would want to settle down with and in any event I am not ready to commit to marriage with anyone yet'. Hearing this mortified me to the point I collapsed in a heap of tears. I have been reduced to a wreck since."

As the heart-wrenching experience of my fellow management consultant shows any matrimonially-perceived dialogue should at the very outset expressly, explicitly and palpably confirm that both the male and female parties about to engage in dialogue are doing so with a view to exploring marriage and not because one of them has this inveterate disposition to increase their circle of friends. The Prophet's advice that "actions shall be judged by their intention" is crucial to establishing whether the dialogue has a matrimonial basis in the first place. A failure to clarify the purpose inspiring the dialogue can leave the "innocent party" disillusioned and heart-broken as was the case with the misled female management consultant above. Her error lies in her failing not to clarify at the very beginning the purpose inspiring her then dialogue with the investment banker; his (the investment banker's) failing stems from deliberately misleading the female party into thinking that they were exploring marriage when all along he had been stringing her along. If "actions are judged by their intention" his deliberate intention to lead her down the garden path was morally bankrupt and tantamount to the most un-Islamic behaviour. His nefarious designs fall nothing short of a moral disgrace! The female's failure in not clarifying the rules of engagement with the gentleman at the very inception of the dialogue effectively compromised her position.

This, however, is not an isolated example. Hundreds of Muslim professionals worldwide have informed Kamran A. Beg Events of similar soul-destroying experiences: where one party innocently thought they were getting to "know each other" with a view to progressing to the wedding altar while the other party vigorously and passionately pleaded their innocence finally resorting to conveniently resting on their laurels by professing that they were unsuspecting of the other party's marriage-based intentions and thought that they had been in regular contact because "I thought you wanted a friend". Quite frankly such lax and remiss behaviour on the part of both parties is Islamically untenable and therefore wholly avoidable.

You can easily avoid the devastating pangs of *'broken-heart syndrome'* by clarifying at the very outset the reality inspiring the animated and colourful dialogue trajectory that is set to follow. As those who have suffered the damaging, debilitating and emaciating consequences of 'broken-heart syndrome' testify every precaution should be taken to insulate and protect the heart against the possibility if it being shattered since a broken heart can take a very long time to heal and that too if you are lucky. Sadly the Muslim professional community is strewn with countless broken hearts as our research evidences, which is all the more reason to be wary of its very real possibility. And even if having endured the tragic consequences of 'broken-heart syndrome' the heart does finally heal sometimes the healing process can last years and perhaps even decades as we have found in the course of our research endeavours. In sum whether you are introduced to someone through the family route or through a non-family conduit such as through the guise of a networking event, which was the case regarding the female management consultant above, asking the right question at the right time, which is at the very beginning, can save untold emotional upheaval and turmoil, which if allowed to precipitate can have terrible consequences for the innocent victim. Suffice it to say make sure that the dialogue is inspired by marriage!

(ii) **Informing the parent(s)/guardian(s) about the dialogue and keeping them abreast of how it is developing:** If the Muslim male and Muslim female who have been introduced for the purposes of a matrimonial dialogue have been introduced through a non-family channel then in the interests of transparency and to safeguard the ethical and moral integrity of that dialogue it is essential for both parties to inform their parent(s)/guardian(s) that they are engaged in a marriage-inspired dialogue with each other. This basic pre-requisite to inform the parent or guardian is a necessary condition to render the dialogue halal. Naturally in the case of a family-based introduction the families are already aware that the male and female are in dialogue since they (the families) effected the introduction in the first place.

A *fatwa* or legal ruling issued by that prodigious centre of Islamic scholarship, Al-Azhar University in Cairo (Egypt), for instance, renders

139

a matrimonial dialogue between a Muslim male and a Muslim female who have met over the Internet through an online matchmaking service, which is an example of a non-family based introduction, as halal provided both parties inform their parent(s)/guardian(s) that they are in dialogue and provided they keep them abreast of how the dialogue is developing, subject to upholding the integrity and ethics that underpin halal Muslim etiquette. The same principle applies to any matrimonial dialogue an individual may be party to whatever the non-family based channel effecting the introduction. For example, as a matter of policy, all Muslim professionals who attend matrimonial events run by Kamran A. Beg Events are required to seek the consent of their families first in order to attend an event and are required to keep them informed of developments when in dialogue with a fellow attendee drawn from our truly outstanding global family of attendees, which to date has generated 100 marriages worldwide.

(iii) **Circumscribing within reason the time over which individual compatibility is gauged:** The Muslim male and Muslim female in dialogue should be given sufficient time to discover whether there is a significant enough measure of compatibility between them at an individual level to merit initiating (in the case of a non-family based introduction) or further expediting (in the case of a family based introduction) direct interaction between their respective parents/guardians and families. However, the

140

dialoguing male and female must not be allowed to fall prey to the ravaging temptation of dating and/or having a pre-marital physical relationship, both of which are Islamically unpalatable and cannot and never will be accommodated by a Muslim value system inspired by the word of Allah (SWT) and gifted to the whole of humanity through the Quran and exemplified by the virtuous life of the Prophet (PBUH). In chapter 1, we expounded in detail on how faith coupled with personal preference should inspire your choice of life partner. The marriage-inspired dialogue framework proposed should impel the Muslim male and Muslim female to terminate dialogue with immediate effect once it is clear that the degree of individual compatibility is insufficient to progress dialogue any further.

To clarify again the two parties pitched in dialogue should be sensitive to the need to initiate (in the case of a non-family based introduction) or revive (in the case of a family based introduction) direct interaction between the families *immediately* after mutually concluding that there is a significant measure of individual compatibility between the two though this too, that is whether the personalities click sufficiently, should be established *as soon as is reasonably possible* after their introduction has been effected. It is very seminal to note that any accountable, transparent and responsible marriage-inspired dialogue framework designed to safeguard the emotional well-being of both dialogue incumbents should circumscribe within reason the time over which the Muslim male and Muslim female in dialogue are allowed to reconcile with the degree to which they click and whether this degree is of sufficient magnitude to initiate (in the case of a non-family based introduction) or revive (in the case of a family based introduction) direct interaction between the families with a view to exploring marriage. If by the expiry of that time period, both parties feel there is currency in progressing matters further the families should initiate (in the case of a non-family based introduction) or revive (in the case of a family based introduction) direct interaction immediately. Where one or both parties is half-hearted or is apprehensive and feels that they need more time the dialogue should be brought to immediate closure.

While individual compatibility is a necessary condition for marriage, it may not in itself be a sufficient condition to sanction a marriage as the extent to which the two family value systems overlap should exercise a significant influence on whether the two parties in dialogue should proceed to marriage. This is in deference to the advice of the Prophet (PBUH) who discouraged marriage where the family values of the male and female are incompatible. See chapter 1 for a more extensive discussion. Thus any marriage-inspired dialogue framework suitable for Muslim consumption must legislate for the individual-cum-family compatibility matrix. It would be devastating for a male and female to dialogue endlessly, as if there was no tomorrow, only to discover that the families were entirely incompatible 6 months after kick-starting their matrimonial deliberations. By then the damage would already have been done. In most of the case studies I have analysed in this regard the male and female have developed strong emotional feelings for one another only to see their nuptial dreams reduced to ruins when the harsh reality of two distinctly incompatible families suddenly hits the radar. This is one tempest too far!

In allowing two individuals to dialogue it is essential therefore that each individual knows as soon as possible whether there is enough individual compatibility to merit initiating (in the case of a non-family based introduction) or further expediting (in the case of a family based introduction) direct family involvement, and if there is the desired degree of individual chemistry to then establish as soon as possible after the families have engaged whether the families are sufficiently similar in outlook and values to warrant progressing a marriage proposal. A health warning to all readers: do not underestimate the importance of the degree to which the families are compatible! A young female economist, aged 26, who contacted me recently to enquire about the services provided by Kamran A. Beg Events described her tortuous experience regarding someone she had been in dialogue with: "I had met a doctor through an online service that I had subscribed to. After exchanging e-mails over the passage of a few weeks we met up and do you know what, we got on like a house on fire. We started talking to and meeting each other on a regular basis and this went on for about a year. I thought I had met my knight in shining armour. We were clear that we wished to marry and got the families involved. The families finally met and everything went belly-up. The families were so not each other – we had so little in common. Despite meeting a few times the families could not get along and it was then that the reality began to set in. There was no way on this here earth I could adjust to his family and vice versa. It will take me a long time to recover and I am shattered. This is so unfair. The man I wanted to marry was equally devastated and it was only when we met in the company of each other's family that the reality of how different we really are at an individual level suddenly hit home."

Many of the eminent child ethologists have shown in their research what John Milton wittily remarked when he stated that "the child is the father to the man". If as most child ethologists contend 70-75% of an individual's personality is shaped, informed and coloured by the experiences they have accumulated in the first five years of their upbringing, then clearly one would be over-presumptuous to say the very least if one assumed one had met one's perfect soulmate before meeting their (the potential soulmate's) family. 81% of the divorcees who have been kind enough to grace the global family of attendees, subscribers and members serviced by Kamran A. Beg Events have acknowledged when interviewed before signing up to one or more of our services, that their marriage had failed because the two families to which they and their then spouse belong were very different and in large measure diametrically opposed in terms of their overarching values and modus operandi. This chasm or 'value gap' had deepened the discomfit felt by the couple towards each other driving a discernible wedge between them, making them increasingly indifferent to each other and heightening tensions to a point where divorce became the only viable lawful remedy.

We are each of us in large measure a personification of our family value system. If 70-75% of one's personality constructs are erected in the first five years of one's life then it is not too difficult to see that the key influencer in terms of shaping one's personality is one's family. 70-75% of Kamran A. Beg was defined by the time the humble writer had reached five and there is no denying that! If one wishes to understand more the party one is in matrimonial dialogue with it is all the more important therefore that one expedites interaction at the family level. We noted in chapter 1 that the Prophet (PBUH) has encouraged families to meet as often as is needed in order to get a firm handle on how compatible the families are, even if that means speaking to acquaintances and friends of the family of the dialogue prospect and eliciting their honest take on the family's character and values. The Prophet (PBUH) further clarified that such inquisitiveness in deference to exploring marriage between two individuals and inevitably two families is in fact a religious duty since ultimately marriage is tantamount to completing half of one's faith and its sacred eminence must not be undervalued by not gauging how congruous the family temperaments are. While individual compatibility is a must to progress the possibility of marriage the Prophet's insightful and timeless advice clearly shows that a marriage is more likely to be sustainable where the families also have much common ground and foster similar basic values (for a more comprehensive discussion see chapter 1). A disconnect at the family level is likely to increase the likelihood of divorce, something which is clearly borne out by our research as highlighted by the experiences of the divorcees who have been magnanimous enough to grace the Kamran A. Beg Events global family. Their feedback clearly testifies to the eternal wisdom contained in the Prophet's counsel that marriage should not be sanctioned where the two families in question are markedly at variance in terms of their basic values!

In conclusion, as Kamran A. Beg Events has always advised Muslim professional singles seeking marriage, it is in the inherent interests of both the male and female in dialogue that they proceed sooner rather than later to a scenario where the families interact directly so that the extent to which the families are congruous in terms of values can be identified as soon as is conceivably possible. This does not necessarily signal that if the two families to which the two individuals in dialogue belong are very incompatible that a marriage between the two individuals will necessary fail assuming that they (the male and female in dialogue) felt that their personalities clicked enough to start off with. However, as the enriching counsel of our beloved Prophet (PBUH) forewarns us and as our research poignantly reveals, the likelihood of divorce is significantly increased when the families are not highly compatible in relation to their values, mores and norms!

(iv) **Eliminating the scourge of dating:** The marriage-inspired dialogue framework should emphasise and place at its very epicentre a system of etiquette that safeguards the integrity of both the Muslim male and Muslim female in dialogue and in particular it must assign maximum exposure to ensuring that the dignity of the female is not violated. It must seek to eliminate the scourge of dating and inhibit any proclivity for the two individuals to date each other and be tempted to partake in a pre-marital physical relationship.

As many of the Muslim professional females interviewed as part of our various research projects contend: "The Muslim community seems to exercise a double standard towards men and women. Men can date and have a relationship only to plead naivety and confess that they innocently and naively succumbed to temptation while Muslim sisters are berated and stigmatised

147

if only for innocently smiling at a Muslim gentleman in the street or in a public place such as a supermarket or restaurant." And without a remote shadow of a doubt as our research irrefutably brings to light, the Muslim community does harbour a double standard in relation to the two genders, which clearly makes the female more vulnerable given the more exacting standards to which she is subjected. I respectfully say to the male folk in our community: please treat other people's daughters in the way you would wish other men to treat your innocent sisters. You cannot have one standard for your friend's sister and a more protective standard for your own sister for they are both equal in the eyes of Allah (SWT) and are both daughters of the same Ummah and are endowed with equally important ownership in the future of the Muslim social imperative, which is intended to cultivate a community enterprise that not only celebrates treating each of its constituents equally but is seen to do so tangibly in practice. Actions speak much louder than words. So let us not pay lip service to according equal respect to the sisters of others. Let us show it in person through the deeds that define how we interact with the females who define the pulse and future of the community. Gentlemen, let us not have one standard for our sisters based on protecting their morality and chastity and an inferior standard for the daughters of other families. Rather, let us seek to apply the same standards of morality and chastity to the entire female fraternity and not just within the ambit of the Muslim community.

The proposed dialogue framework must preserve the integrity of the two individuals in dialogue and their respective families. It should allow them to embrace a progressive medium of dialogue that strikes a workable chord between the traditional values germane to Islam and the values of modernity congruous with Islam. While allowing the male and female in dialogue adequate leverage in halal terms to address whether there is sufficient compatibility at the level of the individual it must not be flexed such that the two parties effectively over-indulge themselves in discussion and eventually get lead astray into the "dating" maze, a labyrinth, which once entered, leaves the incumbent "in a maze". I repeat: the marriage-inspired dialogue framework must have built within its robustness the ability to 'nip the evil in the bud' and to prevent innocent men and innocent women being subsumed by the rampant and repugnant dating culture that has so blighted large sections of the Muslim professional community in their quest to find that all-elusive soulmate.

(v) **Navigating dialogue closure with the utmost sensitivity:** Dialogue construed within the purview of the marriage-inspired dialogue framework should be conducted with honesty and integrity and both parties should seek to accord the other party the maximum degree of sensitivity. Each of us is blessed with an

149

emotional intelligence; surely logic would dictate that the dialogue incumbent should exercise enough intelligence and sensitivity not to encroach the other party's emotional territory and not too cause them any discomfit whatever the dialogue outcome. If the outcome is that one wishes the dialogue to be brought to closure, one should inform the other party in a manner that they are not made to feel rejected, which can otherwise seriously dent their confidence and impede their ability to explore other matrimonial options. As pointed out earlier, if your choice of life partner(s) has already been exercised subject to Allah's will, which it has as the Quranic verse (30:21) cited in chapter 1 reveals, then nobody is in a position to reject anybody in terms of their life partner search as from a Muslim religious perspective this choice has already been made according to a decree preordained by Allah (SWT) Himself. Temporally, we have choices but the outcomes have already been decided subject to a Divine will. We strive to discover the life partner that Allah (SWT) has decreed for us. This is a message that I have communicated directly and indefatigably to many Muslim professionals worldwide as they engage in their life partner search.

85% of our attendees, that is those Muslim professionals who attend matrimonial events run by Kamran A. Beg Events where they are introduced in-person in a halal manner to members of the opposite gender with a view to exploring life partner potential post-event, have lucidly stated in no uncertain terms in their pre-event telephone and written interviews, which are mandatory and designed to select only those applicants who we feel are genuine in seeking a counterpart within the precincts of a halal framework, that they fear enormously the pain of rejection should they wish to initiate post-event dialogue with a party and their keenness or interest is not reciprocated by that party. Well, if your choice of life partner(s) is predestined courtesy of a Divine will, which it is, then the fear of rejection should pale to insignificance. Nobody is in a position to reject or accept anybody as at the Quranic level Allah (SWT) has already preordained the outcome.

If the dialogue outcome is non-progression in terms of marriage it is quintessential that the dialogue be concluded in such a way as not to make the other party feel rejected. Empathy should be at the cornerstone of any and every matrimonial dialogue and each of the two parties should regard it a moral duty not to impair the other party's will or confidence to dialogue with another party once the dialogue is closed. As a London-based 34 year-old architect who attended an event run by Kamran A. Beg Events in Manchester (reference here is being made to Manchester in the UK, which is the case wherever Manchester is mentioned in this book) in February 2006 vented before frequenting the event when recounting his fiendish experience at the hands of a family-based introduction: "I thought I had met the lady of my dreams when I

151

saw her for the first time. We were introduced through the family route. I could hear the wedding bells ringing before the evening was out. Mentally, I had already married her because my heart felt solace in her presence. Three days later we spoke via the phone and she said that she had reflected on the meeting of a few days before and felt that I was not good enough for her and that she was too beautiful for me. In short, she said that I was well below her standard and that had it not been for the modalities associated with having to meet me courtesy of how much her family had made her feel obliged to go ahead with the meeting that she would not have had the time of day for me. In the few minutes we spoke that day, my legs turned to jelly and my confidence was shattered. She had not just crushed my dream; she had crushed me as a person. I was too shocked to tell my parents what had emerged and was reduced to tears. It has taken 6 months of counselling to build my confidence to a point where I can contemplate beginning my search again! If she did not deem me suitable I wish she could have been more polite in her manner. I don't want anyone to feel sorry for me. I want them to treat me as a human being furnished with feelings."

As this gentleman's case testifies there is a certain propriety of manner that needs to be built into the dialogue process. The crime on the part of the lady he had been in dialogue with was not that she did find him compatible; it is her basic Islamic right to end a marriage-based dialogue with any party on the grounds of individual incompatibility. Her crime resides in the lack of propriety and politeness she extended to the gentleman when breaking the news to him; her failing resides in the total insensitivity she displayed in making the male that she had been introduced to feel that she had flatly rejected him because he was inferior in her eyes. That nadir in her etiquette represents the very zenith of arrogance, that is to part company with the person that you have been exploring marriage with in the most unceremonious of ways and to make that person feel belittled, demeaned and inferior. We have a responsibility to conduct dialogue, whatever the conclusion, in a way that does not decimate the other party in the case of closure but leaves the other party feeling respected and honoured.

So, please remember: your ability or inability to dialogue with courtesy and in particular to end a marriage-inspired dialogue with no mileage respectfully and civilly could have a direct impact on the capacity of the other party to explore marriage with life partner prospects after your dialogue with them has been brought to a halt. Dialogue is both an art and a science: the art stems from the ability of an individual to address the other party with sensitivity and civility; the science stems from seeking to explore through intelligent and focused discussion the extent to which there is a connection or click between the two individuals. The science must not be emphasised at the expense of the art otherwise a fate not too dissimilar to that which shook the gentleman above could befall the other party and how then would your conscience wrestle with that?

90% of the Muslim professionals who currently receive matrimonial services from Kamran A. Beg Events have voiced how difficult and unnerving they find the whole terrain of dialogue closure. Granted these individuals are the most outstanding professionals in their own respective fields: dialogue closure and how to negotiate it, however, are akin to "plumbing inside an earthquake zone". As a young female pharmacist attending a Washington, DC matrimonial event for Muslim professionals run by Kamran A. Beg Events admitted boldly in a discussion with me: "I would never wish to end a dialogue making the other person feel he is not good enough for me. That happened to me once. I was at the receiving end. I had been talking to a fellow pharmacist for 4 months. We had been introduced to each other by our parents. One day out of the blue he said that I was not refined enough for him and that he could do much better. That left me in a big mess for a couple of years. Worse still we had dated and nobody questioned that. Our parents just assumed that we were meeting each other and behaving in a decent and urbane manner as professionals apparently do. I am 26 now and even now I feel diffident when talking to men. I fear being put down. Even so, I will not be inhumane and make anyone I do not like feel rejected, not after what I have been through."

Plumbing inside an earthquake zone it may be! Dialogue closure needs to be navigated with the utmost skill and one tool that all dialogue incumbents should absorb into their dialogue toolkit is how to close a marriage-inspired dialogue respectfully, civilly and with the utmost humility and sensitivity! Solecism here could seriously dampen the other party's will to revive their life partner search. In the case of the female pharmacist above it took her two years to transcend that feeling of rejection and begin afresh her life partner search. To extinguish that flame of enthusiasm in the other party because one came across in a highly uncouth, abrasive and uncaring manner, totally insensitive to the other person's feelings, is an expression of conduct most unbecoming. Remember tomorrow that could be you at the receiving end. And rest assured being made to feel rejected represents a distinctly gargantuan sting in the tail that most members of the human fraternity cannot stomach nor should they be compelled to digest. Kamran A. Beg Events urges its attendees, subscribers and members to show empathy, compassion, due care, sensitivity and grace when initiating dialogue closure. Any marriage-inspired dialogue framework should therefore underscore the importance of "empathy, compassion, due care, sensitivity and grace" when plumbing inside the earthquake zone of dialogue closure.

(vi)   **Engendering a progressive, high-trust based working relationship between the dialogue incumbent and their parent(s)/guardian(s):** A marriage-inspired dialogue framework should engender a progressive, high-trust based working relationship between the party in dialogue and their parent(s)/guardian(s). While in our case the two Muslim professionals in dialogue (the same would apply to any two Muslims in dialogue, irrespective of their career background) should be allowed ample leverage within reason to fathom whether there personalities click, at the same time the parents should feel an equal sense of ownership in not feeling excluded from the dialogue process. They should be given regular feedback relating to how the dialogue is evolving. They should feel perfectly comfortable in asking their child from time to time any questions pertinent to understanding the individual their beloved progeny is dialoguing with.

The two individuals in dialogue and their parents are all stakeholders in a marriage-inspired dialogue framework. Each stakeholder should therefore feel a sense of ownership in this all-inclusive framework. No stakeholder should be excluded from its workings. The stakeholder model may also be widened to include other members of one's immediate family; it is only natural for a sibling to enquire how your dialogue is progressing. One should not be inimical to such cordial interrogation. It certainly keeps one very vigilant and on one's toes! It lends constructive urgency to the dialogue!

Be that as it may, many Muslim professionals worldwide attending our matrimonial events have

156

indicated that they feel under great pressure as soon as their dialogue reaches a certain 'critical' point, usually a week after the introduction, whatever the channel through which they have been introduced. Expectations reach fever pitch. Parents get very excited yearning commitment. The child (Muslim professional) unsure of the suitability of the other party becomes inarticulate to express their sense of apprehension as they are still seeking to unearth that all-elusive click. Pressure mounts and before one knows it two camps have developed in the same otherwise usually congenial household: the keen parent hoping for a result and the equally keen child hoping to uncover reality regarding that profoundly cherished click. To satiate both psyches seamless communication is needed at the parent-child interface; this can greatly help to reduce the unfathomable tension that can ensue between the two generations. In addition, expectations can be better managed by coordinating the dialogue between the two dialogue incumbents over a sensible period of time as indicated in (iii) above so that within a reasonable time window of the introduction taking place the Muslim male and Muslim female can expressly determine whether they wish to pursue matters further or not at the family level.

(vii) **Not penalising and showing indifference towards divorcees or widows or widowers:** A marriage-inspired dialogue framework should make it incumbent on all parties to treat divorcees, widows and widowers with dignity, equality and respect. Much to the chagrin of the writer, our research relays a very sad reality particularly endemic to the Muslim community, specifically the existence of blatant widespread ignorance on the part of the mainstay of the community towards divorcees, widows and widowers seeking remarriage with a view to completing half of their faith again. In chapter 1 we dwelled in rigorous detail on widows seeking remarriage, divorce or khula to be deployed as legal remedies in the last resort, the formalities of divorce and subsequently seeking remarriage and the formalities of khula and subsequently seeking remarriage. The reader is advised to consult the opening chapter for more information on each of the afore-stated areas.

It is not a crime to be divorced! In much the same way that Allah (SWT) has willed marriage, He has also willed divorce. Both have been preordained, subject to a Divine will: "And you cannot will unless [it be] that Allah wills, the Lord of Creation" (Quran 81:29). Divorce or khula is stressed by Allah (SWT) as a necessary final resort or legal remedy in the case of marriages where the husband and wife cannot reconcile their differences and reverse the increasing apathy that they have developed towards each other. As Allah (SWT) reminds us in the Quran, the sanctity of any marriage bond is measured according to two limits, namely Allah's limits of 'morality' and 'chastity'. If these limits are likely to be violated it is recommended by Allah (SWT) that the two parties genuinely seek to reconcile any substantive differences first; where such reconciliation is not tenable divorce is declared to be a viable legal remedy. Furthermore these limits must not be violated in favour of preserving the marriage bond. See chapter 1 for more elaboration on the mandatory need to preserve Allah's limits of morality and chastity, which define the very integrity of any marriage tie.

As we stated in chapter 1, the Prophet (PBUH) had 12 wives: Khadija, Sawdah, Aisha, Hafsah, Zaynab bint Khuzayamah, Umm Salamah, Juwayriyah, Zaynab bint Jahsh, Umm Habibah, Safiyyah, Maymunah and Maryam Qibityah. One had been divorced (Zaynab bint Jahsh), two had previously never been married and were virgin wives (Aisha and Maryam Qibityah) and the other nine had been widowed. These "Mothers of the Faithful" as they are reverently referred to in the Quran each played a profoundly landmark role in spreading and propagating Islam. The example of the Prophet (PBUH) is one that should inspire all Muslims. Those never married, divorced (with or without children), widowed (with or without children) were all treated equally during his lifetime and divorcees and widows were not excluded from seeking remarriage but rather motivated by the Prophet (PBUH) to embrace marriage again in deference to completing half of their faith. This is the standard – the Prophet's golden example - we as a Muslim Ummah driven by faith should be seeking to emulate and maintain. Khadija, forty at the time she respectfully proposed to the Prophet (PBUH), was fifteen years his senior when they married for he was twenty-five. She had previously been married twice and widowed before meeting the Prophet (PBUH). She had a son and daughter from her first marriage and a daughter from her second. Khadija bore the Prophet (PBUH) two sons and four daughters with the two sons dying in early childhood. As we further noted in our deliberations in chapter 1 the Prophet (PBUH) exercised polygamy only after Khadija, his first wife, passed away. The Prophet's marriage to Khadija is the finest embodiment of how the Muslim community should treat widows (and divorcees) alike!

However, research conducted by Kamran A. Beg Events alludes to divorcees, widows and widowers generally feeling penalised and excluded by the Muslim community as they strive to find their other half. This degree of alienation is particularly pronounced in the case of divorcees. As one 31 year-old female dentist living in Birmingham (reference here is being made to Birmingham in the UK, which is the case wherever Birmingham is mentioned in this book) with her son observed when reflecting on her experiences in a focus group comprising of divorcees and widows I chaired in May 2006 featuring several Muslim professionals from across the UK: "I was divorced a couple of years ago. My parents are finding it impossible to introduce me to someone on the same wavelength. As soon as we make mention of the fact that I am divorced people just switch off. They are so ignorant and don't want to know you. They make you feel that there is something wrong with you. When I attend weddings or community gatherings, they look straight through me as if I am not there." This sentiment has been echoed by many divorcees, both male and female.

85% of all the divorcees who have subscribed to Kamran A. Beg Events have protested vehemently that the Muslim community penalises and socially excludes them in their search for a life partner because they carry this millstone of divorce round their neck. Furthermore, they indicate the well nigh total absence of a robust and empathetic support network that addresses their concerns. Widows and widowers have similar grievances. 90% of all divorcees, widows and widowers subscribing to our services have argued that they feel stigmatised by and experience perennial social exclusion from within the Muslim community. What a far cry from the example gifted to the Muslim Ummah by the life of the Prophet (PBUH)!

Another female divorcee based in London who contacted our offices in April 2006 tells of her emotionally harrowing woes: "I was introduced to a doctor by a friend. He was based in the same hospital where I was working as a nurse. I had had a very stormy first marriage and was divorced a few years ago. I was 25 then. I am 31 now. The doctor and I hit it off in our first meeting and we continued to talk and meet up regularly. I was seeing him for about 3 months before I popped the question about our families meeting up and getting to know each other. He said he would look into it and let me know in a month or so. A month elapsed and I had received no word though we did continue to meet up and talk. Any way when I broached the topic of the families getting together a month later he was very dismissive and curt in his reply saying that it was too soon to get the elders involved and he needed more time before he could commit. I didn't like what I was hearing but then thought the glass is half full rather than half empty and gave him the benefit. When we confronted the same question again by which time we had been seeing each other 6 months he said that he was sorry and had some bad news. His parents had made it clear to him that he is not to marry a divorcee and for that reason he wished to end things though he wouldn't mind being friends. I was too shocked to say anything. How could he be so cruel and how could his parents be so ignorant, arrogant and un-Islamic?"

To be treated in the way that this nurse was is simply the most dehumanising behaviour that could be meted out to any person. Over the 6 months she was in contact with the doctor the young lady in question developed an intense emotional bond towards the man she was apparently, at least in her own innocent mind, exploring the potential of marriage with. Only after the 6 months had evaporated did she discover to her repugnance that the man had at

162

the very outset decided she was not "marriage-worthy" as her apparent crime lay in her being a divorcee. To use his parents as an excuse after being in regular contact with her for a concerted period of time, which 6 months is, is simply lame and cowardly to put it mildly. To play with someone's feelings and then plead that his parents are not accepting of a divorcee is simply not good enough and smacks of hypocrisy. Granted: his parents may well exercise this prejudice towards divorcees when it comes to their 'golden boy' finding a wife. However, notwithstanding that, what then can we say about the doctor himself? Clearly, he is in no way any less prejudiced towards divorcees than his parents are: if he could not reconcile with the fact that our nurse is a divorcee, if he could not be Muslim-enough to conquer this atavistic bias, why then did he accommodate a dialogue with the nurse only to tell her after half-a-year had gone by that her being a divorcee was an insurmountable constraint! Nobody is debating that we all harbour preferences: however, preference turns to prejudice when someone is lulled into thinking that they are being assigned an equal opportunity when already a preference has penalised their candidature, as was the case with the nurse. Quite simply if the doctor could not tolerate the thought of being married to a divorcee because he has a preference to marry someone who has been 'never married', he should have exercised incisive (excuse the pun!) honesty and revealed that preference to the nurse at the very inauguration of their dialogue. In the first place, one should not penalise a divorcee with a view to marriage; however, if one cannot accommodate the notion of being married to a divorcee, one should not initiate dialogue or accept a request for dialogue with a divorcee when one is already adamant that one's posture in this regard is not likely to be flexed.

As a matter of due care, any marriage-inspired dialogue framework should bring within its fold the urgency to establish at the very beginning of any potential dialogue between a Muslim male and a Muslim female whether a divorcee or widow or widower is likely to be penalised by a party who has never been married and/or their family. At Kamran A. Beg Events we are very upfront in posing this deeply searching question to our attendees, subscribers and members before a dialogue is commenced since our aim is always to preserve the integrity and emotional well-being of each of our service recipients. It is better to embrace reality before indulging in a rudderless dialogue than to experience the appalling fate that befell our unassuming nurse. Such clarification becomes all the more necessary in the case of divorcees with children from a previous marriage where it is crucial to establish whether a potential dialogue prospect will be accepting of the children, not to mention whether they will be able to swallow the fact that the other party is a divorcee.

(viii) **Not penalising and showing indifference towards Muslim reverts:** In much the same way

164

that a marriage-inspired dialogue framework should legislate for how accepting a dialogue prospect is of a potential party who is divorced or widowed, the same logic should be extended to Muslim reverts who as our research shows experience great indifference from the mainstream Muslim community in their quest to seek a counterpart amongst members of the Ummah who were born into the faith. We have already raised this as a deeply worrying concern in chapter 1.

Kamran A. Beg Events interviewed 50 Muslim reverts in the UK between November 2005 and March 2006 to identify their concerns on the matrimonial front. This sample consisted of an even ratio of male and female Muslim reverts drawn from across the UK who had embraced Islam in the new millennium. Each revert featured in the interview programme is a professional single seeking a spouse and is a degree holder. Each has exhibited a huge leap of faith in reverting to Islam, which bears testimony to their unfailing and complete subservience to Allah (SWT). Each is a sterling ambassador for the Muslim community. It is therefore deeply worrying that despite the faith Muslim reverts have shown in the community this faith in large measure is unrequited by the mainstream Muslim community as our research poignantly unmasks. 84% of the Muslim reverts interviewed felt that there is no real support infrastructure that absorbs them into mainstream Muslim life. 86% of the sample felt that their ability to find a life partner within the Muslim community is seriously restricted since, as one revert succinctly put it, "our brethren born into Islam see us as culturally different not recognising that we are all members of the same Muslim family". As one 34 year-old female actuary based in London put it: "I met a Muslim man at work and we took a liking to each other. We met a few times, went out and then he came clean after a couple of months. He said that his parents would not be able to accept me since we belong to different cultures. It hurt me because I had developed feelings towards him and we had seen each over a couple of months." As we can see, the man's failing in this case study resides in his knowing that he and his parents could not fathom the cultural diversity that a potential marriage with the actuary could represent even though as exhorted upon Muslims by the Prophet (PBUH), one should not discriminate against a fellow Muslim on the basis of culture, ethnicity and caste. Such discrimination is strictly prohibited by the Islamic faith. The female's failing stems from not clarifying from the beginning whether culture was likely to be a barrier to expediting progress though in this case she could be excused as this was the first matrimonial dialogue she had entertained after her reversion.

In North America where Islam is easily the fastest growing faith, it has been reported that up to 30% of Muslim reverts are either converting back to their original faith or rejecting faith altogether within 4 years of embracing Islam as they feel excluded from the mainstream Muslim community itself, citing, inter alia, the lack of support received from within the community allowing them to merge more easily and effortlessly into mainstream Muslim life and on account of the gross indifference shown by many Muslims born into the faith towards them when seeking a marriage partner.

All Muslims, whether born into the faith or reverting to Islam, are equal in the eyes of Allah (SWT) and should be treated equally by each other: "Surely the believers are none but brothers unto one another, so set things right between your brothers, and have fear of Allah that you may be shown mercy" (Quran 49:10). The mainstream Muslim community needs to make very concerted and determined efforts to address the needs of Muslim reverts and make them feel an inclusive part of the community. Whilst this theme is not under scrutiny in this book it would be a huge failing on the part of the writer not to acknowledge that there is a serious problem and that it warrants urgent attention otherwise the community may continue to alienate more reverts, which is unacceptable. Marriage is certainly one crucial area where more tolerance needs to be exercised by the majority of Muslims belonging to the mainstream community in how they view and accommodate potential spouses who have reverted to Islam. While there has been some progress in this regard, it is hardly palpable and certainly nothing to write home about.

(ix) **Applying cultural, ethnic, sectarian and racial tolerance when considering Muslim life partner choices:** In the global research study cited at the beginning of this chapter featuring the 500 Muslim professional singles drawn from the UK, Ireland, France, Germany, Australia, the USA and Canada and conducted between March 2005 and March 2006, no less than 77% of the interviewees who contributed to the study acknowledged that their families are not amenable to them seeking a Muslim life partner belonging to a different culture. The singles in question feel that this indifference to other cultures has drastically impaired their ability to find a spouse from within the precincts of the Muslim community and has diminished their efforts to do so greatly in view of the Muslim community being a fragmented minority in each of the seven countries surveyed. It has shrunk the pipeline of potential suitors that they can tap into in their pursuit of matrimonial bliss significantly lending to the increased frustration felt by these professionals.

Insofar as the South Asian interviewees who formed the interview sample were concerned 42% categorically stated that caste or marrying someone whose family descends from the same region as their parents' country of origin was still a compulsory requirement foisted upon them by their inflexible though otherwise loving parents. A 34 year-old teacher, a denizen of Liverpool (reference here is being made to Liverpool in the UK, which is the case wherever Liverpool is mentioned in this book), poignantly states: "This caste barrier has made life impossible for me for every time I introduce someone to my parents if he is not of the same caste as our family he is just treated like a non-entity. I have tried so hard to get them to move away from this blinkered view of the world but all the trying in the world seems to be getting me nowhere. I don't know what to do. I am getting on and to be completely honest I am totally fed up. It is hard enough to find a Muslim husband without having to worry about all these other things."

Another professional, a very dedicated and highly respected 32 year-old IT consultant based in California, vents his frustration describing his 'crushing' experience: "I met a young lady of Arab origin at work and we clicked. My family is from South Asia. We continued to see each other for a few months and felt that we were right in every way possible. However, when it came to the crunch we both got pulverised. Our families were not accepting of a cross-cultural marriage and would not sanction the marriage. It has left our lives in tatters. We both work as IT consultants for the same firm and seeing each other every day at work doesn't do either of us any good. Our cultures should not get in the way: the fact that we both belong to the same faith and are Muslims is all that should count. Why couldn't our parents see it that way? "

As we can infer from the research findings above, sadly caste and culture still appear to play a significant role in screening out worthy suitors.

Islam abhors caste and repudiates the whole concept of caste: Islam forbids the practice of categorising and compartmentalising people on the basis of caste. It has no place within a Muslim social imperative. If caste is prohibited then what does that say of the malpractice that screens potential life partners out because one's family is not amenable to a particular, apparently different caste? As for culture we are not debating that individuals may harbour a particular cultural preference regarding their choice of counterpart; however, if one can exercise a specific cultural preference then surely as a corollary Muslims have every right to exercise a *preference for cultural diversity* in seeking a spouse from the same faith. Cultural difference should not be used to penalise a candidate for marriage. Islam celebrates the esprit de corps encompassed by the concept of the Ummah, a fraternity in which all Muslims, irrespective of their culture, ethnicity, sect and race, are assigned an equal stature and treated with equality: "Surely the believers are none but brothers unto one another, so set things right between your brothers, and have fear of Allah that you may be shown mercy" (Quran 49:10).

While the Muslim community in the west is finally beginning to awaken to how even more challenging finding a Muslim life partner is and while some cross-cultural marriages are beginning to happen, we still have much to do in the way of paving an understanding and building bridges between different cultures, suspending

170

pre-conceived indifferences and progressing marriage proposals out-of-culture. These are hurdles the community can only surmount through revisiting the faith and reviving the levers of equality and fraternity indigenous to Islam. The enlightening life-example of the Prophet (PBUH) is more than adequate to press home the urgency with which we need to do so!

As a 30 year-old surgeon put it: "I had always wanted to marry at the first available opportunity after leaving medical school. Being raised in London, which is cosmopolitan, I thought I had everything going for me. I tried: if it wasn't the caste, it was race; if it wasn't race, it was sect; if it wasn't sect, it was culture. Finally I couldn't take any more and left the scene. I am now married and my wife belongs to a different faith, which falls outside the faith traditions I as a Muslim man am permitted to marry. I have been ostracised from the family and have been reduced to an outcast." As extreme an example as this may appear, I can assure the keen reader this is not a rare exception. Over 200 Muslim professionals worldwide have contacted these humble offices over the past couple of years with similar stories. An analysis of their specific circumstances shows that 184 or a staggering 92% of these Muslim professionals would now be married to fellow Muslim instead if their parents had not excluded potential Muslim suitors that they the professionals wished to progress marriage with. These suitors were un-Islamically dismissed and discounted with disdain along cultural, ethnic, sectarian or racial lines. Such then is the unfathomable price of such deep-rooted indifference towards fellow Muslims!

As a community I would urge all professionals and their parents and families alike, indeed all Muslims, to exercise the highest degrees of *'cultural, ethnic, sectarian and racial tolerance'* when considering Muslim life partner choices per se and when interacting with Muslims in general and to the parents in particular I would respectfully say that it is in your best interests to exercise such tolerance, which is only in keeping with the Muslim value system enjoined upon members of our faith by Allah (SWT) and celebrated through the life of the Prophet (PBUH). We can draw immediate inspiration and comfort from the illuminating example of the Ansar of Madinah and how they welcomed, embraced and accommodated the Muhajirun from Makkah who followed the Prophet (PBUH) during the Hijrah (see chapter 1). Parents and their children should not be averse to Allah's advice, which we repeat again for the sake of emphasis: "Surely the believers are none but brothers unto one another, so set things right between your brothers, and have fear of Allah that you may be shown mercy" (Quran 49:10). As one parent said in her deeply moving letter addressed to me in May 2006: "Had I shown some flexibility on the question of culture, I am sure that my daughter would have been married by now. She is 43. In hindsight, I wish I had agreed to her wish to marry someone from a different culture 12 years ago. I was so mired in this caste and culture thinking that I couldn't see the wood for the trees. My daughter has paid a huge price for my indifference and gross failing as Muslim parent."

A marriage-inspired dialogue framework should therefore make it incumbent on all stakeholders integral to it to exercise the very highest degrees of *'cultural, ethnic, sectarian and racial tolerance'* when considering Muslim life partner choices.

A Summary of the Nine Key Features

We have elucidated in some detail the nine key features that a robust halal marriage-inspired dialogue framework appropriate for both family based and non-family based introductions should be imbued with in deference to the Muslim value system. Case studies have also proved very anecdotal and instructive in emphasising the need to satiate these parameters. These case studies have highlighted some of the pitfalls to legislate for when appropriate safeguards designed to preserve the halal sanctity of a proposed marriage-based dialogue are not erected. Global research conducted by Kamran A. Beg Events has brought to light a rampant "dating culture" that has sadly afflicted a significant proportion of Muslim professionals in their life partner search. If anything such findings have made Kamran A. Beg Events more wary of the need to formulate a robust halal marriage-inspired dialogue framework that seeks to eliminate the anathema of dating, which is Islamically prohibited and therefore haram!

The nine key features integral to a robust halal marriage-inspired dialogue framework suitable for Muslim professionals (and for Muslim consumption in general) are now briefly enumerated below:

(i)   **Making sure that the dialogue is inspired by marriage:** Since "actions are judged by their intention" the marriage-inspired dialogue framework should confirm at the very outset that the Muslim male and Muslim female parties in question genuinely wish to embark on a matrimonial dialogue and that too in a halal manner, which prohibits any penchant to date or have a pre-marital relationship.

(ii)   **Informing the parent(s)/guardian(s) about the dialogue and keeping them abreast of how it is developing:** If the Muslim male and Muslim female who have been introduced for the purposes of a matrimonial dialogue have been introduced through a non-family channel then in the interests of transparency and to safeguard the ethical and moral integrity of that dialogue it is essential for both parties to inform their parent(s)/guardian(s) that they are engaged in a marriage-inspired dialogue with each other. This basic pre-requisite to inform the parent or guardian is a necessary condition to render the dialogue halal. Naturally in the case of a family-based introduction the families are already aware that the male and female are in dialogue since they (the families) effected the introduction in the first place.

(iii)   **Circumscribing within reason the time over which individual compatibility is gauged:** An accountable, transparent and responsible marriage-inspired dialogue framework designed to safeguard the emotional well-being of both dialogue incumbents should circumscribe within reason the time over which the Muslim male and Muslim female in dialogue are allowed to reconcile with the degree to which they click and whether this degree is of sufficient magnitude to initiate (in the case of a non-family based introduction) or revive (in the case of a family based introduction) direct interaction between the families with a view to exploring marriage. The two parties immersed in dialogue should be sensitive to the need to initiate (in the case of a non-family based introduction) or revive (in the case of a family based introduction) direct interaction between the families *immediately* after mutually concluding that there is a significant measure of individual compatibility between the two, which should be established *as soon as is reasonably possible* after their introduction has been effected.

(iv)   **Eliminating the scourge of dating:** The marriage-inspired dialogue framework should emphasise and place at its very epicentre a system of etiquette that safeguards the integrity of both the Muslim male and Muslim female in dialogue and in particular it must assign maximum exposure to ensuring that the dignity of the female is not violated. It must seek to eliminate the scourge of dating and inhibit any proclivity for the two individuals to date each other and be

175

tempted to partake in a pre-marital physical relationship.

(v) **Navigating dialogue closure with the utmost sensitivity:** Dialogue construed within the purview of the proposed marriage-inspired dialogue framework should be conducted with honesty and integrity and both parties should seek to accord the other party the maximum degree of sensitivity. In particular, dialogue closure needs to be navigated with the utmost skill and one tool that all dialogue incumbents should absorb into their dialogue toolkit is how to close a dialogue respectfully, civilly and with the utmost humility and sensitivity! Any marriage-inspired dialogue framework should therefore underscore the importance of "empathy, compassion, due care, sensitivity and grace" when plumbing inside the earthquake zone of dialogue closure.

(vi) **Engendering a progressive, high-trust based working relationship between the dialogue incumbent and their parent(s)/guardian(s):** A marriage-inspired dialogue framework should engender a progressive, high-trust based working relationship between the party in dialogue and their parent(s)/guardian(s). The two individuals in dialogue and their parents are all stakeholders in a marriage-inspired dialogue framework. Each stakeholder should therefore feel a sense of ownership in this all-inclusive framework.

(vii) **Not penalising and showing indifference towards divorcees or widows or widowers:** Any marriage-inspired dialogue framework should bring within its fold the urgency to establish at the very beginning of any potential

176

dialogue between two parties whether a divorcee or widow or widower is likely to be penalised by a party who has never been married and/or their family. Such clarification becomes all the more necessary in the case of divorcees with children from a previous marriage where it is crucial to establish whether a potential dialogue prospect will be accepting of the children, not to mention whether they will be able to swallow the fact that the other party is a divorcee.

(viii) **Not penalising and showing indifference towards Muslim reverts:** In much the same way that a marriage-inspired dialogue framework should legislate at the very outset for how accepting a dialogue prospect is of a potential party who is divorced or widowed, the same logic should be extended to Muslim reverts.

(ix) **Applying cultural, ethnic, sectarian and racial tolerance when considering Muslim life partner choices:** A marriage-inspired dialogue framework should make it incumbent on all stakeholders integral to it to exercise the highest degrees of *'cultural, ethnic, sectarian and racial tolerance'* when considering Muslim life partner choices.

The 3-Dialogue Rule is a Proven Robust Halal Marriage-inspired Dialogue Framework Tempered with Balance and Moderation

The **3-Dialogue Rule**, which has been developed by Kamran A. Beg Events and which so far has successfully guided, subject to the Divine will, 100 Muslim professional couples to the wedding altar since Kamran A. Beg Events came into existence on July 11, 2003, is the **robust halal marriage-inspired dialogue framework** that we strongly recommend as being appropriate for Muslim professionals to deploy when engaged in matrimonial dialogue and, equally, is suitable on a broader scale for general Muslim consumption. The 3-Dialogue Rule is equally applicable to both family based and non-family based introductions.

The 3-Dialogue Rule comfortably satisfies each of the nine attributes identified above as being germane to a robust halal marriage-inspired dialogue framework.

Moreover, as the 100 marriages witnessed so far through Kamran A. Beg Events signal, the 3-Dialogue Rule has proven currency worldwide. It will constitute the focal point in the rest of our deliberations in this book. It is recommended that the Muslim male and Muslim female engaged in marriage-inspired dialogue conform to the spirit and essence of the **3-Dialogue Rule**, which crucially is predicated on the definitive tenets of **balance** and **moderation** integral to the Islamic faith.

We now discuss the 3-Dialogue Rule in the remaining two chapters of this book. Chapter 3 provides a detailed elaboration of what the 3-Dialogue Rule encompasses while chapter 4 shows how well it works in practice and also factors in specific case studies to substantiate this.

3. The 3-Dialogue Rule

The 3-Dialogue Rule is the **robust halal marriage-inspired dialogue framework** that is recommended as the medium through which to orchestrate dialogue between a Muslim male and a Muslim female that is matrimonial in basis. As stated in the previous chapter, since being created in July 2003, Kamran A. Beg Events has had the great honour of seeing 200 Muslim professionals proceed to marriage under its umbrella. The 100 couples that have been generated to date as a courtesy of and subject to the Divine will have each proved to be outstanding exponents of the 3-Dialogue Rule following it in both letter and spirit. Granted these marriages came about as a consequence of non-family based introductions effected through Kamran A. Beg Events. Equally, however, this robust halal marriage-inspired dialogue framework can be applied to family-based introductions as well. Whatever halal channel the marriage-inspired introduction is initiated through the 3-Dialogue Rule's value cannot be underscored enough.

The 3-Dialogue Rule has made and continues to make a significant contribution to the landscape of halal marriage-inspired dialogue between two Muslim professionals, as the 100 marriages that have crystallised through Kamran A. Beg Events thus far clearly bear testimony to and illuminate. It should be noted that 73 of these marriages have taken place in the UK, 3 in Australia, 21 in the USA and 3 in Canada. In each case the dialogue incumbents, each now happily wed, followed the 3-Dialogue Rule.

Islamically, it is seminal to the integrity of any halal matrimonial dialogue that both parties know sooner rather than later whether they will be proceeding to marriage, a decision that cannot be undertaken until the parent(s) or guardian(s) of the Muslim male and Muslim female parties in question have become integrated into the dialogue process. Furthermore, a dialogue is only formally recognised as a dialogue when the parent(s) or guardian(s) of the male and female parties in question have become integrated into the dialogue process. This is made explicitly clear by the 3-Dialogue Rule.

It is my resolute conviction that all Muslim parents and their children alike should be aware of what the 3-Dialogue Rule is, how it works in practice, and how it can safeguard the Muslim male and Muslim female in dialogue and allow them and all other stakeholders integral to the marriage-inspired dialogue process to establish sooner rather than later whether there is any matrimonial currency in a particular dialogue to start off with. While admittedly the 3-Dialogue Rule was originally developed by Kamran A. Beg Events to guide Muslim professionals exploring the question of marriage since Kamran A. Beg Events specifically caters to this clientele of Muslims, the broad appeal, however, of this halal marriage-inspired dialogue framework makes the 3-Dialogue Rule equally suitable for general Muslim deployment.

We will now devote the remainder of this book to focusing on the essence and vitality of the 3-Dialogue Rule.

An Overview of the Matrimonial Services Provided to Muslim Professionals by Kamran A. Beg Events

In the introduction to this book we respectfully noted some of the key milestones that Kamran A. Beg Events has attained so far since its inception. See the introduction for an overview of twelve key milestones achieved to date. Achieving these milestones has fuelled the momentum and vigour with which the organisation has continued to grow and serve the Muslim professional community worldwide.

An overview of the portfolio of marriage-based services provided by Kamran A. Beg Events to Muslim professionals and an appreciation of the non-family based channels used for effecting introductions will greatly assist our discussions about the 3-Dialogue Rule. As we stated in chapter 2: *"By 'Muslim professional' we mean a Muslim who is typically university educated and is either employed by an employer or self-employed."* 98% of the Muslim professionals accommodated by Kamran A. Beg Events hold at least one university degree. Professionals are represented from a diverse spectrum of fields, including, amongst others, medicine, dentistry, nursing, law, accounting, journalism, the media sector, consultancy, IT, marketing, engineering, science, and banking, not to mention individuals running their own enterprises and businesses.

Kamran A. Beg Professional Muslim Singles Evening Events where *attendees* are introduced to one another through a matrimonial event they attend in person, **Kamran A. Beg Professional Muslim Online Matrimonials** where introduction between two Muslim professional *subscribers* is conducted via an online service and **Kamran A. Beg Professional Muslim Marriage Bureau Matrimonials** where *members* are provided with unlimited personalised matching, unlimited online subscription and allowed to attend up to three matrimonial events are each run by **Kamran A. Beg Events**, which is chaired and presided over by Kamran A. Beg, that is the humble writer himself.

Furthermore in the case of Kamran A. Beg Professional Muslim Marriage Bureau Matrimonials all registered members subscribe to **Unlimited Period Membership** of Kamran A. Beg Professional Muslim Marriage Bureau Matrimonials, which is designed to *optimise the member's chances of meeting a life partner* by deploying an *integrated framework* comprising the *personalised matching service* (where our seasoned team of consultants proactively recommend candidates for dialogue based on the member's matrimonial requirements) and the *events* and *online channels* run by Kamran A. Beg Events. This innovative and groundbreaking integrated approach, which originates for the member's needs, has been designed to give members maximum exposure in terms of meeting compatible life partner prospects.

As we noted earlier Kamran A. Beg Events has hitherto built up a global family of 7,000 Muslim professional attendees, subscribers and members, each of whom is committed to the 3-Dialogue Rule.

Insofar as *non-family based introductions* are concerned it is noteworthy to observe that Kamran A. Beg Events has built up an excellent track record in rendering marriage-based introductions among Muslim professionals through *three such channels*, namely through *attendance at matrimonial events*, through *subscribing to the online service* and through *a confluence of the events, online service and personalised matching service resulting in the integrated framework mentioned above*. In each case, attendees, subscribers and members adopt the 3-Dialogue Rule as the marriage-inspired dialogue framework guiding their matrimonial deliberations. This is expressly built into the rules of engagement, which apply to each category of membership. It is suggested that

182

the reader visits, if they have not already done so, the Kamran A. Beg Events web site at www.kamranabegevents.com with a view to learning more about the organisation and each of the services briefly outlined above and seeing first hand the central impact and overriding importance of the 3-Dialogue Rule.

In line with the policy exercised by Kamran A. Beg Events, all prospective attendees, subscribers and members are *vetted* by way of rigorous telephone and detailed written interviews and then extended an invitation to attend an event, subscribe to the online service or become a member of the marriage bureau matrimonials service, subject to their telephone and written interviews being accepted as **appropriate** for the *global family of attendees, subscribers and members* comprising Kamran A. Beg Events. This is to ensure that **only like-minded Muslim professionals** fostering a *compatible mindset* and *geared towards the formalities and etiquette integral to a halal Muslim matrimonial dialogue* are accepted into our family, which is premised on maintaining the very highest standards of *accountability, responsibility, honesty, trust, sincerity, integrity and upstanding etiquette.*

All prospective attendees, subscribers and members are therefore **vetted rigorously** in order to ensure the selection of like-minded, responsible, dignified and upstanding Muslim professionals thereby enhancing the integrity, quality and demeanour underpinning any *marriage-inspired dialogue* that may ensue as a direct consequence of an introduction effected through Kamran A. Beg Events.

Vetting is an imperative key therefore to fostering and accommodating a progressive community of like-minded

183

Muslim professional attendees, subscribers and members and greatly contributes to improving one's chances of finding a life partner. This has certainly been our experience with Kamran A. Beg Events where *vetting* and the application of the *3-Dialogue Rule* form the robust cornerstone on which the very success of our marriage-led enterprise is predicated.

The 3-Dialogue Rule, which amongst other things eliminates the scourge of dating, provides a **dialogue guidance framework** for **members** of **Kamran A. Beg Professional Muslim Marriage Bureau Matrimonials** as it does an **offline dialogue guidance framework** for **subscribers** of **Kamran A. Beg Professional Muslim Online Matrimonials** or a **post-event dialogue guidance framework** for **attendees** of **Kamran A. Beg Professional Muslim Singles Evening Events**. As an organisation, we have seen our global family of vetted Muslim professionals benefit enormously from the added value that the 3-Dialogue Rule provides. This added value has manifested itself tangibly, much to the joy of our attendees, subscribers and members, across all three non-family based introduction platforms provided by Kamran A. Beg Events: *matrimonial events*, *the online service* and *personalised matching*.

How the 3-Dialogue Rule Satiates the Nine Features Underpinning a Robust Halal Marriage-inspired Dialogue Framework

We have detailed in chapter 2 the nine key features integral to a robust halal marriage-inspired dialogue framework suitable for Muslim professionals (and for general Muslim consumption) and will now show how the 3-Dialogue Rule satisfies these conditions. We will do this with reference to a non-family based introduction though the same reasoning can be applied to the case of a family-based introduction. How the 3-Dialogue Rule works in the case of a family based introduction is tackled separately later in this chapter.

The nine features are now recounted below to assist our discussions going forward:

(i) Making sure that the dialogue is inspired by marriage

(ii) Informing the parent(s)/guardian(s) about the dialogue and keeping them abreast of how it is developing

(iii) Circumscribing within reason the time over which individual compatibility is gauged

(iv) Eliminating the scourge of dating

(v) Navigating dialogue closure with the utmost sensitivity

(vi) Engendering a progressive, high-trust based working relationship between the dialogue incumbent and their parent(s)/guardian(s)

(vii) Not penalising and showing indifference towards divorcees or widows or widowers

(viii) Not penalising and showing indifference towards Muslim reverts

(ix) Applying cultural, ethnic, sectarian and racial tolerance when considering Muslim life partner choices

Where we draw reference to the 3-Dialogue rule satisfying these features the feature in question will be referred to as feature followed by the actual feature number in parenthesis. For example, feature (i) would refer to the first of the nine itemised features above constituting a robust halal marriage-inspired dialogue framework.

We shall assume for the purposes of illustration that the Muslim male and female about to engage in a marriage-inspired dialogue have been respectfully introduced to each other via Kamran A. Beg Events through utilising any of the above three non-family based introduction platforms, be it as a result of a *matrimonial event* or through *the online service* or via *personalised matching*, and that some form of appropriate vetting had been performed prior to the introduction being initiated. We have already described in brief the rigorous vetting methodology employed by Kamran A. Beg Events.

Feature (i) of a robust halal marriage-inspired dialogue framework is clearly satisfied by the 3-Dialogue Rule since we would seek to establish at the very beginning that the Muslim male and Muslim female in question genuinely wish to embark on a marriage-inspired dialogue. As strongly stressed in chapter 2 every precaution should be taken to circumvent the odious perils of 'broken-heart syndrome', which is all the more reason to ensure that feature (i) is fully accommodated.

Also, in progressing this marriage-inspired dialogue both parties would be asked pre-dialogue whether any specific preferences were likely to impede the ability of the proposed dialogue to progress productively. **Specifically, the 3-Dialogue Rule would clarify from both potential dialogue incumbents pre-dialogue whether the other dialogue party being a divorcee, widow, widower, or Muslim revert, or being of different cultural, ethnic, sectarian or racial extraction would in any way inhibit the proposed**

dialogue from progressing thereby legislating for features (vii), (viii) and (ix) of a robust halal marriage-inspired dialogue framework. It is of paramount importance to verify that neither party is likely to penalise the other on the basis of any of the aforesaid since the whole intention of the 3-Dialogue Rule is to activate a marriage-inspired dialogue where such preferences cannot be cited as the reason for terminating the dialogue later. **Suffice it to say, if any of the preferences itemised above were likely to inhibit progress the 3-Dialogue Rule would discourage that dialogue to occur in the first place.** This is where clinical honesty is warranted on the part of both individuals before the dialogue is sanctioned. As one 28 year-old female economist of Egyptian origin now living in London who married a 30 year-old dentist of Pakistani origin whom she met at a matrimonial event chaired by the humble writer in Manchester in 2005 stated: "Kamran, before I engaged in post-event dialogue with my soon-to-become husband it was reassuring to know that the 3-Dialogue Rule addressed any question marks I had because you made sure that he had no cultural hang ups about him and me having families from two different cultural backgrounds. This gave me great piece of mind and the confidence to dialogue. I had really been impressed by him at your event and felt that our personalities bounced off each other. It was a good feeling to have. My only concern was that being Egyptian and he being Pakistani could cause a big problem with the families. I had met a chap of Pakistani origin a few years before and despite the fact that we had been in touch for 5 months we had to end everything because his family were not accepting of me being from a different culture. The great thing about the 3-Dialogue Rule is that you put my husband-to-be on the spot before allowing us to dialogue and when he said culture would not be an issue I knew then we could give this dialogue a real go."

Similar sentiments to the female economist are echoed by a divorcee with a son in her feedback to me. The female, a 37 year-old accountant, had attended a London event run by Kamran A. Beg Events in 2005 and was concerned that the previously 'never married' individual (a doctor by profession) she wished to dialogue with and his family may not be accepting of her son, not to mention the fact that she was a divorcee. The male attendee of interest was directly asked by me before allowing the dialogue to proceed whether either of these concerns was likely to impair a dialogue from progressing naturally with the requesting female party. He plainly responded that the lady in question had nothing to worry about and that he was looking forward to speaking to her. I am delighted to inform the enquiring reader that these two graceful and exemplary attendees tied the knot in January 2006 and having spoken to them both recently I can relay that they are enjoying a life of eternal bliss. As the female accountant said to me: "The 3-Dialogue Rule by clarifying where he stood reassured me that being a divorcee with a child would not be held against me. I went into that dialogue knowing that we were both on a level playing field."

The 3-Dialogue Rule makes it incumbent on both parties to inform their parent(s)/guardian(s) that they are in dialogue and to keep their parent (s)/guardian(s) abreast of how the dialogue is developing so fulfilling features (ii) and (vi) of a robust halal marriage-inspired dialogue framework. A 27 year-old female retail banker currently engaged (at the time of writing this book) to a 29 year-old software consultant, both resident in Chicago and introduced by our organisation through personalised matching, writes: "It was really nice to know that he was keeping his parents up to date regarding how we were progressing. Knowing that our parents were aware that we were speaking gave our dialogue a legitimate feel. Whatever the outcome we knew that we existed as far as our parents were concerned. It was also good for my Mom from time to time ask me about him and how I felt. It meant that my Mom valued my decision to talk with him and that she wanted to be as supportive as possible. The thing about the 3-Dialogue Rule is that it makes a dialogue halal because you have to keep your family in the know and that applies for both the male and female. That gives the female respect. So many of my friends have dated men and the guys' families never even knew they had existed." As our retail banker's telling testimonial stresses by making it incumbent on both parties to inform their families that they are in dialogue and of how the dialogue is evolving the 3-Dialogue Rule ensures that neither party is devalued, which would be the case if either or both of the families were oblivious to the dialogue. Since the families are visible to the dialogue it is rendered halal. The 3-Dialogue Rule ensures that the two individuals in dialogue and their parents are all stakeholders in this marriage-inspired dialogue framework. Each stakeholder therefore feels a sense of ownership in this all-inclusive framework representing a win-win scenario for both generations, so helping to bridge the generational gap that can otherwise lead to formidable tensions in the parent-child relationship.

Our two Chicago-based friends will be getting married in December 2006. May Allah (SWT) bless their marriage with eternal matrimonial happiness, Insha'Allah.

Assuming then a dialogue has been initiated through one of the three non-family based introduction platforms (event/online/personalised matching) listed above and sanctioned to proceed, in this case by Kamran A. Beg Events, before direct contact between the parent(s) or guardian(s) of the two Muslim parties is initiated the 3-Dialogue Rule states that the Muslim male and Muslim female parties in question should endeavour to undertake no more than **3 dialogues**, within the purview of a **2-week** time scale, to establish whether there is enough common overlap and compatibility between them to warrant progressing their dialogue to the parent/guardian level. This satisfies feature (iii) of a robust halal marriage-inspired dialogue framework in that the 3-Dialogue Rule circumscribes within reason the time – in this case 2 weeks – and additionally the number of dialogues – in this case 3 dialogues - over which the Muslim male and Muslim female in dialogue are allowed to reconcile with the degree to which they click and whether this degree is of sufficient magnitude to initiate (in the case of a non-family based introduction) direct interaction between the families *immediately* after mutually concluding that there is a significant measure of individual compatibility between the two parties in dialogue. By limiting the time scale over which the two individuals can explore how compatible they are at an individual level to two weeks and by restricting the actual number of dialogues permissible over that timescale to three the 3-Dialogue Rule safeguards the male and female parties in question **against** the spectre of dating and inhibits any proclivity for the two parties to be tempted to partake in a pre-marital physical relationship thereby satisfying feature (iv) of a robust halal marriage-inspired dialogue framework. As we know, dating and having a pre-marital relationship are Islamically prohibited and non-permissible and therefore haram!

A 35 year-old female academic who attended a Washington, DC event run by Kamran A. Beg Events in 2006 writes: "The 3-Dialogue Rule gave me focus. I knew that if by the third dialogue I couldn't feel that connection that it was time to check out of that dialogue. With two weeks to play with and three dialogues to anticipate I knew that we wouldn't become emotionally wrapped up with each other. This is great because there was always a chance that the dialogue could falter and the person I was speaking to may not feel I was right for him. I wouldn't want to be left hurt. Two weeks is ample time to discover if there is any real connection and three dialogues are more than enough to see if there is a substantive enough connection to get the families directly involved with each other. I ended it politely after the third dialogue but it was not like ending a relationship. The 3-Dialogue Rule prevents those sorts of feelings from developing, yet it allows you enough scope to know if there is something there to work on."

As the above submission reveals the 3-Dialogue Rule has built within it a mechanism that safeguards the emotional territory of both dialogue incumbents. While the execution of three dialogues spread over two weeks provides both parties with ample time and dialogue space (meaning the maximum number of dialogues, in this case three) to resolve the degree to which their personalities click, limiting the number of dialogues to three and the time over which they are executed to two weeks ensures that the two parties do not become too emotionally involved or overly consumed with each other otherwise this could exercise a detrimental effect emotionally and psychologically in the event that the dialogue is brought to closure by one or both of the parties.

Since dialogue closure in the case where both parties feel incompatible could occur at the earliest after the first dialogue or at the very latest immediately after the third dialogue and with the dialogue in any event limited in terms of time expended to a maximum of two weeks and the number of dialogues undertaken bounded to a maximum of three dialogues our research shows that the 3-Dialogue Rule also makes it easier and significantly less onerous and discomfiting for the two parties in dialogue to negotiate the very challenging proposition of 'dialogue closure. The 3-Dialogue Rule renders it easier for the two parties in question to fathom 'dialogue closure' with consummate sensitivity and respectfully and civilly, and with the utmost humility and dignity so satisfying feature (v) of a robust halal marriage-inspired dialogue framework. Dialogue closure is a skill that automatically develops as an invaluable part of your dialogue toolkit when deploying the 3-Dialogue Rule.

A Leeds-based (reference here is being made to Leeds in the UK, which is the case wherever Leeds is mentioned in this book) 34 year-old male IT consultant introduced in April 2006 to a 29 year-old property specialist based in London on the basis of personalised matching remarks: "By the second dialogue we were clear that we were not entirely each other's cup of tea. However, we spoke very civilly and when we agreed on mutual closure we were careful not to deflate each other's confidence but rather complimented each other's manner and respected each other's take. We wished each other well and both felt even more rejuvenated regarding continuing our search. Knowing that we had spoken twice allowed us to manage each other's expectations more sensitively and bringing our dialogue to an end was not as difficult as I had thought. We were courteous and parted company on amicable grounds." For the record, the female above in her feedback noted: "He closed our dialogue in the way a gentleman should and if anything made me feel that there is someone out there for each of us and it is just a question of persevering." Need I say anymore: attendees, subscribers and members in their feedback to Kamran A. Beg Events have on the whole maintained that dialogue closure, an area, which for them had previously been equivalent to "plumbing inside an earthquake zone", is much easier to negotiate given the innate quality of the 3-Dialogue Rule to mitigate profoundly the degree to which the Muslim male and Muslim female in dialogue can get emotionally overwhelmed by each other and its predisposition to managing expectations between the two dialoguing parties more intelligently.

Understanding the Time and Frequency of Dialogue Limits Imposed by the 3-Dialogue Rule

It is insightful to note that the 2-week time scale over which to conduct at maximum 3 dialogues within the ambit of the 3-Dialogue Rule was concluded by Kamran A. Beg Events on the basis of a global research project featuring 600 Muslim professional singles based in the UK, Ireland, France, Germany, Australia, the USA and Canada. The sample consisted of 300 males and 300 females respectively. This landmark research was conducted between July 2003 and July 2004 and part of the aim of the research was to *establish the point in time where an emotional bond between the Muslim male and Muslim female engaged in dialogue started developing and intensifying to a point where it then became very difficult emotionally for either or both the Muslim male and Muslim female party to the dialogue to disengage from the dialogue, yet the dialogue had eventually ended in a non-marriage outcome between the two Muslim parties in question.*

We established on the basis of this sample that if on average the Muslim male and Muslim female were in contact for more than 2 weeks they started to develop increasing degrees of emotional dependency on one another, which from a Muslim perspective will get alarm bells ringing if the reason for the parties being in contact in the first place was to explore marriage, yet non-marriage was the outcome. Secondly the research pointed out that the frequency of contact also lends to intensifying the degree of emotional dependency developed between the Muslim male and Muslim female: in short, the more often the two parties speak over the phone, meet in person or communicate via the e-mail the more emotionally-intertwined they become, which again is a major cause for concern if the reason for the two parties being in contact in the first place was to explore marriage, yet non-marriage was the resultant outcome. As our research reveals assuming the Muslim male and Muslim female in question are exploring life partner dialogue the length of time over which the two parties are in contact and the frequency with which they contact each other both correlate significantly with the degree of emotional inter-dependency they develop towards each other during the period they remain in contact with each other. Furthermore our research sample showed that this applies to both family and non-family based introductions.

Our objectives when conducting this research were to establish a suitable time scale over which a Muslim male and a Muslim female could engage in marriage-inspired dialogue and a maximum number of dialogues they could experience over that time period (the dialogue space) such that they could exercise enough leverage to establish whether their personalities clicked without the two parties becoming too emotionally dependent on one another. Whether then the two parties concluded that their personalities did or did not click sufficiently to initiate (in the case of a non-family based introduction) or further expedite (in the case of a family-based introduction) direct family involvement we would nonetheless have one pleasantly satisfying consolation, namely significantly mitigated emotional dependency between the Muslim male and Muslim female. This is important for as we have noted in chapters 1 and 2 even if the personalities click until it has been confirmed that there is a significant degree of overlap between the two family value systems the marriage is likely not to be sanctioned by the powers that be since individual compatibility of itself is not a sufficient condition to ensure that a potential marriage between the two parties would be sustainable. Therefore it was clear to Kamran A. Beg Events when conducting the research study described that whether the two parties progressed their dialogue to the family level or not the degree of emotional bonding and dependency developed between the two individuals during the phase of ascertaining whether the degree of individual compatibility was significant would in fact need to be contained.

Moreover, what we discovered through the professionals interviewed was that if the two Muslim parties were in dialogue for more than 2 weeks and the two parties had not activated direct family interaction at the very latest by the end of the second week after initiating contact with each other either via the telephone or through meeting in person there was a **95% probability** that direct interaction between the families with a view to exploring marriage would **never**

occur irrespective of how long the two individuals remained in communication after the 2-week watershed. **This translates into a non-marriage scenario for the two Muslims in question and applies equally to both family and non-family based introductions!**

Having identified this crucially vital cut-off point we then revisited the professionals who had so kindly formed the research sample and asked them the very direct question: "Hand-on-heart, assuming you are exploring marriage, how many dialogues do you need to have with a fellow Muslim professional to establish whether your personalities click enough to get your families involved?" Here, one dialogue can either be a telephone conversation or a meeting where you see that individual in person. 84% of the respondents indicated that they would need no more than three dialogues but that three dialogues would give both Muslim parties enough exposure to one another to know if there was a significant enough click provided they met at least once in person during the course of the dialogue process. 10% of the respondents said two dialogues would suffice provided they met at least once in person during the course of the dialogue process but the sizeable majority (84%) of our sample was of the opinion that three dialogues were a sensible number of dialogues to undertake over which to come to a firm decision on whether the two Muslim personalities were sufficiently compatible at an individual level to get the families involved provided at least one of these dialogues took the form of a meeting where the Muslim male and Muslim female met each other in person.

What the 3-Dialogue Rule States

The groundbreaking research above therefore allowed Kamran A. Beg Events to define two key parameters that would need to be allowed for when formulating a robust halal marriage-inspired dialogue framework for two Muslims in dialogue:

(i) Dialogue between a Muslim male and Muslim female should be limited to a maximum of 2 weeks to mitigate the degree of emotional dependency and bonding that may be developed between the two parties.

(ii) The number of dialogues undertaken over this time scale should be capped at a maximum of three to allow the parties enough 'dialogue space' to establish the degree to which their personalities click.

Thus we can now state the 3-Dialogue Rule:

The 3-Dialogue Rule states that the Muslim male and Muslim female exploring the question of marriage should endeavour to undertake no more than **3 dialogues**, within the purview of a **2-week** time scale, to establish whether there is enough common overlap and compatibility between them to warrant progressing their dialogue to the parent/guardian level.

The 3-Dialogue Rule Clearly Distinguishes Between Dialogue, which is Halal, and Dating, which is Haram

Through the 3-Dialogue Rule, we are now in a position to make a tangible distinction between *'marriage-inspired*

197

dialogue' featuring a Muslim male and Muslim female that is halal and permissible and *'dating'*, which is Islamically prohibited and non-permissible and therefore haram!

Provided, as stated in the 3-Dialogue Rule above, the two Muslim dialogue incumbents endeavour to undertake no more than **3 dialogues**, within the purview of a **2-week** time scale, to establish whether there is enough common overlap and compatibility between them to warrant progressing their dialogue to the parent/guardian level then the dialogue is 'halal' and 'permissible'. This applies equally to both family and non-family based introductions. If by no later than the third dialogue, subject to a 2-week time scale, the two individuals agree that there is sufficient compatibility between them to warrant progressing their dialogue to the parent/guardian level then direct interaction between the families should be activated *immediately* and *any future dialogues between the two individuals would need to be sanctioned by both families once the families had engaged directly.*

If, however, the two Muslim individuals are still in communication such that the 2-week time limit has been overstepped and they have not activated direct interaction between the families at the very latest by the end of the second week after initiating contact with each other either via the telephone or through meeting in person the two parties are effectively dating according to the limits imposed by the 3-Dialogue Rule. This is evidenced by our research, which categorically discloses that if a Muslim and a Muslim female are in dialogue for more than 2 weeks such that they have not expedited direct family interaction at the very latest by the end of the second week after initiating contact with each other either via the telephone or through meeting in person that there is a **95% probability** that direct interaction between the families with a view to exploring marriage would **never occur** irrespective of how long the two individuals remain in communication after the 2-week watershed. This translates into a non-marriage scenario and applies equally to both family and non-family based introductions!

The 3-Dialogue Rule entreaties both the Muslim male and Muslim female particular to the dialogue to be wary of the above distinction between *dialogue* and *dating*. We note that this delineation between when two individuals are in halal dialogue vis-à-vis when they are dating specifically applies to Muslim professionals (and by extension to Muslims per se) as the original research was based on analysing marriage-inspired introductions experienced by Muslim professionals in dialogue with fellow Muslims. Quite simply: if you and the other person have been left to your own devices for more than 2 weeks and your families have not been engaged with a view to exploring the question of marriage at the very latest by the end of the second week after which you and the other party had initiated contact with each other either via the telephone or through meeting in person you are dating since the limits imposed by the 3-Dialogue Rule would have been violated.

Pertinently therefore, as our insightful research brings to light, if you are exploring life partner potential with any Muslim party to whom you have been introduced through a *non-family based channel* and you have been in communication with that individual for more than 2 weeks after initiating communication with that party either via the telephone or through a meeting in person and you and that individual have not encouraged your parents to contact each other at the very latest by the end of the second week after you had initiated contact with that individual either via the telephone or through a meeting in person then you and the other individual are according to the limits imposed by the 3-Dialogue Rule dating as in such circumstances there is a 95% probability that your respective parents will never engage with a view to exploring marriage between you and your fellow Muslim meaning that there is a 95% probability that you and that individual will not be proceeding to marriage. The cards then are heavily stacked against you both. Surely, it is better to heed the advice of the 3-Dialogue Rule and play it safe then to be sucked into what can reasonably be predicted as a marriage-wise non-productive situation, not to mention one that could leave you and the other party emotionally jaded and thoroughly bemused.

The same wisdom would apply to a *family-based introduction*. That is, if you are exploring life partner potential with any Muslim party to whom you have been introduced through a family-based introduction and you have been in communication with that individual for more than 2 weeks after initiating communication with that party either via the telephone or through a meeting in person and you and that individual have not encouraged your parents to revive contact with each other at the very latest by the end of the second week after you had initiated contact with that individual either via the telephone or through a meeting in person then you and the other individual are according to the limits imposed by the 3-Dialogue Rule dating as in such circumstances there is a 95% probability that your respective parents will never re-engage with a view to exploring marriage between you and your fellow Muslim meaning that there is a 95% probability you and that individual will not be proceeding to marriage.

The 3-Dialogue Rule Eliminates the Tempest of Dating

The **3-Dialogue Rule**, which is tempered with **balance** and **moderation**, clearly safeguards the two individuals in dialogue against the ominous perils of dating. Following the 3-Dialogue Rule does not necessarily mean that the Muslim male and Muslim female in question will proceed to marriage if they do activate family engagement in accordance with the limits imposed by the framework. As we have already noted the degree to which the two families harbour similar values would also exercise a significant influence on the likelihood of a marriage outcome. In the event that the families were engaged, the 3-Dialogue Rule would clearly allow the families to engage sooner rather than later thereby allowing an outcome to be determined as soon as possible, which can only help to safeguard the emotional sensitivities of the two individuals central to the dialogue. However, the luxury that the 3-Dialogue Rule does confer is that the two individuals partaking in dialogue will know sooner rather than later, subject to the limits imposed by the 3-Dialogue Rule, whether their personalities click sufficiently to warrant family involvement and if not to terminate the dialogue sooner rather than later subject to the limits imposed by the 3-Dialogue Rule. In other words, you have at the most until the end of the second week and if that click does not register at the very latest by then the 3-Dialogue Rule entreaties dialogue closure so preventing the tempest of a dating scenario from evolving. It effectively eliminates the possibility of dating if properly adhered to!

A 32 year-old female management accountant in May 2006 recounts: "Until signing up to a Kamran A. Beg Events event in Manchester I did not have the faintest idea when to draw the line under a dialogue. My parents introduced me to a nice man last year. They said it would be sensible for us to develop an understanding and take things from there. They wanted us to get to know each other before progressing things between the families. My mother was insistent that she did not wish to put too much pressure on me. The problem we had was that we had no structure to follow. We were just told to get on with it and see how things worked out. We talked for about 6 months and met up at alternate weekends. We both kept our parents informed as best we could but things turned out a bit pear-shaped towards the end. He started seeing me more as a friend and to be honest as much as I willed myself to see us both growing old together it just wasn't happening. It started to drain me after a while and then finally he called it off. The whole thing was grinded to a halt. Much to my relief, I might add! Had I known about the 3-Dialogue Rule we would have been honest enough to draw the same conclusion much sooner. That would have saved the agony. The good thing about the 3-Dialogue Rule is that you've got to come clean within 2 weeks. It is sad that our parents are not aware of the need to give a structure in the way the 3-Dialogue Rule does." As this example poignantly illustrates, it is not just the two individuals in dialogue that need to be guided in terms of how a halal marriage-inspired dialogue framework should work. The parents too need to be enlightened of an appropriate dialogue structure their children can adopt to avoid being put into a position where they are unnecessarily prolonging contact with a party with whom there is insufficient personal mileage, not to mention being rescued from the possibility of a dating scenario.

Many Muslim professionals when speaking of their experiences in focus groups conducted by Kamran A. Beg Events have readily admitted that their parents innocently encourage them to spend time 'getting to understand' the other party but that no concrete guidance as such is provided in terms of how long to spend in dialogue with the other party before making a decision whether to progress matters to the next level or not. No real steer is provided on this seemingly 'grey area': by not providing appropriate guidance it is clear to see why dating could prevail and in part be a consequence of parents not providing suitable time scales over which to delimit interaction between the two individuals. To the parent community I say this respectfully: encouraging your children to develop an understanding with someone you have introduced them to without providing appropriate time scales over which contact between the two individuals is allowed amounts to giving a free hand to dating! And that really is the most avoidable own goal!

In a session that I convened with a group of Muslim parents in March 2006 in Manchester where our offices are housed it was clear to me that safeguarding their children from being sucked into the maelstrom of dating was a serious concern. Recognising that the interface between east and west needs to be straddled with a lot of sensitivity and care does mean throwing in the towel to dating. Yet what pleasantly surprised the parents who attended a very lively session was how the inherent logic built into the 3-Dialogue Rule not only straddles that interface pragmatically but more pertinently how it also eliminates the risk of dating from happening. Leverage between the two individuals within the purview of the 3-Dialogue Rule is not rendered at the expense of compromising those values that are deeply intrinsic to the Islamic faith; rather leverage is inspired by seeking to preserve those values that define the essence of the Muslim personality. 80% of the parents in attendance during that magnificently insightful and at times overwhelmingly lively and extremely dynamic session acknowledged that they could see that by not imposing a limit on the time the two individuals in dialogue are given to fathom whether there is a connection how this could contribute to an increased propensity to become embroiled in a dating scenario.

Most of the parents in attendance, however, were averse to how taxing mentally and emotionally unbridled marriage-wise non-productive dialogue could ultimately prove for their child. What was deeply encouraging, however, was the open-mindedness the above parents showed to embracing the 3-Dialogue Rule pledging to disseminate the word among family and friends and enthusiastically confirming that they would strongly encourage any of their children seeking marriage to adopt it. As one of the parents featured in this focus group said: "With the 3-Dialogue Rule you come to terms with the reality of an introduction sooner, not later. The parents have the peace of mind of knowing within 2 weeks whether the dialogue between their child and the other party has any life to it. My wife and I can sleep at night knowing that by making use of the 3-Dialogue Rule my daughter will not be innocently dragged into the frightening vortex of dating."

As the female management accountant above further pontificates: "I kick myself for not getting out sooner. If you sign up to the 3-Dialogue Rule getting out of a dialogue with no tomorrow is made so much easier for you. You stop living in self-denial because it keeps your mind trained on the question of compatibility. You get out of the dating game. That can save a lot of precious time, heart-ache and stress!"

The Need for the Muslim Female Party to Have a Mahram or Chaperone or Third Party and the 3-Dialogue Rule's Absolute Insistence on it

In the context of the 3-Dialogue Rule, one dialogue can either be a telephone conversation with the individual you are exploring marriage with or a meeting where you see that individual in person and where notably and absolutely crucially the female party is accompanied by a *mahram* or chaperone or third party in keeping with the traditional Muslim values at the heart of Islam and designed to safeguard the integrity and sanctity of the male-female interaction contained within that marriage-inspired dialogue. A mahram for the sake of clarification is a chaperone or third party that the female cannot marry (Al-Omar, 1999). The chaperone must be present with a Muslim female when the female meets a Muslim male with a view to exploring marriage as Islam clearly prohibits the male and female in question (two unmarried individuals) from either meeting alone in a closed room where no third parties are present or from going out alone. Getting to know each other in either of the two afore-stated ways is simply out of the question: it has no place within a value system inspired by Islam! There is a specific hadith, which explicitly warns that when the male and female dialogue incumbents are alone with no third party to watch over them the third party present is *Shaytan* or Satan meaning that the two unsupervised parties could possibly surrender to the lure of temptation representing a further violation of the Islamic value system. Cutting to the chase: not having a chaperone in place makes the two

205

unmarried people in dialogue more vulnerable to dating and falling prey to the lure of a physical relationship. Since Islamically there is no legal relationship between the male and female in dialogue it is essential that a chaperone be factored into any meeting. *Khulwah*, which is the scenario where the male and female who are in dialogue are left to their own discretion to meet alone with the chaperone omitted from the meeting, is expressly forbidden and is therefore haram.

Islam fully respects and celebrates the right of the Muslim male and Muslim female exploring the possibility of marriage to meet each other in person as otherwise there is no real way of fathoming to what extent the personalities connect with one another, be it physically, mentally, religiously, intuitively and otherwise. See chapter 1 for a detailed exposition on how a blend of faith and personal preference define your life partner choice. Physical attractiveness, as we have borne witness to in chapter 1, is not denigrated or relegated to being inconsequential making the need to meet all the more urgent and necessary. As the Prophet (PBUH) encouraged: "Look at her, for it is more likely to establish affection between you" (Ahmed, Abu Dawud, Tirmidhi, Nisai and Ibn Majah). However, in the same breath the Prophet (PBUH) clarified that: "No man should be allowed to meet a woman alone in privacy except when she is accompanied by a mahram" (Bukhari and Muslim). Temperance is at the heart of the Muslim social imperative and while the Prophet (PBUH) encouraged the male and female exploring the possibility of marriage to engage in a transparent discourse and to meet provided the intention actuating the meeting was to explore the question of marriage at the same time the Prophet (PBUH) insisted on such meetings being tempered through the inclusion of a mahram. It is this harmonious confluence of harbouring a genuine intention to explore marriage and the incontrovertible insistence on the presence of a mahram, which inextricably dovetail to ensure the halal integrity of the meeting or meetings informing the dialogue.

As the 3-Dialogue Rule indicates, at least one of the three dialogues should take the form of a meeting in person assuming the two parties progress beyond the seismic first dialogue, which is typically a telephone conversation. In the case of a meeting, the chaperone would typically break the ice and kick-start the meeting between the two parties reminding the two parties about the purpose inspiring the meeting. Meetings should be organised in a public place such as a café or a restaurant. After spending say 15-20 minutes with the Muslim male and Muslim female in dialogue the chaperone could leave them for some time to engage in dialogue in the public place where the meeting had been arranged to return perhaps an hour or two later as the meeting is reaching an end. Note this would not represent a violation of basic Muslim values since the chaperone had in the actual physical presence of the male and female initiated the meeting thereby testifying to the fact that they had not met alone and moreover leaving them to dialogue in a public place to return later as the meeting was heading to a close would not compromise the two unmarried people not being alone as other people would also be present in the vicinity of the meeting place – cafés and restaurants are after all public arenas that seldom suffer from a shortage of customers! The chaperone could be a sibling or a friend and should be sufficiently mature to set the stage, to break the ice and to politely remind the male and female yearning to dialogue why they are meeting.

Having got the ball rolling and the 'razor-sharp' minds of the two persons keenly trained on the task at hand, which is to gauge how much life partner potential that dialogue holds, chaperones can endearingly excuse themselves after a short interval and leave the two dialoguing parties to converse only to return later typically as the meeting is drawing to a close. Alternatively, the chaperone could remain present throughout the entire duration of the meeting. *In either case, the chaperone should not be viewed as a restrictive social protocol severely handicapping the ability of the male and female to dialogue; on the contrary the chaperone is a halal social necessity inspiring the male and female to dialogue in a focused manner where they assess each other's potential as a prospective spouse for one another and where their energies are allied to and remain primed on seeking to fathom this tantalisingly challenging proposition.*

The existence of a chaperone makes the meeting halal, lends sanctity to the meeting, helps to preserve the female's integrity, provides the female with a more safe, robust and secure social environment in which to accommodate dialogue, ensures that the two people in dialogue are singing from the same 'hymn sheet' not losing sight of the matrimonial purpose inspiring the meeting in the first place and significantly reduces the propensity of the two parties to surrender to the ravages of dating. Since "actions are judged by their intention" insisting on the inclusion of a chaperone helps to keep the minds of the Muslim male and Muslim female focused not only on the driver catalysing the meeting, namely to explore further the possibility of life partner potential between them, but additionally and equally importantly maintains an urbane ambience where the basic formalities associated with good Muslim etiquette are upheld.

Note all attendees, subscribers and members of Kamran A. Beg Events are required as a matter of policy in accordance with our rules of engagement to abide by the chaperone system in deference to the Islamic faith. *Insistence on a chaperone accompanying the female in question is mandatory and is a pre-requisite of the 3-Dialogue Rule, which stresses that the inclusion of a chaperone at a meeting between the two parties in dialogue is mandatory, non-negotiable and cannot be compromised!*

Our research, however, gives visibility to the worrying trend that a very significant proportion of Muslim professionals have become accustomed to meeting the other party alone entirely oblivious to the need to have a chaperone in place or dismissive of having a third party present for fear that the third party may invade the sovereignty of their meeting space as their privacy would be encroached. This 'going it alone' approach seems to have become extremely fashionable and sadly the norm; this, however, does not mean it is religiously acceptable, which it is not! Suffice it to say, it does not sit well with Islam, which unequivocally warrants the maintenance of a chaperone system to ensure the halal integrity of the dialogue.

In chapter 2, we reported on a global research study conducted by Kamran A. Beg Events between March 2005 and March 2006 featuring 500 Muslim professional singles who were interviewed to identify the extent to which dating had impacted the Muslim community. The sample comprised 250 females and 250 males with participants drawn from the UK, Ireland, France, Germany, Australia, the USA and Canada. We recount that 80% of all Muslim professional males interviewed confirmed that they had dated by age 30 and furthermore 70% acknowledged that they had engaged

209

in some form of physical relationship with a female drawn from the Muslim faith by the same age. 78% of all Muslim professional females interviewed confirmed that they had dated by age 30 and furthermore 68% acknowledged that they had engaged in some form of physical relationship with a male drawn from the Muslim faith by the same age. Furthermore, we additionally report that only 5% of the total pool of interviewees making up this research study gave an affirmative when asked whether they had been party to meetings with a dialogue prospect where the female party had been escorted by a chaperone. **This well nigh total disregard for a chaperone at such meetings in large measure explains the increased tendency for the male and female to fall foul of the repugnant spectre of dating and its associated consequences! Thus all the more need to heed the excellent counsel of the Prophet (PBUH), which we stress again: "No man should be allowed to meet a woman alone in privacy except when she is accompanied by a mahram" (Bukhari and Muslim).**

Contrary to what some Muslim professionals may think chaperones do not impair the ability of the two individuals to engage in a transparent marriage-inspired discourse. They do not encroach on the privacy the two parties may wish to exercise when having an open, personal and frank exchange regarding their suitability as marriage counterparts. The ability to dialogue is not stifled because a chaperone is party to the deliberations. On the contrary the presence of a chaperone makes the meeting halal, which is of paramount importance and moreover induces an appropriate sense of urgency that allows the male and female partaking in dialogue to remain primed on the marriage-inspired prerogative underpinning the dialogue itself!

The Definitive Question Underpinning the 3-Dialogue Rule - "Will the person with whom I am exploring a marriage-based dialogue allow me to complete half of my faith?"

We now establish the definitive question underpinning the three dialogues that constitute the 3-Dialogue Rule. This question acts as a constant reference point for the Muslim male and Muslim female exploring the prodigious question of marriage. The Muslim male and Muslim female are after all party to marriage-inspired dialogues meaning that the two parties exploring life partner potential should never lose sight of the definitive or overarching question underpinning the dialogue, specifically: **"Will the person with whom I am exploring a marriage-based dialogue allow me to complete half of my faith?"** This question follows directly from the Prophet's (PBUH) insistence that marriage is tantamount to completing half of one's faith, which we explained at length in chapter 1: "When a servant [i.e. individual] marries, he has completed half of his religion, so let him fear Allah concerning the other half" (Bayhaqi). Allah (SWT) Himself enjoins marriage on the Ummah through an express commandment: "Marry those of you that are single" (Quran 24:32). We also recall from chapter 1 that the Quran (4:21) reminds us that marriage constitutes a mithaaq or solemn covenant between husband and wife therefore making it absolutely incumbent to document the marriage in writing. Marriage is not a casual matter and certainly not for the faint-hearted. In consenting of their own free will to the sacred institution of marriage the Muslim male and Muslim female must intend unmitigated commitment or permanence: if the *action* is *marriage* then the *intention* must be to observe *permanence*. Anything less in terms of one's commitment to the other party when

211

agreeing to marriage will not do and is strictly forbidden by Islam. For a more in-depth treatment of the above areas the reader is invited to consult chapter 1.

Each of us harbours a unique chemistry. Unless we fathom and come to terms with what constitutes that chemistry we cannot with any plausible conviction even begin to appreciate a suitable choice of life partner. The reader is referred to chapter 1 where a rigorous discussion is provided on how faith in conjunction with personal preference should help to define your life partner choice. Total honesty is needed to understand your own person before you begin to contemplate the type of personality you may wish to embrace in wedlock. Nobody for a moment even is suggesting that discovering that unique chemistry, which resonates and interlocks with yours, is going to happen overnight or suddenly surface with consummate and ambidextrous ease. However, what is clear is that we can make this at times frustrating, painful, deeply challenging and exhausting process of discovery less frustrating and less onerous by raising the right question from the very outset. Whatever our chemistry, whatever the impeccable constitution of that all-elusive - yet to be discovered, subject to the Divine will - endearing soulmate for whom we mortals all yearn, we can make the taxing journey that lays ahead easier by keeping our mind trained on the pivotal question that should guide at all times a marriage-inspired dialogue between a Muslim male and a Muslim female irrespective of the halal channel – be it family-based or non-family based - through which they are introduced to each other:

"Will the person with whom I am exploring a marriage-based dialogue allow me to complete half of my faith?"

This then is the definitive question that drives the 3-Dialogue Rule. Answering this question allows us to perceive with greater clarity the type of personality we may wish to embrace through marriage. It allows us to identify more readily that unique blend of physical, mental, religious, intuitive and other compatibilities we seek in a prospective spouse with a view to enjoying a harmonious marriage that allows one to complete half of one's faith. In other words your choice of life partner governed by that unique mix of faith and personal preference (see chapter 1) allied to your constitution should register an affirmative against this definitive question; only then can you assess whether that mix of faith and personal preference you identify in any prospective marriage prospect would indeed allow you to complete half of your faith. The right question surely has to be the one that is asked in deference to our faith-tradition for marriage as Allah (SWT) reveals in the Quran and as the Prophet (PBUH) reinforced elegantly ultimately and crucially boils down to a question of faith! See chapter 1 for more detail.

While the 3-Dialogue Rule requires both the Muslim male and Muslim female in dialogue to scrutinise their marriage-inspired dialogue against the backdrop of the above question at the same time the 3-Dialogue Rule clearly recognises that until the families engage directly, assuming the two persons decide to proceed further after executing the 3-Dialogue Rule, only then can the definitive question of whether the other party will allow you to complete half of your faith be more rigorously and fully answered. As we have acknowledged in chapters 1 and 2 the degree to which the two families are compatible in terms of values and their basic temperament also has a very significant part to play in determining the feasibility of a particular marriage tie and therefore has a major part to play in helping to answer the above question. That given, the question, however, should allow the two individuals embarked on the 3-Dialogue Rule to identify whether there is sufficient mileage to take things further at least in relation to whether their personalities overlap enough at an individual level. The question though can only be more conclusively answered once the families engage directly!

The point to underscore is that however advanced a marriage-inspired dialogue is between a Muslim male and Muslim female, that is whether the dialogue be at juncture where they are still trying to establish if there personalities click sufficiently to warrant direct family involvement or whether the dialogue has actually matured to direct family engagement, the fundamental question above, that is, *"Will the person with whom I am exploring a marriage-based dialogue allow me to complete half of my faith?"*, must always remain at the very forefront of the dialogue with a view to identifying more clearly and resolutely the feasibility of a particular marriage outcome.

Kamran A. Beg Events beseeches all the Muslim professionals seeking marriage through its services and indeed all other members of the Muslim Ummah seeking a counterpart to adopt wholeheartedly and unreservedly the definitive question - ***"Will the person with whom I am exploring a marriage-based dialogue allow me to complete half of my faith?"*** – in order to inspire their life partner search, a question stemming from the need for a Muslim to totalise their faith in deference to Allah (SWT), a question inspired by the hadith stated at the beginning of this section, a question formulated to help guide, focus, enlighten and drive their life partner search!

214

What the 3-Dialogue Rule Encompasses in Practice: The Case of a Non-family Based Introduction

The **3-Dialogue Rule**, which is tempered with the quintessential attributes of **balance** and **moderation**, has been followed outstandingly well by the Muslim couples who have so graciously proceeded to marriage courtesy of Kamran A. Beg Events. As we have already stated since being founded on July 11, 2003, Kamran A. Beg Events has witnessed 100 marriages hitherto with marriages having occurred in the UK, Australia, the USA and Canada. At the time of going to press ten more marriages have been confirmed, which coupled with the 100 that have materialised to the present represents an exceptionally prodigious and laudable feat on the part of our exemplary global family of attendees, subscribers and members. Each marriage has inspired this growing global family to attain even greater heights and the story continues with the confirmation of ten more marriages subsequent to achieving the definitive century landmark on May 21, 2006, in the writer's beloved home city, that modern acropolis, the world's first true modern industrial city, that megalopolis of unparalleled splendour, Manchester, which is the global hub, indeed the endearing epicentre of Kamran A. Beg Events!

The 3-Dialogue Rule states that the Muslim male and Muslim female exploring the question of marriage should endeavour to undertake no more than **3 dialogues**, within the purview of a **2-week** time scale, to establish whether there is enough common overlap and compatibility between them to warrant progressing their dialogue to the parent/guardian level.

We assume for the purposes of illustration a **non-family based introduction** arising through a halal channel, in this case Kamran A. Beg Events, though the same principles would apply equally to a *family-based introduction* as we shall see shortly. Assume, for example, a Muslim male and a Muslim female have been introduced to each other on the basis of attending a matrimonial event or through personalised matching, which are two of the three non-family channels of introduction provided by Kamran A. Beg Events. The specific case of how the 3-Dialogue Rule is articulated for an online introduction (a further non-family channel provided by Kamran A. Beg Events) will be discussed later in this chapter.

In the context of the 3-Dialogue Rule one dialogue can either be a telephone conversation with that individual or a meeting where you see that individual in person such that the female party is accompanied by a *mahram* or chaperone or third party in keeping with the requirements of the Muslim value system as expounded earlier in this chapter.

Throughout the dialogue process the key question informing the marriage-inspired dialogue between the Muslim male and Muslim female would be: *"Will the person with whom I am exploring a marriage-based dialogue allow me to complete half of my faith?"*

In the case of a non-family based introduction the 3-Dialogue Rule would proceed along the following lines.

1. The Muslim male and Muslim female parties in question should endeavour to engage initially in one 'exploratory' telephone conversation, effectively the first dialogue, and then spend the next few days

reflecting on how much overlap surfaced during that dialogue – the first dialogue - before deciding whether they wish to proceed to a second dialogue. *Was enough mileage derived from the first dialogue to warrant a second dialogue?* If one or both parties feel they do not wish to proceed further they should inform Kamran A. Beg Events who will respectfully inform the other or both parties accordingly or alternatively the two parties could inform each other directly though the former option is always more advisable. In either case, dialogue closure should not be treated lightly. "Empathy, compassion, due care, sensitivity and grace" should be assigned when closing a dialogue as already discussed in chapter 2.

2. Assuming the two parties wish to proceed to the second dialogue they could arrange to meet in a public place though Kamran A. Beg Events would respectfully advise that the female party must be accompanied by a chaperone. The two parties should then spend the next few days reflecting on how much overlap surfaced during that dialogue - the second dialogue - before deciding whether they wish to proceed to a third dialogue. *Was enough mileage derived from the second dialogue to warrant a third dialogue?* If one or both parties feel they do not wish to proceed further they should inform Kamran A. Beg Events who will inform the other or both parties accordingly or alternatively the two parties could inform each other directly though the former option is always more advisable.

3. Assuming the two parties wish to proceed to the third dialogue they could either engage in a further telephone conversation or arrange to meet in a public place for a second time though Kamran A. Beg Events would respectfully advise that the female party must be accompanied by a chaperone should the latter option be preferred. The two parties should then spend the next few days reflecting on how much overlap surfaced during that dialogue - the third dialogue - before deciding whether there is enough common overlap and compatibility between them to warrant progressing their dialogue to the parent/guardian level. *Was enough mileage derived from the third dialogue to warrant direct interaction between the families with a view to exploring marriage?* If one or both parties feel they do not wish to proceed further they should inform Kamran A. Beg Events who will inform the other or both parties accordingly or alternatively the two parties could inform each other directly though the former option is always more advisable.

Having undertaken one dialogue, it is important to note that between dialogues the 3-Dialogue Rule *discourages* regular or extensive communication between the Muslim male and Muslim female exploring marriage. The two parties need a few days to analyse critically and conscientiously the dialogue they have just been party to so that their focus is not distracted from the central question: *"Will the person with whom I am exploring a marriage-based dialogue allow me to complete half of my faith?"* This is not an easy question to answer. Nobody said it would be! Our research, however, shows that both parties 'need their own space' after a dialogue to collect their own thoughts and to reconcile them with this overarching question so that they can decide more clinically and honestly whether they wish to proceed to the next dialogue and if so for the right reasons. Bombarding one another with an endless stream of text messages and partaking in endless discussion is discouraged by the 3-Dialogue Rule and in any event clearly contravenes it: the two parties must not overstep the three-dialogue mark, subject to the 2-week time limit. That precious space the two parties need to train their agile mind on the crucial question above should not be invaded by such impetuous and naïve behaviour, which, as experience evidences, invariably leads to *apathy* developing between the two individuals causing the dialogue to *atrophy* and eventually surrender to its *demise*.

If by no later than the third dialogue, subject to a 2-week time scale, the two individuals agree that there is sufficient compatibility between them to warrant progressing their dialogue to the parent/guardian level the 3-Dialogue Rule states that direct interaction between the families should be activated *immediately* and *any future dialogues between the two individuals would need to be sanctioned by both families once the families had engaged directly.*

If the two parties have not agreed, at the very latest by the third dialogue, subject to the 2-week time limit, that there is enough mileage and compatibility between them for their parent(s)/guardian(s) to become involved the 3-Dialogue Rule categorically states that that dialogue should be brought to honourable closure with immediate effect with empathy, compassion, due care, sensitivity and grace informing the whole process of dialogue closure. Immediate dialogue closure here is a logical outcome and follows directly from our research, which has demonstrated that if two Muslim parties are in dialogue for more than 2 weeks such that they have not expedited direct family interaction at the very latest by the end of the second week after initiating contact with each other either via the telephone or through meeting in person that there is a **95% probability** that direct interaction between the families with a view to exploring marriage would **never occur** irrespective of how long the two individuals remain in communication after the 2-week watershed. This translates into a non-marriage scenario and applies equally to both family and non-family based introductions!

In sum, the 3-Dialogue Rule entreaties both the Muslim male and Muslim female exploring the question of marriage to decide by no later than the third dialogue, subject to a 2-week time limit, whether they wish to progress their dialogue to the parent/guardian level or whether they wish to bring honourable closure to the dialogue itself.

The Role of Dialogue Mentors

At Kamran A. Beg Events, all dialogues are coordinated and monitored by our experienced consultants who will monitor how the dialogue is progressing and who are available to guide and advise the Muslim male and Muslim female in dialogue accordingly at any stage during the execution of the 3-Dialogue Rule. The consultants in effect provide the two parties with invaluable impartial points of reference and allow the two individuals to remain alert to addressing the key question informing the 3-Dialogue Rule: *"Will the person with whom I am exploring a marriage-based dialogue allow me to complete half of my faith?"*

At Kamran A. Beg Events, we view the two individuals in dialogue as **dialogue investors**. I have coined this term to emphasise how important it is for the dialogue incumbent to extract maximum return on investment from any marriage-inspired dialogue. In much the same way that an investor may wish to secure a good return on investment from investing in the stockmarket a dialogue incumbent should similarly aspire to derive maximum mileage from the dialogue process with a view to addressing the above fundamental question and therefore establishing as soon as possible, subject to the limits of the 3-Dialogue Rule, whether there is any real life in progressing dialogue with the other party further. This clearly requires a considerable quantum of investment in terms of time and energy on the part of both individuals. Whether the actual outcome of applying the 3-Dialogue Rule culminates in activating direct interaction between the families or dialogue closure it is germane to the learning curve experienced by the Muslim male and Muslim female exploring marriage that they both extract a maximum return on investment from that dialogue scenario by refining and building on their ability to explore the possibility of a marriage tie against the backdrop of the central question propelling their dialogue: *"Will the person with whom I am exploring a marriage-based dialogue allow me to complete half of my faith?"*

Our consultants effectively operate as **dialogue mentors**. Interaction with a dialogue mentor allows the **dialogue mentees** (the Muslim male and Muslim female in dialogue) to put their thoughts into perspective, to consolidate their impressions gained of the other party after engaging in any of the three dialogues with them permitted courtesy of the 3-Dialogue Rule and to fathom with greater clarity and conviction the life partner potential thrown up by the other party. It is not uncommon for the two parties to use a dialogue mentor as a sounding board against which to 'think aloud' as they are deciding whether enough overlap has been sensed to progress the dialogue to the next dialogue in the trilogy of dialogues that constitute the dialogue space afforded by the 3-Dialogue Rule.

As a very eclectic and articulate 34 year-old nurse working in London related reflecting on her dialogue with a 41 year-old surgeon based in Birmingham whom she met at one of our matrimonial events in London in 2006: "With the 3-Dialogue Rule I knew there was no time to squander. We had to cut to the chase. I had to discipline my mind to focusing on marriage through constantly reminding myself about how much I really believed the surgeon could help me to realise half my faith. That question allows you to digest what you are really looking for in that someone special. Your thinking becomes more harnessed. Your mind cannot afford to waver. Making a decision becomes tonnes easier. After our first phone conversation I called Kamran (reference here is being made to the writer) and gave him my feedback. This allowed me to discuss more broadly the pros and cons of the initial dialogue. Kamran kept my attention fixed on analysing the marriage potential offered by the surgeon in terms of meeting half my faith. That was the key. After meeting the surgeon a few days later I felt buoyant and positive. My friend who sat in also gave encouraging feedback. I was seeing marriage through a different light. We got our parents involved after that meeting. Things have gone like a dream. We will be getting married in December, 2006."

As the above example highlights the role of a dialogue mentor is crucial to providing the two dialoguing parties with a reliable and trusted reference point – someone who acts as a confidant(e) allowing them to get things off their chest but who unfailingly asks them to be clinically honest when assessing the other party's life partner worth through dissecting the key question relating to the potential of the other party to allow them to complete half of their faith.

We recommend that all dialogues should fall under the vigilant and empathetic eye of dialogue mentors. This approach has stood the attendees, subscribers and members of Kamran A. Beg Events in very good stead. Even in the case of family-based introductions, both parties would be better served if, at every stage of dialogue progression, they consulted with a member of their own family or another designated individual acting in the capacity of a dialogue mentor in much the same way that they would consult with one of our consultants had that introduction stemmed from Kamran A. Beg Events.

Dialogue mentors exercise a very calming influence on the two dialogue incumbents who should never be made to feel isolated or on their own as they strive to appreciate one another's marriage potential. All dialogues have their ups and downs; dialogues tend to be very serrated at times. Dialogue mentors help the two parties rapt in dialogue to put the dialogue into perspective, to not defocus when it comes to looking at the bigger picture and to remain loyal to addressing the definitive question of evaluating the marriage potential of the other individual against the backdrop of achieving half of one's faith.

Direct Interaction Between the Two Families Following the Conclusion of the 3-Dialogue Rule: The Cooling Off Period, the Sanctioning of Future Dialogues Between the

Muslim Male and Muslim Female Exploring Marriage and the 3-Dialogue Rule's Insistence on Family Compatibility to Inspire a Marriage Outcome

If by no later than the third dialogue, subject to a 2-week time scale, the Muslim male and Muslim female party to the marriage-inspired dialogue agree that there is sufficient compatibility between them to warrant progressing their dialogue to the parent/guardian level then direct interaction between the families should be activated *immediately* and *any future dialogues between the two individuals would need to be sanctioned by both families once the families had engaged directly.* The 3-Dialogue Rule discourages any further dialogue between the Muslim male and Muslim female once they have progressed matters to the family level until the families have engaged directly and agreed to any future dialogues between the two individuals be they telephone conversations, meetings in the presence of the two families or meetings away from the families where again the female party should be accompanied by a mahram or chaperone or third party to preserve the halal integrity of the dialogue, which must never be compromised at any stage during the dialogue process. Note, however, the families could engage directly after the first dialogue or indeed following the second dialogue though three dialogues tend to represent the norm based on the marriages arising from Kamran A. Beg Events. Of the 100 marriages that have emanated so far through introductions generated among Muslim professionals via Kamran A. Beg Events 86% of the marriages transpired after direct family engagement was facilitated following the execution of the third dialogue within the remit of the 3-Dialogue Rule.

As implied above, we strongly advise a cooling off period between the final dialogue executed within the precincts of concluding the 3-Dialogue Rule and the point when the two families engage directly. This added precaution also continues to safeguard the two individuals central to the marriage-inspired dialogue from developing too intense an emotional connection with each other as a marriage outcome is by no means a certainty and also acts as a powerful deterrent to the continued very real threat of dating, which must never be underestimated. It should be noted that dating and the temptation to be lured into a physical relationship could still rear their ugly head at any time. Emotions still need to be tempered and expectations need to be managed once the 3-Dialogue Rule has been applied since agreeing to direct family involvement following the conclusion of the 3-Dialogue Rule does not necessarily signify that the Muslim male and Muslim female in dialogue will definitely proceed to marriage. That would be premature to conclude to say the least!

As we have already noted in chapters 1 and 2 the degree to which the two families harbour similar values would also exercise a significant influence on the likelihood of a marriage outcome. The family values, mores and norms held by the two families in question, which personify the very character of those two families, that is the male's family and the female's family, exercise a very formidable impact in terms of how comfortable the male and female parties in question and their parent(s)/guardian(s) feel that marriage between the two persons is indeed a tenable outcome. Marriage from an Islamic perspective is not just a marriage between two individuals; it is also a marriage between two families, one that should strengthen the ties and build on the amity between the two families, a composite that in turn should feed favourably into the marriage bond experienced by husband and wife (see chapter 1): "If a man and a woman belong to families that share close or partial similarities in their views on morality, religion, social behaviour and the day to day house-hold management, they are more likely to develop a bond of love and compassion. Their marriage tie can be expected to bring the two families closer together" (Maudoodi, 2000: pp.12-13). For two families to foster a compatible temperament it goes without saying that their values, mores and norms should in large measure be congruous.

If, as we have gathered from the first two chapters, a staggering 70-75% of one's personality is shaped by one's upbringing in the first five year's of one's life then it is not too difficult to deduce that one's family is the key influencer responsible for shaping one's personality. That is, no matter how much you might think you click with someone until you meet that individual's family you truly cannot calibrate the degree to which you and that individual are compatible in terms of a potential marriage. The luxury that the 3-Dialogue Rule does confer is that the two individuals partaking in dialogue will know sooner rather than later, subject to the limits imposed by the 3-Dialogue Rule, whether their personalities click sufficiently to warrant family involvement. *However, at the same time, the 3-Dialogue Rule also stresses the centrality of family compatibility to inspiring a marriage outcome and explicitly legislates for a cooling off period between concluding the 3-Dialogue Rule and the families engaging directly for such interaction or social transaction is vital in order to ascertain the degree of family compatibility.*
This cooling off period is in complete recognition of the overriding need to maintain the halal integrity of the

226

dialogue as any future dialogues between the Muslim male and Muslim female would require the express consent of the two families, which could only result once the two families had become directly involved subsequent to the 3-Dialogue Rule being concluded. This would apply equally in the case of non-family based and family-based introductions: in the former case the two individuals would **initiate** family involvement having exercised the 3-Dialogue Rule; in the latter case they would **further expedite** family involvement having executed the 3-Dialogue. Whatever the mode of introduction there should be a cooling off period between concluding the 3-Dialogue Rule and initiating (in the case of a non-family based introduction) or further expediting (in the case of a family-based introduction) direct family involvement. This is necessary to ensure that the marriage-inspired dialogue between the Muslim male and Muslim female remains halal! Any future dialogues between the two individuals, subsequent to concluding the 3-Dialogue Rule, would therefore need to be sanctioned by both families once the families had engaged directly and would thus follow the cooling off period.

Clearly then given the paramount importance of family compatibility in determining the likelihood of two individuals proceeding to marriage, it is only through the process of direct family engagement that we can answer conclusively the pivotal question that is at the very heart of any marriage-inspired dialogue between two Muslims:

"Will the person with whom I am exploring a marriage-based dialogue allow me to complete half of my faith?"

As we explained in the first two chapters of this book, 81% of the divorcees who have accessed the services offered by

Kamran A. Beg Events have affirmed that their marriages had failed because the chasm or 'value gap' between their and their then spouse's family value systems could not be bridged and this irreconcilable difference had fed unfavourably into the husband-wife relationship culminating in the marriage tie being severed.

We noted in chapter 1 that the Prophet (PBUH) encouraged families to meet as often as is needed in order to get a firm handle on how compatible the families are, even if that means speaking to acquaintances and friends of the family of the dialogue prospect and eliciting their honest take on the family's character and values. The Prophet (PBUH) further clarified that such inquisitiveness in deference to exploring marriage between two individuals and inevitably two families is in fact a religious duty since ultimately marriage is tantamount to completing half of one's faith and its sacred eminence must not be undervalued by not gauging how congruous the family temperaments are. While individual compatibility is a must to progress the possibility of marriage the Prophet's insightful and timeless advice clearly shows that a marriage is more likely to be sustainable where the families also have much common ground and foster similar basic values (for a more comprehensive discussion see chapter 1). A disconnect at the family level is likely to increase the likelihood of divorce, something which is clearly borne out by our research as highlighted by the experiences of the divorcees who have been magnanimous enough to grace the Kamran A. Beg Events global family. Their feedback clearly testifies to the eternal wisdom contained in the Prophet's counsel that marriage should not be sanctioned where the two families in question are markedly at variance in terms of their basic values!

As the enriching counsel of our beloved Prophet (PBUH) forewarns us and as our research poignantly reveals, the likelihood of divorce is significantly increased when the families are not highly compatible in relation to their values, mores and norms!

It is only when both families have directly engaged in discussion, exchanged several visits and extensively consulted third parties knowledgeable of the other family - all in aid of developing a more in-depth appreciation for that family's true character - can a more reliable impression be formed of the family of the marriage prospect with both families and the two individuals remaining loyal throughout the process to answering the pivotal question above. Any dialogues that the Muslim male and Muslim female enter into once the families do engage directly would need to be approved by the two families be they telephone conversations, meetings in the presence of the two families or meetings away from the families where again the female party would be accompanied by a mahram or chaperone or third party to render the dialogue halal. If then this process of discovery reveals that there is a significant degree of overlap between the values and temperament of the two families and the Muslim male and Muslim female simultaneously feel through further exchanges after the families have engaged directly that they have built favourably on the individual compatibility that was palpable during the course of executing the 3-Dialogue Rule then this favourable conflux of individual and family compatibilities would reinforce the case for the two individuals to proceed to marriage, subject of course to the Divine will.

Adopting the **3-Dialogue Rule** at the very outset of the marriage-inspired dialogue process clearly allows the outcome, **that is whether the Muslim male and Muslim**

female integral to that specific dialogue will be proceeding to marriage, to be determined sooner rather than later! This outcome is notably gauged without compromising the integrity – emotional, family, community or otherwise - of the Muslim male and Muslim female party to the dialogue, with the integrity of the two individuals and their respective families maintained on account of the halal ethos that constantly reinforces the entirety of the dialogue process. **In particular, adherence to the 3-Dialogue Rule safeguards the Muslim female and her family.** It also safeguards the male and female in question **against** dating and having a relationship, both of which are Islamically prohibited and non-permissible! Throughout the dialogue process the two individuals supported by their respective families must continue to remain steadfast in addressing the definitive question informing the marriage-inspired dialogue: *"Will the person with whom I am exploring a marriage-based dialogue allow me to complete half of my faith?"* Only then can the feasibility of a particular marriage prospect be properly assessed!

As a 32 year-old female doctor who recently (February 2006) married after meeting her prospective husband (a 34 year-old finance specialist) at a matrimonial event chaired by myself in Manchester in 2005 pointed out in her very considered feedback: "The 3-Dialogue Rule stops you from beating about the bush. It alerts you to the pressing need to extract maximum value from each dialogue interaction. It reminds you of the importance of marriage by not allowing you to forget that this is a commitment, which allows you to master 50% of your faith. I always kept this in mind as I was trying to come to terms with the suitability of the gentleman to whom I had been introduced through the event. My milestone for each interaction was to figure out to what

230

extent the gentleman that I was talking to could meet the demands becoming of allowing me to complete 50% of my faith. I was looking for my knight in shining armour but for that knight to shine his chemistry would have to lend to my conviction that we could both cross that bridge of faith in unison together. At the same time the 3-Dialogue Rule meant that I kept my emotional climate in check as the crunch would come when our families met. You don't really know if you have clicked until the families get involved. The 3-Dialogue Rule prepared me mentally to accept that while we may hit it off individually we should not unduly raise our expectations until the families get together. That would be the real test! By doing that the 3-Dialogue Rule doesn't allow you to become a hostage to your own emotions, which can otherwise prove a real nightmare to control. It is this in-built safeguard that protects your emotional constitution! When the families did meet the question of faith that had driven the 3-Dialogue Rule allowed for more direct and upfront discussion between the families. It made a decision so much easier. Previously when I had been introduced to someone we had been left to our own devices to get on with the business of working out whether we should get married. There was no structure. Our parents just left us to see whether marriage could result. I had been searching for a soulmate since graduating, yet had nothing concrete to hold on to in the way of a practical framework guiding my matrimonial deliberations. With the 3-Dialogue Rule and the family interaction that followed there was always one underlying theme at the hub of this marriage-inspired journey: whatever the degree of chemistry between myself and the gentleman I was examining the possibility of marriage with would he for all his many qualities allow me to complete half of my faith. That was the foothold in my life partner search I had lacked previously and that my family were ignorant off until I encountered the 3-Dialogue Rule. And this time round it made all the difference. The 3-Dialogue Rule gave me that solid foothold. Two months after initiating the 3-Dialogue Rule we got married!"

What the 3-Dialogue Rule Encompasses in Practice: The Case of a Family-based Introduction

In the case of a **family-based introduction**, we would recommend the Muslim male and Muslim female to apply the 3-Dialogue Rule in much the same way that it applies to a non-family based introduction. The 3-Dialogue Rule would kick in once the two families had introduced the Muslim male and Muslim female to each other ideally at an initial meeting where both families and the two individuals in question were present, such that after that initial meeting the two individuals on reflection had agreed to engage in a marriage-inspired dialogue. In cases where such an initial meeting is not possible an initial telephone conversation between the Muslim male and Muslim female after the parent(s)/guardian(s) of the two parties have spoken to each other on the phone would act as a substitute for such an initial meeting with the 3-Dialogue Rule kicking in after that initial telephone conversation had been concluded assuming the two individuals in question on reflection had agreed then to engage in a marriage-inspired dialogue.

In the context of the 3-Dialogue Rule one dialogue can either be a telephone conversation with that individual or a meeting where you see that individual in person such that the female party is accompanied by a *mahram* or chaperone or third party in keeping with the requirements of the Muslim value system as expounded earlier in this chapter.

Throughout the dialogue process the key question informing the marriage-inspired dialogue between the Muslim male and Muslim female would be: *"Will the person with whom I am exploring a marriage-based dialogue allow me to complete half of my faith?"*

The 3-Dialogue Rule would clearly allow the two individuals to identify sooner rather than later, subject to the limits specified by the 3-Dialogue Rule, if there is any mileage in taking the matter forward and whether to further expedite direct family involvement. If the dialogue did warrant reviving direct family engagement a cooling off period as outlined in the case of a non-family based introduction would similarly be recommended until the families engaged directly again. Any further dialogues between the Muslim male and Muslim female following the completion of the 3-Dialogue Rule would then need to be sanctioned by their respective families once engagement between the families had been revived and all the formalities intrinsic to halal dialogue would require to be observed.

Briefly, in the case of a family-based introduction the 3-Dialogue Rule would proceed along the following lines.

1. The Muslim male and Muslim female parties in question should endeavour to engage initially in one 'exploratory' telephone conversation, effectively the first dialogue, and then spend the next few days reflecting on how much overlap surfaced during that dialogue – the first dialogue - before deciding whether they wish to proceed to a second dialogue. *Was enough mileage derived from the first dialogue to warrant a second dialogue?* If one or both parties feel they do not wish to proceed further

they should inform their parent(s)/guardian(s) who will respectfully inform each other accordingly or alternatively the two parties could inform each other directly though the former option is always more advisable. In either case, dialogue closure should not be treated lightly. "Empathy, compassion, due care, sensitivity and grace" should be assigned when closing a dialogue as already discussed in chapter 2.

2. Assuming the two parties wish to proceed to the second dialogue they could arrange to meet in a public place though the female party must be accompanied by a chaperone. The two parties should then spend the next few days reflecting on how much overlap surfaced during that dialogue - the second dialogue - before deciding whether they wish to proceed to a third dialogue. *Was enough mileage derived from the second dialogue to warrant a third dialogue?* If one or both parties feel they do not wish to proceed further they should inform their parent(s)/guardian(s) who will respectfully inform each other accordingly or alternatively the two parties could inform each other directly though the former option is always more advisable.

3. Assuming the two parties wish to proceed to the third dialogue they could either engage in a further telephone conversation or arrange to meet in a public place for a second time though the female party must be accompanied by a chaperone should the latter option be preferred. The two parties should then spend the next few days reflecting on how much overlap surfaced during that dialogue - the third dialogue - before deciding whether there is enough

common overlap and compatibility between them to warrant progressing their dialogue to the parent/guardian level. *Was enough mileage derived from the third dialogue to warrant reviving direct interaction between the families with a view to exploring marriage?* If one or both parties feel they do not wish to proceed further they should inform their parent(s)/guardian(s) who will respectfully inform each other accordingly or alternatively the two parties could inform each other directly though the former option is always more advisable.

In the case of a family-based introduction, the 3-Dialogue Rule entreaties both the Muslim male and Muslim female exploring the question of marriage to decide by no later than the third dialogue, subject to a 2-week time limit, whether they wish to progress their dialogue to the parent/guardian level and therefore further expedite direct family involvement or whether they wish to bring honourable closure to the dialogue itself.

What the 3-Dialogue Rule Encompasses in Practice: The Case of an Online Introduction

In chapter 2 we noted that a *fatwa* or legal ruling issued by that prodigious centre of Islamic scholarship, Al-Azhar University in Cairo (Egypt), renders a matrimonial dialogue between a Muslim male and a Muslim female who have met over the Internet through an online matchmaking service, which is another example of a non-family based introduction, as halal provided both parties inform their parent(s)/guardian(s) that they are in dialogue and provided they keep them abreast of how the dialogue is developing, subject to upholding the integrity and ethics that underpin halal Muslim etiquette.

In the case of an online introduction, the 3-Dialogue Rule would kick in once the Muslim male and Muslim female had agreed to undertake their first telephone conversation. We shall assume for the sake of illustration that the Muslim male and Muslim female have been introduced through our online service, Kamran A. Beg Professional Muslim Online Matrimonials. All our subscribers are expected to observe the 3-Dialogue Rule. Furthermore we strongly recommend subscribers to the online service to have at least one initial telephone conversation after exchanging dialogue online before deciding whether they wish to accommodate a meeting in-person.

In the context of the 3-Dialogue Rule one offline dialogue can either be a telephone conversation with that individual or a meeting where you see that individual in person such that the female party is accompanied by a *mahram* or chaperone or third party in keeping with the requirements of the Muslim value system as expounded earlier in this chapter.

Throughout the dialogue process the key question informing the marriage-inspired dialogue between the Muslim male and Muslim female would be: *"Will the person with whom I am exploring a marriage-based dialogue allow me to complete half of my faith?"*

The 3-Dialogue Rule would clearly allow the two individuals to identify sooner rather than later, subject to the limits specified by the 3-Dialogue Rule, if there is any mileage in taking the matter forward and whether to initiate direct family involvement. If the dialogue did warrant initiating direct family engagement a cooling off period would again be recommended until the families engaged directly with any future dialogues between the Muslim male and Muslim female sanctioned by their respective families and all the formalities intrinsic to halal dialogue observed.

Briefly, in the case of an online introduction the 3-Dialogue Rule would proceed along the following lines.

1. The Muslim male and Muslim female subscribers in question should endeavour to engage initially in one 'exploratory' telephone conversation, effectively the first offline dialogue, and then spend the next few days reflecting on how much overlap surfaced during that dialogue – the first offline dialogue - before deciding whether they wish to proceed to a second offline dialogue. *Was enough mileage derived from the first offline dialogue to warrant a second offline dialogue?* If one or both parties feel they do not wish to proceed further they should inform each other accordingly. Dialogue closure should not be treated lightly. "Empathy, compassion, due care, sensitivity and grace" should be assigned when closing a dialogue as already discussed in chapter 2.

2. Assuming the two parties wish to proceed to the second offline dialogue they could arrange to meet in a public place though the female party must be accompanied by a chaperone. The two parties should then spend the next few days reflecting on how much overlap surfaced during that dialogue - the second offline dialogue - before deciding whether they wish to proceed to a third offline dialogue. *Was enough*

mileage derived from the second offline dialogue to warrant a third offline dialogue? If one or both parties feel they do not wish to proceed further they should inform each other accordingly.

3. Assuming the two parties wish to proceed to the third offline dialogue they could either engage in a further telephone conversation or arrange to meet in a public place for a second time though the female party must be accompanied by a chaperone should the latter option be preferred. The two parties should then spend the next few days reflecting on how much overlap surfaced during that dialogue - the third offline dialogue - before deciding whether there is enough common overlap and compatibility between them to warrant progressing their dialogue to the parent/guardian level. *Was enough mileage derived from the third offline dialogue to warrant direct interaction between the families with a view to exploring marriage?* If one or both parties feel they do not wish to proceed further they should inform each other accordingly.

In sum, the 3-Dialogue Rule entreaties both the Muslim male and Muslim female subscribers exploring the question of marriage to decide by no later than the third offline dialogue, subject to a 2-week time limit, whether they wish to progress their dialogue to the parent/guardian level or whether they wish to bring honourable closure to the dialogue itself.

The Case of Several Marriage Prospects Arising Simultaneously

238

Muslim professionals and their very keen and dedicated parents when contacting Kamran A. Beg Events often pose the following perennial question: What is ethically viable in terms of how to pursue marriage-inspired dialogue if a Muslim male or Muslim female have several marriage prospects to consider simultaneously? We now discuss how they should proceed such that they uphold the ethical values inspiring a marriage-inspired dialogue in the first place and give justice to each dialogue prospect. We now touch on how they should follow the 3-Dialogue Rule in the case of several dialogue prospects arising concurrently.

Let us assume that you encounter the rather privileged position whereupon you have been inundated with several marriage prospects simultaneously. We recommend that you have one telephone conversation with each marriage prospect and then decide which one you would like to pursue further dialogue with in terms of completing the 3-Dialogue Rule, subject to the limits imposed by the 3-Dialogue Rule. The initial phone conversation would represent the first dialogue in each case.

That is you would have a phone conversation with X dialogue prospects where X>1 but after this initial phone discussion with each prospect – representing the first dialogue in each case - you would pick just the one dialogue prospect to partake at maximum in a further two dialogues with within the context of the 3-Dialogue Rule since the limits imposed by the 3-Dialogue Rule would need to be observed. If this dialogue with your first preferred marriage prospect did not bear fruition then you could revisit dialogue with one of the other marriage prospects effectively reviving the marriage-inspired dialogue process with that prospect at the second dialogue point. The key is to be in "3-Dialogue

239

dialogue" with only one marriage prospect at any one time, subsequent to the initial telephone conversation, which represents the first dialogue as indicated above.

The above advice assumes that after the initial phone conversation you conclude that you would like to pursue further dialogue in the first place with any of the marriage prospects that have transpired simultaneously. We have assumed that the first dialogue in each case is a phone conversation. Note the first dialogue could be a meeting in a public place though the female party must be accompanied by a chaperone. After having experienced an initial dialogue with each marriage prospect assuming you still wish to pursue further dialogue with any of the prospects you should pursue the 3-Dialogue Rule with only one prospect at any one time, subject to the limits stipulated by the 3-Dialogue Rule being fully respected. If dialogue with that prospect is brought to closure then you can revisit the possibility of dialogue with one of the other marriage prospects. In this way you assign due respect to the integrity of each marriage prospect and preserve the halal sanctity underpinning the marriage-inspired dialogue process!

Ten Questions that Allow the Definitive Question Underpinning the 3-Dialogue Rule - "Will the person with whom I am exploring a marriage-based dialogue allow me to complete half of my faith?" - to be Answered

As we have already gathered in this chapter the pivotal question at the heart of a marriage-inspired dialogue between any two Muslims should be: *"Will the person with whom I am exploring a marriage-based dialogue allow me to complete half of my faith?"* This is the quintessential question that drives the 3-Dialogue Rule. It is through unmitigated allegiance to resolving where you stand in relation to this most seminal and definitive question that you as a Muslim exploring marriage with a fellow Muslim can fathom with greater clarity and immediacy the degree to which your personalities click and if that click is sufficiently palpable to warrant direct family engagement. You may well feel "physically, mentally, religiously, intuitively and otherwise" attracted to the Muslim you are engaged in marriage-inspired dialogue with. You may well feel a click but there is only way sure way of calibrating that click and that is to relate the degree of connection you feel with the person you are exploring marriage with to the central consideration that should always prevail when considering marriage within the Muslim faith: *"Will the person with whom I am exploring a marriage-based dialogue allow me to complete half of my faith?"* This question must always inform your analysis of someone's marriage-worthiness. Both the Muslim male and Muslim female directly party to exploring marriage with each other and their respective families assuming the dialogue is referred to the family level once the 3-Dialogue Rule has been executed should never fall foul of assessing the appropriateness of a possible marriage tie against the backdrop of this crucial question.

241

Kamran A. Beg Events has conducted extensive research into ascertaining the primary types of questions that the two individuals in dialogue should certainly seek to examine, albeit amongst a whole host of others, when discharging the 3-Dialogue Rule with a view to grappling with the definitive question that should constantly inspire their matrimonial deliberations: *"Will the person with whom I am exploring a marriage-based dialogue allow me to complete half of my faith?"* We are not suggesting that the proposed questions that follow and which allow this definitive question to be tackled are the only questions that should surface during the dialogues that compose the family of dialogues integral to the 3-Dialogue Rule. How many questions to ask of the other party would not be too dissimilar to asking how long is a piece of string? Clearly you and your fellow dialogue incumbent will exercise discretion in terms of the actual questions raised for discussion and the number of questions you each respectfully venture for reflection. What is key here is that the questions that are thrown up for discussion allow the Muslim male and Muslim female who have been introduced to one other to assess the degree to which they click with each other in the context of the definitive question and whether that click is of sufficient magnitude to extend deliberations to the families of the two individuals concerned.

It is important to reinforce that the 3-Dialogue Rule gives the Muslim male and Muslim female the licence to have an open, transparent and uninhibited marriage-inspired dialogue configured to allow them to assess the extent to which their personalities click and whether there is sufficient mileage there to get the families directly engaged. At the same time the 3-Dialogue Rule emphatically stresses that the two persons in dialogue should never take their eye of the ball.

242

They should remain conversant with gauging each other's suitability for marriage in deference to the definitive question: *"Will the person with whom I am exploring a marriage-based dialogue allow me to complete half of my faith?"* It is total commitment to answering this question that allows for such transparent dialogue to be cultivated in the first place between the Muslim male and Muslim female exploring marriage. We will expand on this in chapter 4 through some very insightful feedback that the reader will find positively instructive and distinctly encouraging!

At Kamran A. Beg Events we advise attendees, subscribers and members subscribing to our organisation to engage in informed dialogues, which allow them to derive maximum worth in terms of forming a clear view as quickly as possible, subject to exercising the 3-Dialogue Rule, on how compatible they feel certainly at the individual level with the other person albeit recognising that the marriage-worthiness of that individual can only fully be explored when the families are brought into the picture. As the Muslim male and Muslim female are executing the 3-Dialogue Rule Kamran A. Beg Events advises that the following ten questions, admittedly amongst others that may enter the fray, be brought under the scrutiny of the two discussants as they will greatly contribute to shedding light on forming a position on the definitive and overarching question, which forms the central plank of the dialogue process: *"Will the person with whom I am exploring a marriage-based dialogue allow me to complete half of my faith?"* Our research shows that asking such questions allow a dialogue incumbent to identify sooner rather than later whether there is sufficient overlap with the other person to engage the families. These ten questions enable two Muslims to gauge the degree of individual compatibility that may be present in deference to the definitive question and also give the Muslim male and Muslim female a much-needed initial steer on each other's family values though the latter area cannot be more substantially evaluated unless the families engage directly. The ten questions that we recommend, which our attendees, subscribers and members and other Muslim professionals worldwide have found very germane to fathoming someone's life partner potential, are enumerated below.

1. How would your best friend describe your personality in three phrases and why?
2. What are your favourite interests and hobbies?
3. What are the primary qualities you are looking for in a spouse?
4. What do you regard as the primary responsibilities of a Muslim husband and a Muslim wife?
5. What shared responsibilities should a Muslim husband and a Muslim wife exercise?
6. Once married when ideally would you like to have a family?
7. What part does Islam currently play in your life?
8. How do you see yourself growing in terms of your faith in partnership with your life partner once you have settled down?
9. What three values does your family cherish above all and why?
10. Once married what sorts of things would you do in order to act as a bridge between the two families and to bring our families closer together?

Our research has indicated that the responses generated by the other individual to these questions allow you to grasp relatively quickly, subject to observing the 3-Dialogue Rule, whether there is enough "common currency" between you and that person to further explore the question of marriage with the families engaged directly. Asking these ten questions in particular allows you to come to terms with whether you really feel enough of a click "physically, mentally, religiously, intuitively and otherwise" to merit that click being ventured for further scrutiny with the families brought on board. These ten questions should form a major part of your deliberations when you partake in marriage-inspired dialogue. These are the sorts of very direct and upfront questions that should help to define the pulse of such dialogue and which should enter the fray with relative immediacy and urgency. These questions, which allow you to address the definitive question, can be analysed further in the light of family involvement once the green light is given to progress discussions with the marriage prospect to the next step. We recognise that the Muslim male and Muslim female exploring marriage may well wish to add to this list of questions. This is entirely encouraged but the key is to ensure that whatever additional questions are raised they help you to answer the definitive question underpinning the entirety of the marriage-inspired dialogue process: *"Will the person with whom I am exploring a marriage-based dialogue allow me to complete half of my faith?"*

The first question gives you an insight into the key aspects of the other individual's personality as seen through the eyes of a third party. The second question provides you with more data on the dialoguing party's personality as you develop some feel for their interests and hobbies. These two questions set into train a thought process that allows you to start putting the marriage prospect's personality into context and how it might relate to your personality.

The third, fourth, fifth and sixth questions are directly marriage-related. The third question gets the ball rolling with some clarity provided in terms of the principal qualities that the other person is seeking in a potential life partner. This immediately triggers a process of reflection where as the recipient of this specific response you begin to reconcile at some basic level with how the attributes specified relate to the key qualities that define your disposition and whether you can see yourself subscribing to the marriage personality sought by the individual you are in dialogue with. This clarity is then amplified through the fourth question, the aim of which is to furnish you with a deeper insight into precisely how in the mind of the marriage prospect the responsibilities assigned to a husband and a wife are compartmentalised. This take is then further expanded through the fifth question as the discussion here provides you with an understanding of how the marriage prospect views the whole concept of "partnership in marriage". In chapter 1 we provided a basic overview of the rights of the wife, the rights of the husband and the mutual rights shared by the couple, which should allow you to put into context the responses given by the other party to the fourth and fifth questions. The sixth question gives you a direct feel for how keen the other person is to have a family – is it something that is on the cards immediately after marriage or is there an expectancy to stagger having a family and if so for how long? The question needs to be asked and directly so. One should not feel even a modicum of embarrassment when bringing it up for discussion. It is vital to get to grips with the aspirations of the marriage prospect for having a family and how these fit in with your own wishes. The themes examined through the third, fourth, fifth and sixth questions therefore enable you to develop some visibility on what

246

marriage to that individual would entail and how that model for marriage resonates with the vision you have in mind.

Whilst the responses generated up to this point would have given you some feel for that individual's Islamic awareness questions seven and eight get to the heart of the matter directly. Question 7 gives you an appreciation of the role Islam presently plays in the other person's life: it allows you to home in on whether the religious inclination of that person currently synchronises with where you are in terms of practising your faith, which albeit is a personal contract between you and Allah (SWT). You may have certain expectations in terms of where ideally you would expect your potential life partner to be in terms of their faith. Question 7 allows you to get to the point. Question 8 then allows you to comprehend the importance assigned by the marriage prospect in the way you both as a potential couple would be expected to grow Islamically. Again you would assess how this corresponds with your expectations. Since marriage is equivalent to mastering half of your faith the need to broach faith directly through asking questions 7 and 8 cannot be overemphasised. Transparency in regard to understanding the other individual's religiosity is essential if you are to establish whether the marriage prospect has all the credentials needed to allow you to potentially complete half of your faith.

Question 9 gets you to talk about each other's family values directly. Again some light may already have been shed on this theme through responses proffered to some of the earlier questions but a direct line of enquiry is always encouraged. Through raising the question directly you get an appreciation for the (three) key values that inspire the marriage prospect's family and how these relate to your own family. As we have

247

already mentioned you cannot develop a thorough insight into someone's family values until the families engage directly but nonetheless you can derive at least a basic feel for them through this question. Question 10 then permits you to understand in more detail the importance the marriage prospect assigns to marriage reaching beyond a union of two individuals and extending to a union of two families. Does the marriage prospect understand the need to act as a bridge between the two families? Do they understand how to foster a good ambience between the families? If you are a female you could also ask the male party whether you would be required to live with your prospective in-laws, which in any event the male should clarify in his answer to question 10. We recall The Igloo Test from chapter 1 and how it demonstrates that there is no correlation between a wife living with her in-laws and divorce but that there is a significant correlation between the spouses being the products of two different family value systems and divorce. Question 10 also allows you to develop some understanding of how the individual you are in dialogue with intends to balance the rights of their spouse vis-à-vis the rights of their parents, which is a theme that we alluded to in chapter 1. This is a balancing act that needs to be performed with great sensitivity and the utmost responsibility and it is always insightful to decipher the degree to which the person you are exploring marriage with has thought this through. Questions 9 and 10 in effect allow you to develop some initial insight into how congruous your family values may be though as already stressed this area can only be tackled more rigorously once the two families engage directly.

While the above list is not meant to be exhaustive the ten questions certainly provide you with enough data to come to terms with what potential there is for further dialogue against

248

the backdrop of the definitive question: *"Will the person with whom I am exploring a marriage-based dialogue allow me to complete half of my faith?"* Is there enough of a click between your personalities to explore dialogue at the family level? Whether you feel physically attracted to the marriage prospect is a question that only you can wrestle with having met that individual in person. That said that conclusion combined with the discussion generated courtesy of these ten questions should give you plenty of food for thought and allow you to establish whether you feel sufficiently "physically, mentally, religiously, intuitively and otherwise" connected to the marriage prospect to take things to the next stage. Admittedly there will inevitably be other questions that would enter the arena of discussion depending on your concerns and particular circumstances. Adding to this list is encouraged. For example, in the case of a divorcee with children we encourage them to decipher exactly how accepting the marriage prospect is of children from a previous marriage. There is only one way to come to terms with that and that is to ask the question directly. The whole point to having a list of questions in mind is to give the marriage-inspired dialogue a sense of direction. Certain questions will come to mind off the cuff. However, you should have some key questions in mind before you embark on dialogue, subject to the 3-Dialogue Rule, so that once you have expired the Rule you are in a position to conclude decisively whether you feel there is enough mileage certainly at an individual level to progress matters to the next stage. If the families engage directly this list of ten questions can be further analysed and supplemented with yet other questions in order to further examine the degree of individual compatibility between the Muslim male and Muslim female exploring marriage whilst the two individuals and their families simultaneously endeavour to establish the degree of family compatibility.

Marriage-inspired dialogue fostered by the 3-Dialogue Rule is stimulated by a concerted intention on the part of the Muslim male and Muslim female undertaking the dialogue to evaluate one another's life partner potential on the basis of each other's suitability to allowing them to subscribe to negotiating half of their faith. Given the revered stature that marriage inevitably carries within the Muslim faith the need for transparent discourse between the two persons exploring marriage is absolutely essential. The 3-Dialogue Rule empowered by a question of faith inherently invokes such conspicuousness. The 3-Dialogue Rule buoys the ability of the two persons locked in matrimonial discourse to broach such themes readily and not apprehensively. Pertinently these ten questions help you to develop a clear view on whether you wish to expand on the dialogue you have had with a particular individual through engaging the family channel once you have expired the 3-Dialogue Rule. They, however, are not exclusive to developing that view but certainly play a major role in allowing you to decide whether to refer dialogue to the next stage. Such questions should form an inextricable part of your dialogue toolkit for marriage-inspired dialogue. It may well be that you tailor other questions to lend to your dialogue toolkit – that is all fine and well but do remember to keep these ten questions in mind. They invariably have this inveterate tendency to allow you to gauge sooner rather than later whether there is any point in progressing deliberations with that person further. These ten definitive questions allow you to analyse someone's life partner potential very clearly and quickly as they are inspired by the pivotal concern: *"Will the person with whom I am exploring a marriage-based dialogue allow me to complete half of my faith?"* This view is corroborated by the overwhelmingly affirmative feedback we have received not just from Muslim professionals subscribing to Kamran A. Beg Events but also from Muslim professionals generally who are not currently signed up to our services but who have kindly contacted our offices to elicit advice on how to dialogue with a marriage prospect after hearing about the 3-Dialogue Rule.

A 30 year-old Muslim female investment banker based in Paris was introduced to the 3-Dialogue Rule by a female friend, a 32 year-old lawyer resident in London, who has attended various matrimonial events for Muslim professionals convened by Kamran A. Beg Events in London. The investment banker was keen on acquiring an appreciation for the sorts of questions to ask when in dialogue with a potential suitor. On her friend's advice she dropped me a line in February 2006. I sent her a list of the ten questions above asking her to be wary of them when exploring marriage. Feedback the investment banker e-mailed to me in April 2006 is self-explanatory and positively receptive of the advice that was sent her way. She encouragingly wrote: "Applying the 3-Dialogue Rule makes asking those ten key questions so easy – it gives you the nerve to tackle the question of marriage head on and not to be afraid of asking those ten specific questions, which otherwise you would ordinarily be too nervous to ask. Before you know it more questions are rolling off the tip of your tongue effortlessly. But those ten questions put everything into perspective when it comes to working out someone's marriage suitability." More will follow in chapter 4 on how the very nature of the 3-Dialogue Rule makes it easier for a Muslim male and Muslim female to partake in less inhibited dialogue insofar as exploring each other's life partner potential is concerned.

Always Remaining Loyal to the Definitive Question - "Will the person with whom I am exploring a marriage-based dialogue allow me to complete half of my faith?"

The 3-Dialogue Rule states that the Muslim male and Muslim female exploring the question of marriage should endeavour to undertake no more than **3 dialogues**, within the purview of a **2-week** time scale, to establish whether there is enough common overlap and compatibility between them to warrant progressing their dialogue to the parent/guardian level.

As we have seen in the course of this chapter adopting the **3-Dialogue Rule** at the very outset of the marriage-inspired dialogue process clearly allows the outcome, **that is whether the Muslim male and Muslim female integral to that specific dialogue will be proceeding to marriage**, to be determined sooner rather than later! This outcome is notably gauged without compromising the integrity – emotional, family, community or otherwise - of the Muslim male and Muslim female party to the dialogue, with the integrity of the two individuals and their respective families maintained on account of the halal ethos that constantly reinforces the entirety of the dialogue process.

The 3-Dialogue Rule is equally applicable to both family-based and non-family based introductions, as we have discussed in detail in this chapter.

Throughout the dialogue process the definitive question informing the marriage-inspired dialogue between the

252

Muslim male and Muslim female should be: *"Will the person with whom I am exploring a marriage-based dialogue allow me to complete half of my faith?"*
In discharging the 3-Dialogue Rule a list of ten definitive questions are recommended by Kamran A. Beg Events as being germane to the dialogue incumbent's dialogue toolkit, which may well encompass other questions. These ten questions, which have been dissected in chapter 3, are listed below.

1. How would your best friend describe your personality in three phrases and why?
2. What are your favourite interests and hobbies?
3. What are the primary qualities you are looking for in a spouse?
4. What do you regard as the primary responsibilities of a Muslim husband and a Muslim wife?
5. What shared responsibilities should a Muslim husband and a Muslim wife exercise?
6. Once married when ideally would you like to have a family?
7. What part does Islam currently play in your life?
8. How do you see yourself growing in terms of your faith in partnership with your life partner once you have settled down?
9. What three values does your family cherish above all and why?
10. Once married what sorts of things would you do in order to act as a bridge between the two families and to bring our families closer together?

These ten questions enable the Muslim male and Muslim female exploring marriage to fathom each other's life partner potential very clearly and quickly since they are motivated by the definitive question underpinning marriage-inspired dialogue: *"Will the person with whom I am exploring a marriage-based dialogue allow me to complete half of my faith?"* These ten questions help to address the definitive question stated, which the Muslim male and Muslim female in dialogue should always remain loyal to during their marriage-inspired deliberations. Naturally the themes raised by these ten questions would be subjected to further scrutiny should the Muslim male and Muslim female having discharged the 3-Dialogue Rule conclude that there is sufficient mileage to warrant engaging the families directly.

In particular, adherence to the 3-Dialogue Rule safeguards the Muslim female and her family. It also safeguards the male and female in question **against** dating and having a relationship, both of which are Islamically prohibited and non-permissible! Throughout the dialogue process the two individuals supported by their respective families must continue to remain steadfast in addressing the definitive question informing the marriage-inspired dialogue: *"Will the person with whom I am exploring a marriage-based dialogue allow me to complete half of my faith?"* Only then can the feasibility of a particular marriage prospect be properly assessed!

We now move into the final chapter of this book, namely chapter 4, to appreciate how well the 3-Dialogue Rule works in practice.

4. The 3-Dialogue Rule Works

Since being founded on July 11, 2003, Kamran A. Beg Events has experienced 100 marriages worldwide amongst Muslim professionals subscribing to our services. These marriages bear the indelible insignia of the 3-Dialogue Rule, which we elaborated on in extensive detail in chapter 3, with each marriage ultimately manifesting the will of Allah (SWT).

Armed with a comprehensive understanding of the 3-Dialogue Rule we are now in a position to examine how well the 3-Dialogue Rule works in practice and how it irons out some of the problems commonly encountered by Muslim professionals when seeking a life partner with a view to completing half of their faith.

We recall that the definitive question informing the marriage-inspired dialogue process is: *"Will the person with whom I am exploring a marriage-based dialogue allow me to complete half of my faith?"* In this chapter we will gather the profoundly positive impact that this question has exacted in guiding exponents of the 3-Dialogue Rule. This overarching question should form the very cornerstone of any marriage-inspired dialogue featuring a Muslim male and a Muslim female and its central importance simply cannot be stressed enough. It is this question that truly defines the soul of a genuine marriage-inspired dialogue between two Muslims who fully recognise the sacred stature assigned to marriage by Allah (SWT), a theme we explored in detail in chapter 1.

The 3-Dialogue Rule as Experienced by Two Specific Couples Resulting from Kamran A. Beg Events: The Inspiring Cases of Umer Majid and Aisha Janjua, and Dr Ashraful Mirza and Andleeb Anwar

In this chapter we discuss the experiences of some of the couples generated through Kamran A. Beg Events who have applied the 3-Dialogue Rule.

Two of the couples we feature were interviewed for the CNN feature on Kamran A. Beg Events, which was originally featured on the edition of 'Inside The Middle East' broadcast by CNN International on September 30, 2005. The feature received excellent reviews worldwide reflecting very creditably and exceptionally well on our outstanding global family of attendees, subscribers and members who at the time of the feature being aired had accounted for, subject to the will of Allah (SWT), 88 marriages, since when we have had a further 12 marriages allowing the century mark to be registered on May 21, 2006.

The feature was produced by one of CNN's most distinguished journalists, Robyn Curnow, whose consummate professionalism was a delight for each of us to experience who participated in the making of the programme.

Umer Majid and Dr Ashraful Mirza were both interviewed for the feature, each of whom got married as a result of finding a wonderful bride through the matrimonial events programme run for Muslim professionals by Kamran A. Beg Events. Umer Majid and Aisha Janjua were married on January 2, 2005, and Dr Ashraful Mirza and Andleeb Anwar were married on September 11, 2005: may Allah (SWT) bless both couples with every matrimonial bliss, Insha'Allah. We now share their experiences of the 3-Dialogue Rule with the reader.

(i) The Inspiring Case of Umer Majid and Aisha Janjua Discussed: Umer Majid, entrepreneur, and Aisha Janjua, solicitor, neither of whom had been previously married, were introduced to each other at the professional Muslim singles matrimonial event convened in Manchester on February 21, 2004. Umer and Aisha's families are both originally from Pakistan.

I had the great honour of chairing that auspicious event, which would subsequently generate three marriages, subject to the Divine will. Post-event Umer and Aisha engaged in an initial telephone conversation on February 22, 2004, building on the individual compatibility they had sensed at the event. The 3-Dialogue Rule was conducted under my event guardianship with both Umer and Aisha providing me with detailed feedback at every step of the dialogue process and having access to me directly as their dialogue mentor. Before we got the ball rolling Umer and Aisha respectfully informed their parents and families that they were about to enter a marriage-inspired dialogue under my guardianship.

Having reflected on their first dialogue for a couple of days, the feedback I received from Umer and Aisha was very favourable, with both individuals being careful to assess the matrimonial merits of the other on the basis of the central question that should propel any marriage-inspired dialogue: *"Will the person with whom I am exploring a marriage-based dialogue allow me to complete half of my faith?"* In fact before Umer and Aisha embarked on their first dialogue both had the courtesy to discuss with me the implications of

257

this question and how to go about addressing it. As Aisha reported back after their inaugural post-event dialogue: "Since we are seeking a life partner on the basis of completing half our Deen or faith our opening dialogue was very focused. We broached areas of discussion germane to how we both perceive marriage. This has allowed Umer and me to be more upfront rather than skirting around the issues. I never thought it was possible to have such a transparent discussion regarding marriage so quickly. The ten questions Kamran A. Beg Events encourages to be looked at provided both Umer and me with a good base to operate from and also allowed us to develop other themes relevant to our dialogue." We therefore note that the urgency induced by aligning themselves to viewing marriage as a question of faith gave Umer and Aisha a licence to ask questions relating directly to a marriage-inspired dialogue readily at the very outset of the dialogue process, which is perfectly Islamic. We also note Aisha's reference to the list of ten questions that we discussed at the end of chapter 3 and which we suggested would provide a good foundation for a marriage-inspired dialogue actuated by a question of faith. These questions had provided Umer and Aisha with a useful springboard from which to ask yet other relevant questions. They did not feel inhibited in asking such questions and furthermore such questions came to them naturally. As Umer clarified: "In our phone discussion I made it clear to Aisha that I saw marriage as a sacred institution that would allow me to complete half of my faith and act as a bridge between two families and that I wished for both our families to be close to one another. It was good to be able to discuss things that are so directly relevant to marriage within a few minutes of starting our discussion. Those ten questions Kamran A. Beg Events recommends for discussion made it easier for the dialogue to develop a good natural flow, which in turn made it much easier to discuss other important areas relevant to assessing each other's life partner potential."

Umer and Aisha then proceeded to a second dialogue on February 29, 2004, which took the form of a meeting at a local restaurant in Manchester, a city which the reader will note has an outstanding reputation for Muslim cuisine. Umer and Aisha are both from the north west of England. Aisha was chaperoned by her siblings and the dialogue was sanctioned and signed off by me personally. Between their first dialogue and their meeting Umer and Aisha had no contact with each other in keeping with the spirit of the 3-Dialogue Rule. As Aisha said to me at the time: "This respite has given me time to put our discussion into perspective and to think about the next set of questions I would like to explore with Umer." However, in the run up to the meeting I spoke to both of them separately being their perennial point of reference. Umer telephoned me on the eve of that meeting and indicated that he was very upbeat and positive about the meeting the following day and that having no contact with Aisha since their first dialogue had allowed him to get a handle of the issues that he wished to tackle. As he also said: "The space between dialogues gives you time to evaluate the currency of the dialogue you have just had. You get time to clear your mind and to reconcile yourself with working on a list of questions for the next dialogue and what issues you would like to examine in more detail. Again that list of ten questions Kamran A. Beg Events stresses is very useful in helping to earmark a list of particular issues you would like to look at more closely. By not contacting Aisha after the first conversation I feel that I have respected Aisha and her family's dignity."

The meeting that took place the following day proved to be a resounding success. Aisha's siblings sat through the first part of the meeting at the restaurant and then left Umer and Aisha to converse for an hour before returning and drawing the meeting to a reluctant close. During that meeting Umer and Aisha established that they had highly compatible personalities. They got on like a house on fire. Umer in his feedback after the meeting exclaimed: "Meeting Aisha and her siblings made me realise not just how complementary our personalities are but that we belong to two families that can pull on with each other." Umer, who is an exceptionally articulate, eclectic and highly respected member of the Muslim community in Manchester, sung Aisha's praises in a way that only a consummate gentleman could when he and I spoke the next day. On the same day, Aisha, who bless her is a communitarian at heart, remarked: "Subject to our families meeting each other and getting on with each other Umer can help me to complete half of my faith." This sentiment was echoed by Umer himself in his ecstatic feedback of the previous day's deliberations: "Knowing that marriage will allow me to consolidate my faith has allowed me to come to terms more quickly with the soulmate I need. I can now fathom that chemistry more perspicuously. Aisha has that chemistry and I will leave the rest to the will of Allah (SWT)."

Within the space of two dialogues Umer and Aisha ascertained that their personalities were highly compatible and declared their wish to me to get their families to engage directly. In this case, all three of us concluded that a third dialogue would not be necessary. The two dialogues they had had post-event were spaced apart by one week and by March 1, 2004, eight days after the first dialogue and well within the 2-week time limit permitted by the 3-Dialogue Rule, the two families were asked to engage directly.

The families initially met for the first time on March 7, 2004, with both Umer and Aisha present. Umer's parents spoke to Aisha's parents for the first time on the Wednesday before that meeting. That initial phone conversation set the stage for the families to meet. Umer and Aisha had no contact with each other after concluding the 3-Dialogue Rule until the families met. After exchanging visits a couple of times each the two families confirmed that their values are indeed highly similar and compatible, with the question of Umer and Aisha completing half of their faith constantly guiding both families as well as Umer and Aisha through out the course of this brilliantly executed marriage-inspired dialogue. As we noted in chapter 1, family compatibility was stressed by the Prophet (PBUH) as the additional layer of compatibility that should overlay the individual compatibility necessary for two Muslims seeking marriage. That was clearly the case with Umer and Aisha. During this time Umer and Aisha were allowed to meet with Aisha chaperoned as before and engage in phone conversations but only after the families had met initially and sanctioned future contact between Aisha and Umer in keeping with the tenets celebrated by the Muslim value system (see chapter 3). Furthermore Umer and Aisha both performed Istikhara (see chapter 1) along with their parents after the families had met the first time and by the time the families had exchanged two sets of visits each Umer and Aisha and their parents had experienced a very favourable response. As Umer remarked: "After performing Istikhara in order to consult Allah (SWT) for His counsel on my intention to marry Aisha I awaited Allah's guidance. After Istikhara I was totally at peace with myself and knew that this symbolised an affirmative from

261

The Lord Most High." Umer's sentiment was echoed by his parents both of whom experienced the same harmonious feeling after performing Istikhara. Aisha echoed Umer's feeling saying to me: "After Istikhara my heart and mind are one. Istikhara has confirmed that Umer is that special person I have been seeking who will allow me to complete half my Deen. My parents feel the same and are at ease after performing Istikhara."

Umer's family formally requested Aisha's hand-in-marriage in late March 2004. Aisha's family accepted their proposal for marriage and Umer and Aisha proceeded to marriage on January 2, 2005. I had the great privilege of attending their beautiful marriage. Umer shortly before the marriage spoke to me pointing out that the 3-Dialogue Rule and its emphasis on completing half of one's faith had allowed him to appreciate fully the enormity of marriage and to remain focused in his dialogues with Aisha on the key questions germane to exploring marriage in that sacred light. As Umer said: "We never lost sight of the question of faith. The 3-Dialogue Rule drummed that into both of us. That made for more discerning family interaction."

Umer and Aisha are now both happily settled in Manchester, Alhamdulillah. This dynamic and enterprising couple have done much to encourage other Muslim professional singles to find matrimonial sanctuary. Since getting married Umer and Aisha have made several appearances at various Muslim professional matrimonial events run by Kamran A. Beg Events in the UK where they have featured as memorable guest speakers enlightening attendee groups of their experiences of the 3-Dialogue Rule and the halal integrity that propelled them to the wedding altar. They continue to receive, and deservedly so, the most outstanding feedback from attendees who in turn have been motivated by their heart-warming story. As I have often remarked in my travels worldwide in the capacity of chairing Kamran A. Beg Events, Umer Majid and Aisha Janjua are undoubtedly an impeccable personification of the definitive Muslim couple and serve as an inspiration for the Muslim Ummah at large!

(ii) The Inspiring Case of Dr Ashraful Mirza and Andleeb Anwar Discussed: Dr Ashraful Mirza, doctor, and Andleeb Anwar, civil servant, initially met at a professional Muslim singles matrimonial event held in Manchester on June 19, 2005. The reader by now would have picked up the heart-warming revelation that the Manchester venue has this delectably inveterate disposition for generating marriages galore. Whilst chairing events worldwide I have frequently been given to describing Manchester as the dynamic hub of our global organisation, which indeed it justifiably is. Of the 100 marriages, which have occurred through Kamran A. Beg Events at the time of going to press, 31 emanate from introductions secured amongst Muslim professionals who had been in attendance at a Manchester event. For those of you who have not had the honour of visiting Manchester rest assured firmly ensconced in the soothing knowledge that it really is the centre of the universe, apart from being the writer's home city of course!

Ashraful, from London, is an exceptionally thorough and polished gentleman who has for many years engaged in community-related initiatives in keeping with his very giving and altruistic nature. He very strongly believes in putting something back into the community. Andleeb, from Manchester, is a very dynamic and open-minded person blessed with profound compassion and whose consummate appreciation for the true spirit with which Islam should be propagated is something truly unique to behold. Ashraful was a divorcee with a daughter from a previous marriage. Andleeb had previously never been married. At the event they both attended it was clear that there appeared to be a very encouraging connection between their respective personalities, a good pretext on which to initiate post-event dialogue.

Before the first post-event dialogue was sanctioned I, in my humble capacity, as the event guardian to both Ashraful and Andleeb was required to clarify two key issues. Firstly, would the fact that Ashraful was a divorcee with a child in any way penalise the ability of the dialogue to progress smoothly? Secondly, the fact that Ashraful and Andleeb are of two different cultural backgrounds needed to be broached directly with both parties, including their families, and confirmation was then sought that cultural diversity would not serve as an impediment later, which Islamically it is not. Ashraful's family originates from Bangladesh while Andleeb's family stems from Pakistan.

As we noted in chapter 2, a marriage-inspired dialogue framework should underscore the need not to penalise and show indifference towards divorcees and moreover should make it incumbent on all stakeholders integral to it to exercise the very highest degrees of cultural tolerance when considering Muslim life partner choices. Andleeb and her family citing the example of the Prophet (PBUH) confirmed that Ashraful would be assessed for marriage on the basis of his personality and whether he and his family values made him a potential suitor for Andleeb with a view to allowing her to complete half of her faith. Ashraful being a divorcee with a child would not in any way affect their assessment of whether he was a suitable match for Andleeb who along with her graceful family was accommodating of Ashraful not just being a divorcee but also accepting of the fact that he had been gifted with a child from his first marriage. Furthermore both Ashraful and Andleeb indicated with express clarity that culture was not an issue for either of them and that their families were open to cultural diversity, which Islam celebrates enormously. Have received confirmation on both fronts the 3-Dialogue Rule was put into effect under my guardianship.

At the end of their first dialogue, a lively telephone conversation, both parties provided me with very encouraging feedback. This gave momentum to two more dialogues, with all three dialogues completed within the 2-week time limit reserved for the 3-Dialogue Rule. As Ashraful pointed out after the very first dialogue: "That list of ten questions cultivated by Kamran A. Beg Events in respect of whether a marriage prospect can help you to master half of your faith has really got our dialogue off to a flying start. It provides a fertile landscape for marriage-inspired dialogue to blossom from."

Between dialogues Ashraful and Andleeb did not contact each other and their point of reference was myself. Both called me several times and e-mailed me feedback and their general thoughts on how they felt the dialogue was beginning to mature into that "dialogue of a life time". I vividly recall with great glee Ashraful's comment to me after the third dialogue where Andleeb and he had met at a café in a chaperoned setting: "Andleeb is a very pious, Allah-fearing and devout Muslim. She and her family have respected me for the person I am. She has never once made me feel uncomfortable because I am divorced with a child. She really is that someone special who can help me to complete half of my Deen. Her Islam shows in her graceful humility." Let Andleeb's Islamic-broadmindedness and fairness serve as a reminder to the Muslim community of the dignity and humanity with which Muslims should treat divorcees. Her inspiration is clearly derived from the life of the Prophet (PBUH) and bears testimony not just to her but also to her excellent upbringing as a model Muslim.

In no time at all after concluding their third dialogue within the time precincts of the 3-Dialogue Rule Ashraful and Andleeb engaged their families directly. As Ashraful admitted in his feedback on meeting Andleeb's family he was overwhelmed by how similar the families are in terms of temperament and how seamless the communication between them was. This was the final piece in the jigsaw puzzle and after the families exchanged one set of visits Ashraful and his family concluded that Andleeb was blessed with all the qualities and more that Ashraful had yearned for in a wife. Throughout this process Ashraful and Andleeb along with their families had remained true to the pivotal question of faith: *"Will the person with whom I am exploring a marriage-based dialogue allow me to complete half of my faith?"* Both Ashraful and Andleeb and their respective families performed Istikhara (see chapter 1 for more detail) after that initial meeting of the two families, with all parties receiving a brightly positive response having undertaken Istikhara!

As Ashraful acknowledged in a phone conversation with me shortly before his family requested Andleeb's hand in marriage: "The 3-Dialogue Rule tests your commitment to the other person. You know that if there is a spark the families have to get involved immediately. That spark can only be calibrated by asking yourself time and time again

266

whether that person will enable you to negotiate 50% of your Deen. That question crosses over to when the families get talking. Your whole psyche is disposed to answering that one question with tireless urgency. But you cannot contend fully with this question until the families meet. The 3-Dialogue Rule gets you to that stage as soon as is reasonably possible. Only then can you put that click into perspective!"

Ashraful and Andleeb were married on September 11, 2005. Andleeb lives with her in-laws and has made it abundantly clear that provided the two families resemble each other significantly from the point of view of their respective values living with the in-laws can be a very positively uplifting experience. Ashraful's parents are very fond of Andleeb and admire her majesty and grace as a person. All three get on like a dream and as Andleeb said to me: "It is an Islamic duty of the highest virtue to support one's husband in enabling him to honour his parents. If a Muslim woman can live her parents all her life until she gets married then living with her future in-laws is not as unfathomable an option as many Muslim professional females mistakenly tend to make out since the key is to marry someone whose family values are compatible with yours to start off with. In my in-laws I have found an extra set of parents and our relationship is based on mutual love, trust and respect. My in-laws have absorbed me into their family in the most loving manner and treat me like their own daughter. Their values are the values on which I was raised by my parents and the values that run through my family." And so The Igloo Test, which we discussed at length in chapter 1, wins the day! This analogy shows that it is not residing with the in-laws as such, which leads to the increased likelihood of marital breakdown; rather it is a marked variance in the family values of the two spouses, which exercises an adverse influence on the ability of a marriage to flourish thereby making divorce a more likely outcome. As Ashraful remarked in May 2006: "Andleeb and I come from very similar families. It is always a joy when the families get together. We do everything we can to support each other in upholding the highest respect for our families and for each other's families." Thus Ashraful and Andleeb have both mastered how to balance the rights of the spouse with the rights of their parents in the spirit we conveyed in chapter 1.

Ashraful and Andleeb now live in London and their exemplary marriage continues to act as a beacon of hope for many other Muslim professional singles seeking marriage. Ashraful's speeches at various UK-based Muslim professional matrimonial events run by Kamran A. Beg Events have been received very amenably and have always generated the most ecstatic and memorable applause from our attendees. Dr Ashraful Mirza and Andleeb Anwar have been described by their friends as the pulse of their community in London and as a wonderfully inspiring couple, which they indubitably are!

The 3-Dialogue Rule as Viewed by a Chaperone to the Female Party: Surrya Jabeen's Perspective

In 2006, Kamran A. Beg Events was respectfully shortlisted for the Lloyds TSB 2006 Public Service Excellence Asian Jewel Award, which is widely recognised as a very highly prestigious award in the UK. This nomination was steered with great professionalism, dedication, enthusiasm and energy by Surrya Jabeen, Tasleem Ali and Tazim Ali, who were the joint co-chairs for the nomination, which was supported, inter alia, by a whole volume of testimonials received from Muslim professionals belonging to our global family of attendees, subscribers and members and also by submissions forwarded by various couples generated, subject to the Divine will, through Kamran A. Beg Events.

The category in which Kamran A. Beg Events received a shortlisting was won by Mohammed Afzal Khan, Lord Mayor Manchester, with the shortlist itself comprising of four nominees in total, including Kamran A. Beg Events.

Our progression to the shortlist for this award reflects exceptionally well on our model global family of attendees, subscribers and members and moreover on the formidable and groundbreaking mark they have made worldwide, with their global footprint serving as an inspiration to the whole of the Muslim community.

Surrya Jabeen, cited above, merits a special mention! Surrya was also interviewed for the CNN feature we referred to at the very beginning of this chapter. Her sterling contribution to that programme received outstanding plaudits from viewers worldwide, which still continue to flood in incessantly. Surrya is one of the very finest attendees that Kamran A. Beg Events has had the distinguished honour of serving. An entrepreneur blessed with a rare flair and abundantly eclectic Surrya who lives in London is a great ambassador for the Muslim community. Over the years Surrya has worked tirelessly to serve the Muslim community and her contributions have touched the lives of many. In particular she has allowed countless Muslim professional females to come to terms with their real potential and to excel to even greater heights not just professionally but on all fronts. Surrya has been endowed with a distinctively prodigious understanding of Islam and straddles the east-west interface with the most virtuous and consummate Islamic majesty, modesty and integrity. Without a doubt she is a remarkable role model for the Muslim community and her monumental sense of compassion is firmly anchored on her complete faith in Allah (SWT).

In addition to being one of our most revered attendees Surrya has also acted as an exemplary chaperone to several female attendees subscribed to Kamran A. Beg Events and also other female friends when they have been engaged in the joys of marriage-inspired dialogue. She is a great advocate of the 3-Dialogue Rule!

In a discussion that I had with Surrya in March 2006 she pointed out in her inimitably articulate manner: "A lot of Muslim professionals have got caught up in the dating racket, innocently or otherwise. They think that getting to know someone over a protracted period of time automatically increases their likelihood of marrying that someone. Well it simply doesn't! The 3-Dialogue Rule gives you a viable halal alternative. It gets rid of dating and gets you into dialogue that is driven by one sole intention: marriage. And do you know what? It is so overdue because dating is ruining so many Muslim professionals' chances of getting married."

Furthermore having chaperoned several Muslim females pursuing marriage-inspired dialogue Surrya has been able to confirm the tangibly accentuated sense of purpose that the 3-Dialogue Rule has conferred upon the Muslim male and Muslim female party to those dialogues. In her opinion the 3-Dialogue Rule has allowed the outcome to transpire at the earliest possible time thereby mitigating the extent to which the emotional temperament of the two individuals in question has been impacted and interwoven. She has noticed the increased sense of urgency shown at the meetings that she has attended in the capacity of a chaperone where as she puts it: "The male and female are both more direct in their take on what they are looking for in marriage and waste no time at all before thrashing out the key issues. The 3-Dialogue Rule gives them a licence to discuss things relevant to marriage more immediately and openly. Knowing that marriage will result in allowing you to negotiate half of your religious faith allows the two parties to be more forthright in giving expression to their feelings on marriage and what they are really looking for in their other half." What is interesting to decipher in this feedback that Surrya has provided is her incisive observation that the 3-Dialogue Rule makes the dialogue incumbents feel less inhibited in cutting to the chase and giving vent to their matrimonial expectations. That nervous apprehension, which otherwise ordinarily hinders the male and female from being so transparent initially, is channelled into harnessing a heightened sense of positive urgency where the male and female seek to extract the maximum mileage from the meeting with a view to assessing the marriage-worthiness of the other party. Whatever chemistry endears you as someone in relentless pursuit of your soulmate with the 3-Dialogue Rule you calibrate the marriage-worthiness of the other person literally from the word 'go'. Your whole psyche is conditioned to addressing the burning question: *"Will the person with whom I am exploring a marriage-based dialogue allow me to complete half of my faith?"*

Commenting on some of the burning issues then that have been raised at meetings where she has chaperoned the female party Surrya gleefully notes: "Questions such as, for

271

example, what are you looking for in a life partner?, how large a family would you like to have?, how do you see our families integrating if marriage did result?, where would you live assuming we got married? and what values does your family cherish? are not untypical at a first meeting. With the 3-Dialogue Rule asking these questions comes naturally to both the male and female. You don't feel held back." Inhibition therefore transmutes to a zeal to remain loyal to gauging the suitability of the other party as quickly as possible, which translates into an urgency, which inspires both dialogue incumbents to wrestle with the key issues with greater immediacy. This allows the male and female in dialogue to establish as soon as possible whether they connect without compromising their emotional territory. Remaining true to the above definitive question allows the male and female to remain true to themselves and that in turn allows them to remain true to each other.

What could be more relevant to a marriage-inspired dialogue than discussing issues germane to marriage and pertinent to grasping the suitability of the other party as a potential life partner vis-à-vis their potential to allow you to complete half of your faith. Those questions that you would normally hesitate to ask flow off the tip of your tongue more freely. These are the very questions you need to contemplate to assess the viability of the other party in terms of marriage. These are the very types of questions and themes that drive dialogue executed through the medium of the 3-Dialogue Rule. Rather than second-guessing the person you are in dialogue with you tackle the issues directly. In chapter 3 we recommended that you ask ten key questions, albeit amongst others you may wish to explore, when executing the 3-Dialogue Rule in order to ascertain sooner rather than later whether you feel there is enough individual compatibility to progress your deliberations to the family level. These questions as we noted allow you to discern whether the individual you are in dialogue with has the potential of allowing you to negotiate half of your faith and therefore allow you to establish reasonably quickly and with greater incisiveness whether there is any potential in furthering discussions with the marriage prospect once the 3-Dialogue Rule has been deployed and exhausted. Earlier in this chapter we noted how useful these questions can prove through the enlightening experiences of two couples we have seen emerge through Kamran A. Beg Events, namely Umer Majid and Aisha Janjua and Dr Ashraful Mirza and Andleeb Anwar. Asking such questions is made all the more easier since they help you to assess directly whether the marriage prospect has the potential to allow you to complete half of your faith and are therefore inspired by the central question of faith invoked and celebrated by the 3-Dialogue Rule. Since the 3-Dialogue Rule stresses the need for transparent discourse between the Muslim male and Muslim female exploring marriage asking such questions and any other questions that you may regard as material to the cause come all the more readily and with greater ease.

Getting to the point is what the 3-Dialogue Rule demands of the two people exploring marriage. There is no getting away from getting to the point and that too sooner rather than later. As Surrya testifies: "The nature of the 3-Dialogue Rule forces the male and female in dialogue to come clean as quickly as possible. It conditions the psyches to do so."

Making both parties cognisant so quickly of the other person's life partner potential makes the 3-Dialogue Rule uniquely quintessential as a robust halal marriage-inspired dialogue framework. With the psyches avidly trained on

273

homing in on the other party's marriage-worthiness as quickly as possible at least in terms of individual compatibility the purposeful dialogues that ensue within the bounds of the 3-Dialogue Rule inevitably radiate a certain intensity, which importantly stems from the increasing urgency of the Muslim male and Muslim female to partake in directly relevant transparent discussion designed to grapple speedily with the other person's suitability for marriage. As the Muslim male and Muslim female derive more and more information in terms of understanding whether they click individually with each other almost seamlessly and with effortless resolve the dialogue incumbents find themselves asking basic questions allied to discovering more about each other's family values though admittedly in the knowledge that a complete or more thorough analysis related to family compatibility can only occur once the families engage directly. In the list of ten questions that we recommended in chapter 3 as being integral to a marriage-inspired dialogue toolkit when executing the 3-Dialogue Rule we recount that questions 9 and 10 deal explicitly with acquiring some visibility on the family values of the marriage prospect before the families are engaged directly. It is this unswerving loyalty then to fathoming the other party's marriage worthiness that instils dialogues conducted within a 3-Dialogue Rule framework with a distinctive and palpable urgency, a constructive urgency that is amplified by virtue of the two parties engaged in dialogue constantly reconciling with viewing marriage as a sacred conduit through which to complete half of their faith. Whatever that unique combination of faith and personal preference (see chapter 1) you may seek in a potential counterpart in the way of that special chemistry you yearn for knowing that that chemistry should allow you to master half of your faith raises the stakes no end. Suddenly the two individuals in dialogue acclimatize their thinking to acknowledging that the attributes they value, if identified in a potential soulmate, are of themselves not sufficient to register that much sought after click. Simply these attributes are subservient to a further check: having found what you are looking for vis-à-vis a compatible chemistry does that person necessarily have the right temperament to allow you to complete half of your faith?

As Surrya elaborates: "Having chaperoned several females who have applied the 3-Dialogue Rule it is clear that the meeting was not just about whether the female in question and the male she was in dialogue with felt comfortable in terms of the usual checklist: looks, education, professional compatibility, similar outlook and values. Here there is a question of Deen: having possibly identified a chemistry that you can relate to in someone in a matrimonial light does that necessarily mean that you will complete half of your faith if you proceed to marriage with them?" As we can adduce from Surrya's telling observations and as we have already intimated earlier the stakes then are clearly raised and it is this constant reference to a question of faith that allows you to fully acknowledge whether having identified that elusive chemistry that you yearn for whether that chemistry as embodied by the other individual has the potential to allow you to cross that bridge of faith, a question that you can only contend with more fully once the families are engaged directly. Calibrating a marriage-inspired dialogue against this overriding question of faith is what propels the 3-Dialogue Rule and what should run through the heart of any family interaction that may follow. In reminding the dialogue incumbents of the importance of marriage the 3-Dialogue Rule also impresses on the Muslim male and Muslim female in dialogue that they should not take

275

marriage lightly and should at all times be wary of its religious connotations. This is why marriage represents such a huge undertaking in the Muslim community: it goes beyond a union of two individuals and two families. Most significantly, it allows you to take that vital step closer to Allah (SWT), subject to the Divine will, a definitive step that renders the completion of half of your faith thereby allowing you to contribute in very large measure to exercising the horizontal and vertical dimensions of faith expounded in chapter 1. Knowing that places an additional heightened responsibility on the shoulders of both the Muslim male and Muslim female party to a marriage-inspired dialogue. This great responsibility extends to their families. You cannot afford to be remiss or nonchalant when it comes to appreciating the very sacred eminence associated with marriage: being allied to it lends clarity to the decision-making process and culminates in a decision inspired by the right motivation!

An Analysis of the Dialogue Trajectories of the 100 Couples Emerging from Kamran A. Beg Events Hitherto

An analysis of the dialogue trajectories followed by the 100 couples Kamran A. Beg Events has generated so far through introductions secured among Muslim professionals subscribing to our services is very revealing. On average each of these Muslim professionals referred 2.3 dialogue prospects to their families for direct family engagement after progressing the dialogues in question through the 3-Dialogue Rule. We note then that there was a probability of 0.43 or almost 50% of a 'marriage' outcome once a referral had been made to the families. There was a 0.57 probability of a non-marriage outcome. What the 3-Dialogue Rule imparted in these cases was the ability to identify as soon as possible, subject to the families subsequently becoming directly engaged in the marriage-inspired dialogue progress on expiry of the 3-Dialogue Rule, the actual outcome itself: marriage or non-marriage.

In the cases where non-marriage was the outcome 84% of the Muslim professionals party to such marriage-inspired dialogues acknowledged that the key hindrance inhibiting a marriage outcome was the lack of compatibility between the actual families of the Muslim male and Muslim female who had been engaged in dialogue. This then is one of the endearing features of the 3-Dialogue Rule: it allows you to gain visibility on how compatible the families are in a time wise efficient manner designed to safeguard both the individuals in dialogue and their respective families.

The 3-Dialogue Rule Extinguishes the Vile Tempest of Dating

As a very eclectic 32 year-old female investment banker based in London put it: "It was third time lucky. I had already referred two men on to my family through Kamran A. Beg Events. The good thing is that the 3-Dialogue Rule made it possible for the families to get involved as quickly as possible and we knew within a month of my first dialogue with either of these men that marriage would not be the end-result. The families were too different and that made me and my family feel uneasy about taking things forward. And then when I referred the third introduction to the family and the families met things ran very smoothly. We were all comfortable with each other. Within a month of initiating the 3-Dialogue Rule the families gave their blessings to our engagement and now we are married. The 3-Dialogue Rule totally cuts out dating." Seminally, outcomes are established without being preyed upon by the menacing tempest of dating since dating is entirely expunged from the equation of male-female interaction governing a marriage-inspired dialogue predicated on the 3-Dialogue Rule. Muslim professionals worldwide in their feedback to Kamran A. Beg Events have consistently acknowledged that the 3-Dialogue Rule not only provides a halal framework for marriage-inspired dialogue but that it equally importantly identifies the key risk of dating, mitigates the effects of this risk and eliminates it entirely from the landscape of male-female interaction construed within the ambit of exploring the other party's marriage potential. Circumventing dating as it does, the 3-Dialogue Rule makes dating unthinkable and renders it totally redundant. All Muslims know that dating is Islamically prohibited and therefore haram: those in the Muslim community who have been remiss about this and have thought it to be fashionable think again. You can know the outcome without being subsumed by the perils of dating! The 3-Dialogue Rule gives you that assurance and if you are a female reader nothing could be more comforting than knowing this. Truly, the 3-Dialogue Rule has replaced diamonds, and more recently pearls, as a girl's best friend!

The vast majority of Muslim female professionals who contact Kamran A. Beg Events are very keen to point out that they wish to explore marriage-inspired dialogues without being sucked into the vortex of dating, which is entirely understandable in view of how prevalent dating has become among Muslim professionals as evidenced by our research elaborated in chapter 2. As a 26 year-old female economist residing in New York recently remarked: "So many of my Muslim friends are dating – they see it as a way of getting to know the other person. Ironically very few of them are marrying. What the 3-Dialogue Rule does is it strips dating out of the equation altogether. It shows you that it is possible to gauge the suitability of the other person without surrendering to the sad dating culture, which can be seen throughout the Muslim community." What this observation demonstrates is that dating sadly is a reality that has hit the Muslim community hard. The 3-Dialogue Rule, however, distinctively eliminates this risk, as we have already seen in chapter 3.

A 31 year-old pharmacist based in Leeds writes: "I was introduced to someone through a friend. I wasn't sure how to handle speaking to him until one day I was asked by a friend of mine to read about the 3-Dialogue Rule created by Kamran A. Beg. It gave me direction. I had not at the time subscribed to a service provided by Kamran A. Beg Events. After reading the rule on the company web site I contacted its author directly – Kamran himself - who clarified it to me. Getting back to the person I had been introduced to, a 35 year-old microbiologist, we had three dialogues spread over the two weeks stipulated by the rule. After the third dialogue I had wanted to proceed to the family stage. The microbiologist did not see eye to eye with me on this asking for another month of getting to know each other. I had remembered that if by the third dialogue the families did not get involved directly that any future contact between he and I would amount to dating and on top of that there was a 95% chance that our families would never meet if they did not speak immediately after the third dialogue we had both had. I terminated the dialogue and said to him that I was not prepared to wait another month. The 3-Dialogue Rule gave me that conviction: it saved me from another month of uncertainty and above all from being pushed into a dating scenario. I then got into dialogue with another chap and after our second dialogue we agreed that there was enough overlap between our personalities to get the families involved. I am now married to him. The thing to underscore here is that the 3-Dialogue Rule provides a framework that allows you to grapple with the true marriage potential of anybody you are introduced to without becoming too emotionally preoccupied with that person. It nips dating in the bud and protects the female's integrity." As this testimonial articulates the 3-Dialogue Rule does not allow dating to rear its ugly head. From a Muslim perspective dating is an anathema: the 3-Dialogue Rule is a definitive panacea for the dating affliction that has so penetrated and blighted the heart of the Muslim community. To live in self-denial and not acknowledge the degree to which dating has become fashionable in Muslim professional circles is tantamount to giving dating a free hand or carte blanche to run havoc with the essence of the Muslim value system. The 3-Dialogue Rule as our two case studies above illustrate gets the bull by its horns and not only mitigates the effects of dating but goes one step further – it eliminates dating from any landscape on which a marriage-inspired dialogue respectful of Muslim values is painted. It stares dating in the face and says a firm "No" to it. The 3-Dialogue Rule signifies the demise of dating and jettisons it altogether – lock, stock and barrel - from the arena of marriage-inspired dialogue that a Muslim male and Muslim female should be party to, the precincts of which should always be safeguarded in deference to the dialogue retaining its halal quintessence!

At Kamran A. Beg Events where we have witnessed 100 Muslim marriages so far we exercise zero tolerance when it comes to the tempest of dating. Since our inception on July 11, 2003, we have banned 102 Muslim female and 75 Muslim male professionals at the time of going to press largely on account of their propensity to not take heed of our advice to steer clear of dating. In fact more specifically 60 of these females and 51 of these males have been relieved of their subscription to our organisation on account of dating! For this I make no apologies. From an Islamic perspective dating is off limits and we as a community cannot afford to exercise complacency in this regard. This is explained in meticulous detail to our Muslim attendees, members and subscribers before they sign up for the relevant service. If after signing up any individual accessing our services dates a fellow attendee, member or subscriber and we can demonstrate that beyond reasonable doubt then in subservience to the elegant Muslim value system, which at all times must be preserved and not compromised, that particular Muslim individual and the Muslim party they have dated are respectfully banned from any future association with Kamran A. Beg Events. The writer does not pay lip service to the perdition that dating has caused to the Muslim professional community. We formally relieve individuals who depart significantly from the tenets of palatable Muslim etiquette from any future association with our organisation or membership as our vision is inspired by the need to safeguard the integrity of a halal marriage-inspired dialogue as manifested by the 3-Dialogue Rule in keeping with the values integral to Islam. Dating is a significant violation of what is Islamically tenable and as a large proportion of the 102 females and 75 males banned above have discovered it will not be tolerated by Kamran A. Beg Events nor will we at Kamran A. Beg Events turn a blind eye to it.

281

Having said that though we have up to the present juncture in time accommodated 7,000 vetted attendees, members and subscribers worldwide (see the introduction) and the 177 Muslim professionals banned from any future association with Kamran A. Beg Events represent a very small fraction (2.5%) of the total global membership we have served so far, which overall consists of the most outstanding ambassadors for the community. Those specifically banned for dating amount to 111 in total so far representing 1.6% of the total number of Muslim professionals we have serviced thus far. This sends out a clear and unequivocal message to the rest of our global family: whatever the outcome of a marriage-inspired dialogue that outcome can be fathomed without being afflicted by the ravages of dating. Islam prohibits dating: there are no two ways about that. Islam celebrates balance and moderation in everything that we as Muslims discharge. Dating impels the Muslim male and Muslim female caught up in its throes to the precarious states of imbalance and immoderation and is alien to what is acceptable within a Muslim social perspective. Those Muslim professionals trapped in the dating maze think again: Islam prohibits it and do you know what our research conclusively demonstrates that in the Muslim community there is no correlation between dating and proceeding to the wedding altar! If anything dating throws you way of course and makes securing that all-vital marriage tie to complete half of your faith increasingly elusive. In the Muslim community dating is as far removed from getting married as being ignorant of algebra is to becoming a seasoned mathematician. The 3-Dialogue Rule diminishes the stature of dating to being totally inconsequential: predicated on balance and moderation in keeping with the need to propagate a robust halal marriage-inspired dialogue the 3-Dialogue Rule eliminates dating entirely from the whole fold of male-female marriage-inspired interaction. Crucially, the 3-Dialogue Rule allows the Muslim male and Muslim female to establish whether there is any mileage in progressing their marriage-inspired dialogue to the family level without surrendering to the devastating excesses of dating!

I recall very vividly a telling discussion I had with a Muslim female attendee at the end of a matrimonial event for Muslim professionals that I chaired in London in 2006. At the event I had spent some time explaining the 3-Dialogue Rule and delineating between marriage-inspired dialogue that is halal and dating, which as we all know is un-Islamic. The young lady, a teacher by profession, approached me and courageously confessed: "Until encountering the 3-Dialogue Rule I had not realised that I had actually been dating the man that I met through a friend six months ago. Sadly that got nowhere and we parted company a month ago. By then I had been going out with him for five months. Our families never once spoke. It just wouldn't work – the harder I tried the more we drifted apart. I now realise that I should have informed my parents at the beginning, restricted my interaction with him to the 2-week limit endorsed by the 3-Dialogue Rule before parting company with him and seen him only in the presence of a chaperone. I have so many Muslim friends who are dating, who think that by dating and getting to know the other person they are improving their chances of getting married. Not one of them has reached a stage where the families have got together. Most of them have been going out for three to six months." Well, as we already know the 3-Dialogue Rule gives us a stark warning. If the families of the Muslim male and Muslim female exploring marriage have not engaged at the very latest by the end of the second week after initiating contact with each other either via the telephone or through meeting in person there is a 95% probability that direct interaction between the families with a view to exploring marriage will never occur irrespective of how long the two individuals remain in communication after the 2-week watershed. This translates into a non-marriage scenario (and applies equally to both family and non-family based introductions!). Clearly it does not take much in the way of inference to conclude that based on the observations regarding her friends that the teacher has made that they (her friends) are dating, which is forbidden by Islam, not to mention have palpably violated the 3-Dialogue Rule and are therefore highly likely not to tie the knot with the parties they are talking to.

The female in question subsequently engaged in dialogue with a male attendee from the same event. The dialogue was terminated after they had had their third dialogue as they mutually concluded that the all-vital connection they were looking for was not quite there. In her feedback to me after dialogue closure the teacher said to me in a very memorable telephone conversation: "The 3-Dialogue Rule calls a spade a spade: you know where you stand with the other person by the third dialogue. If you see eye-to-eye that's fine – the families get involved and then you get a better handle on each other's suitability. If not that's fine too – you move on but you move on without hurting each other's feelings and getting emotionally involved. You can then focus more attentively on the next person and give justice to that person rather than living in the past." Living in the past, as this female attendee stated, is a very powerful metaphor for having a relationship and the whole notion of a pre-marital relationship is prohibited in the Islamic faith. Yet as her initial testimony above and indeed as our research discussed in chapter 2 show dating and having a relationship have become almost fashionable in the Muslim professional community and are clearly not confined to a very negligible or insignificant minority of Muslim professionals.

As we reported in chapter 2, research conducted by Kamran A. Beg Events featuring 500 Muslim professional singles drawn from the UK, Ireland, France, Germany, Australia, the USA and Canada and interviewed over the period March 2005 to March 2006 displayed the piercing prevalence of dating within the Muslim professional community. The sample contained as many males as females. We recall that 80% of all Muslim professional males interviewed confirmed that they had dated by age 30 and furthermore 70% acknowledged that they had engaged in some form of physical relationship with a female drawn from the Muslim faith by the same age. Moreover, 65% of the males interviewed indicated that they had dated and/or experienced a physical relationship with females drawn from other faiths. As for the female contingent interviewed the research is equally revealing. 78% of all Muslim professional females interviewed confirmed that they had dated by age 30 and furthermore 68% acknowledged that they had engaged in some form of physical relationship with a male drawn from the Muslim faith by the same age. Moreover, 50% of the females interviewed indicated that they had dated and/or experienced a physical relationship with males drawn from other faiths. We also concluded on the basis of this research that dating and/or experiencing a pre-marital relationship are gender neutral and more or less equally preponderant amongst both Muslim males and Muslim females, certainly in terms of the participants who bravely featured in the research undertaken.

In sum dating in the Muslim professional community is a real issue and cannot be ignored and conveniently brushed under the carpet rug. Nor will the problem simply dissipate if the Muslim community continues to adopt that stance and remains averse to its deleterious consequences. Dating and having a pre-marital relationship can never occupy a legitimate position within the Muslim social value system enjoined upon Muslims by Allah (SWT) through the Quran and manifested by the life of the Prophet (PBUH). Such behaviours as represented by dating and partaking in a pre-marital relationship violate the sacred boundaries of acceptable Muslim male-female social interaction and are frowned upon from an Islamic perspective. Moreover, as our research further demonstrates there is no correlation between dating in the Muslim community and getting married. Dating derails you from marriage! Or put more simply the more you are attracted to the prospect of dating the more you encumber your chances of securing a marriage tie with a fellow Muslim. So why then impair your chances of finding a Muslim life partner by going down the slippery road of dating?

As we recount from chapter 3 the 3-Dialogue Rule makes an express distinction between a 'halal marriage-inspired dialogue' and 'dating': "If, however, the two Muslim individuals are still in communication such that the 2-week time limit has been overstepped and they have not activated direct interaction between the families at the very latest by the end of the second week after initiating contact with each other either via the telephone or through meeting in person the two parties are effectively dating according to the limits imposed by the 3-Dialogue Rule." The case then for the 3-Dialogue Rule is all the more compelling as it clearly defines dating, strongly discourages it and definitively extinguishes any possibility of dating from the horizon of Muslim male-female interaction underpinning a halal marriage-inspired dialogue designed to establish ultimately whether the person you are in dialogue with has the life partner potential to allow you to complete half of your faith and therefore enable you to discharge that prodigious undertaking 'most sacred'.

In April 2006, having returned to the office after chairing yet another momentous and groundbreaking matrimonial event for Muslim professionals, this time in Manchester, that eminent megalopolis where Kamran A. Beg Events is gracefully headquartered, I was greeted by a very revealing e-mail from a young Muslim female doctor based in Toronto. She had just turned 30 and had with untold exuberance and contemplation embarked on that all-exciting fourth decade, still nostalgic though and understandably so about her adventurous 20s. Nothing is more rejuvenating than thinking about the glorious decade that was! The doctor alluded to how a friend of hers who had attended a matrimonial event for Muslim professionals that I had chaired in New York in 2004 had told her about the intrinsic social value of the 3-Dialogue Rule. She admitted in her e-mail that she had explored marriage with three males over the two years prior to embracing the 3-Dialogue Rule and in each case she and the other party had never quite reached the stage where "our families got to talk". She described a "dating urge" as having derailed and consumed her efforts to find a genuine husband as so many of her "Muslim friends are predisposed to dating", "not knowing how otherwise to be certain" that she "had connected with the man" she was "seeing at the time" before getting the families involved. Having familiarised herself with the basics of the 3-Dialogue Rule she had set about transforming the modus operandi that she applied to any future situation where she was introduced to a marriage prospect and had been practising the 3-Dialogue Rule religiously since January 2006. She confessed that initially she found the whole transition to the 3-Dialogue Rule very taxing and a major upheaval in her life as it "represented a whole new way of dissecting the compatibility equation". But she persisted and her persistence had paid off. She noted: "The 3-Dialogue Rule has helped me to kick the dating bug. You can make a measured judgement about how compatible you are with the other person without resorting to seeing them endlessly and aimlessly. The 3-Dialogue Rule really kicks dating in the teeth! It allows you to engage in marriage-led discussion with an introduction without surrendering the most precious asset that any Muslim has: their faith. It helps you to tame your emotions and you do not get sucked into a relationship. You remain true to safeguarding your faith because you know full well that marriage is all about finding half your faith. The 3-Dialogue Rule never lets you forget that."

Having read her very moving testimonial I felt obliged to phone her, which I did the same evening as luckily she had provided a contact number in her e-mail. I congratulated her on her exemplary application of the 3-Dialogue Rule. Our discussion reinforced her very positive experiences stemming from deploying the 3-Dialogue Rule. She concluded the conversation by remarking: "I haven't found the man of my dreams yet. But be sure of one thing. Whoever I'm introduced to now I make it clear to him that we're going to follow the 3-Dialogue Rule. And if they're not comfortable with that - no hard feelings - I don't progress that opportunity. Since becoming a 3-Dialogue Rule exponent I've been introduced to four men and every time I've been able to draw a conclusion – that we're not right for each other - without falling prey to dating and without letting my feelings get the better of me. Who needs dating when you've got the 3-Dialogue Rule?"

A natural corollary therefore of the 3-Dialogue Rule is the demise and extinction of dating. If you are a Muslim reader and are caught up in the 'dating game' think again. Religiously it is forbidden! Our research highlights that there is no correlation between dating and getting married to a fellow Muslim. On the contrary you are making it increasingly difficult to tie the knot with someone drawn from within the Muslim community the longer you remain entrapped by the emaciating lure of dating. Do not allow the tempestuous sea of dating to drown your aspirations of finding a Muslim life partner. The 3-Dialogue Rule provides a plausible robust halal marriage-inspired framework for dialogue that allows you to avoid the deplorable curse of dating. It extinguishes the vile tempest of dating! It allows you to identify the marriage potential of the other person sooner rather than later without compromising the basic tenets of the Islamic faith tradition. It allows you to cut to the chase and make an informed decision predicated not just on the degree of individual compatibility between you and the dialogue prospect but also inspired by an initial feel for the extent to which the family values of the two families might converge. Above all the 3-Dialogue Rule keeps your keen mind trained on the sacred majesty of marriage by providing a constant reminder that marriage is equivalent to realising half of your faith and must therefore never be derided by being treated casually and nonchalantly and must always be assigned the greatest importance and the utmost reverence.

The 3-Dialogue Rule De-emphasises the Undue Importance Attributed to Relocation

Just how important is it for you to find that elusive soulmate and take your nuptial vows? Would you move to the other side of the world to enjoy matrimonial bliss? Or is relocation a thorny issue when it comes to taking that gargantuan leap of faith? Should relocation even enter the fray given the sacred eminence assigned to marriage by Islam? True you may be comfortably ensconced in your profession; true your profession may not allow you the immediate geographical mobility that you would ideally like should you meet that someone special outside your immediate geography. But should your profession or more specifically your professional career aspirations interfere with or curtail your ability to explore marriage with that very compelling, charismatic and mesmerising personality who you had prayed day and night for and who has suddenly surfaced especially if joining that individual at the wedding altar should warrant relocation either in the same country or even to another country, not to mention another continent?

I recall with great fondness when I chaired my very first matrimonial event for Muslim professionals in Manchester on July 11, 2003, a female doctor in attendance at the event, who had just turned 32 at the time, intimated that she was not prepared to consider any marriage prospect outside Manchester. True the splendour of Manchester is irresistibly enchanting and as a city it has no parallel. That said and despite my own objective view that Manchester is the centre of the universe I had proceeded to impress upon the doctor that she needed to broaden her horizons and not write off possibilities further afield. However, she was adamant in her seemingly immoveable stance and her rejoinder as I so clearly recall bore unfailing testimony to her laudable allegiance to this unique and homely megalopolis. Having now turned 34, we meet the same female attendee at a matrimonial event in London. This particular event had occurred on July 3, 2005, almost two years on. I had the honour of chairing it. Immediately the discerning reader would have noted that the doctor's renewed vigour to find her knight in shining armour had caused her to consider pastures anew as she was now frequenting an event in an entirely different city. This anecdote already throws up some very interesting connotations!

In her case the journey to London proved to be a highly productive one. At the event she met a management consultant from New York who at the time had been assigned to a client project in London. They are now married and wait for it... settled in New York! From Manchester to New York was the Divine fate that had always awaited the doctor who only two years earlier had vowed never to abandon the tranquillity of Manchester. However, as time had gently persuaded her, marriage, and not being restricted to a particular geography, is a solemn covenant that allows you to complete half of your faith and as long as you remain wary of that relocation suddenly becomes second nature assuming you have met the right person subject to the right family temperament. If she could boldly transcend continents in her pursuit of matrimonial bliss then surely relocating to a different part of the same country cannot be as intractable as many would initially be led to believe. When I spoke to her recently (March 2006) she commented: "Living in New York is no big deal. Fine I have to take some professional examinations since I will be practising medicine in another country. But that is nothing compared to the worry of not being married. When I came to the London event that was a huge step for me. It was an admission on my part that I needed to be more practical, change my thinking and re-evaluate my approach to finding a life partner. I never thought I would marry someone from the US. But married I am. So many of my Muslim friends have blown away good opportunities for marriage because they have placed their career first. No one is saying pack in your profession. You have every right to pursue your professional ambitions. But you can always find a way forward on the professional front. The same cannot be said for meeting that someone right. And if you are fortunate enough to meet that someone special do not let geography and profession cloud your judgement otherwise you might be in for a very long wait before the next Mr Right turns up and that too if you are lucky. The thing that the 3-Dialogue Rule invokes in your thinking on marriage is that it aligns your mind to viewing marriage through the prism of mastering half of your faith. When you do that you get your priorities right."

Given the prodigious sacred stature Islam attributes to marriage to allow factors then such as professional convenience and geographical inflexibility to impair your desire to complete half of your faith is nothing short of de-prioritising the importance of marriage. Not for a second is the writer suggesting that you should surrender your professional dreams lock, stock and barrel. Those dreams can still be fulfilled as in the case of the female doctor above but by re-positioning them about a tenacious determination to get married and that too to the right person and for the right reason. Getting married may well involve a significant upheaval in terms of relocation or rethinking your career options. But Muslim female readers relocation does not mean an end to your career should you have to relocate to a different city or a new country as a result of marrying someone. Should you wish to pursue your career after getting married that is your fundamental Islamic right and the example of the female doctor above should inspire you – there is always "a way forward"! The question that must always propel a marriage-inspired discourse is whether the person you are exploring marriage with has what it takes to allow you to negotiate half of your faith. Being resolved to getting to the bottom of this question is what propagates the 3-Dialogue Rule and puts everything else into perspective. Being a management consultant or economist or doctor does not correspond with completing half of your faith. Marriage does! And therefore marriage should constitute the epicentre about which you should endeavour to revolve your decision-making. Moving to another city or a different country does not distance you from your family; if anything securing a marriage tie helps you to build bridges between two families irrespective of how near or far you live to your family of origin and in real terms brings you closer to your family. Being married and living in New York has not undermined the female doctor's relationship with her parents and siblings. As she said in an e-mail sent to me in April 2006 shortly after visiting her family in Manchester from her newly adopted home, New York: "Never have I felt so close to my parents. Being married makes me feel even closer to them."

In April 2006 Kamran A. Beg Events sent out a survey to 200 Muslim professional female singles subscribed to Kamran A. Beg Events and based in the UK to get to grips with how flexible attitudes are in relation to the burning question of relocation. All credit to the research sample for generating such a good response rate. 172 surveys were returned accounting for an 86% response rate and the results make interesting reading. In terms of the respondents who did answer the survey 121 females or 70.3% of the total number of respondents acknowledged that the 3-Dialogue Rule had prompted them to rethink the basis on which to progress a marriage-inspired dialogue: thinking of marriage in the context of completing half of their faith had compelled them to prioritise marriage in a different light. 116 females or 67.4% of the respondents said that they were entirely flexible in terms of relocating anywhere in the UK to be with their other half. 26 females or 15.1% of the respondents said that they would be prepared to move to another country if that meant being with the gentleman of their dreams. Similar research conducted by Kamran A. Beg Events in April 2004 featuring 200 different Muslim professional female singles subscribed to Kamran A. Beg Events and based in the UK had cast a different light and showed that only 31% of the respondents were flexible in terms of relocating anywhere in the UK to be with their other half and 11% were not averse to moving to another country to be with their knight in shining armour.

Over the two years separating the two surveys we note quite a significant jump insofar as flexibility is concerned in connection with relocation certainly with regard to relocating to anywhere in the UK. There is clearly an increasing realisation on the part of Muslim professional females based in the UK that exercising flexibility in terms of entertaining marriage prospects from other parts of the UK is likely to help the matrimonial cause even though that would inevitably involve relocation should the outcome be marriage. The proportion of female respondents amenable to relocation to a different part of the UK in aid of finding a suitable life partner has more than comfortably doubled since the time of the first survey. As one of the female participants – an investment banker by profession - in the April 2006 survey summed up: "Before I signed up to Kamran A. Beg Events the thought of moving outside London and away from my family was unthinkable. The 3-Dialogue Rule has caused me to revisit and revise my earlier ideals. True ideally I would like to meet someone based in London but if that doesn't happen it's not the end of the world. If someone special is going to help me to secure half of my faith then I am quite prepared to marry that person anywhere and not just in the UK. The 3-Dialogue Rule has taught me one invaluable lesson. Don't be distracted from the main question running through any marriage-based deliberation: Will the person whom I have been introduced to help me to fathom half of my Deen? If so where you live and any professional discomfit or upheaval you experience become manageable. You can always get another job or find a fix to maintaining your professional ambitions but you can't guarantee that you will meet the right person again. That is too big a risk to take. I don't want to be 40 and unmarried because Birmingham was too far or because my career was too important!"

The "invaluable lesson" that the investment banker above has alluded to is grasping the definitive question, which defines the very pith and marrow of any Muslim marriage-inspired dialogue, a question that is the at the very heart of the 3-Dialogue Rule: *"Will the person with whom I am exploring a marriage-based dialogue allow me to complete half of my faith?"* For it is this definitive question and remaining consistently focused on answering it when exploring marriage with any person that will allow you to see the wood for the trees and order your priorities correctly. Relocation, your professional aspirations, no longer weigh down your ability to rationalise the suitability of a particular marriage prospect because at stake is much more than the possibility of moving to a different city or a new country or rethinking your career options. At stake is your determination to realise half of your faith through the sacred gateway of marriage and that is a vision that the 3-Dialogue Rule never allows you to surrender!

The 3-Dialogue Rule Mitigates the Effects of Urban Tribalism

In May 2005 I had the memorably pleasant privilege of being contacted by a young Muslim female postgraduate student based in New York who at the time was compiling a dissertation centred on reviewing what options are available to the Muslim community in the west for seeking out life partners. I agreed to be interviewed on behalf of Kamran A. Beg Events as part of her gallant research effort. I attended to a number of telephone interviews during the course of which the very dedicated researcher rightly in the spirit of inquisitive scholarship, which should always be encouraged, unleashed a whole gamut of very searching questions germane to her research. We had by now reached the third and final interview and just as this trilogy was nearing conclusion she suddenly regurgitated the following very notable remarks: "On a lighter note I was introduced to a pleasant enough fellow a few months ago but my friends didn't take a liking to him. I didn't think he would fit in and things were brought to a halt." I innocently enquired what was it about this gentleman – clearly a marriage prospect – that her entourage of friends had found objectionable. She proceeded to explain: "We're very close. My friends and I do spend a lot of time together – we go shopping, enjoy going to the theatre, adore visiting museums and art galleries and every other Sunday we have brunch together. We're always there for each other. I just couldn't see him fitting in."

What the researcher referred to in her truly enlightening reply is what Ethan Watters famously describes as an "urban tribe" – for more animated detail on this fascinating subject the reader is encouraged to visit www.urbantribes.net. An urban tribe is basically a group of friends who spend time with each other on a reasonably regular basis, who partake in shared activities together, who consult each other on many key decisions concerning their individual lives and who provide each other with that vital pillar of emotional bankability. Your urban tribe is essentially your family of 'single' friends and together you constitute a coherent social network, which significantly influences your life particularly between completing your studies and getting married. People look to their urban tribe or this family of 'single' friends for, amongst other things, reassurance, emotional comfort, reinforcement, affirmation, clarity and compassion.

We all have a best friend. We all have a circle of friends. But if you are single that circle of friends or urban tribe typically and predominantly comprises of fellow singles, which in sum create this coherent, dynamic and hospitable community that exercises a palpable and tangible impact on your life between university and marriage. It is not unknown for a person who has been introduced to a marriage prospect to consult their best friend to bounce off them exactly what they are really thinking regarding that introduction. The best friend often acts as a sanity check. Sometimes you may broaden your appetite for soul searching and speak to a few friends. You are in pursuit of that affirmation and testing the waters to see whether the person you are submerged in marriage-inspired dialogue with is likely to gain the unequivocal acceptance of your best friend or your urban tribe. In the case of the researcher above we note that the gentleman she had been exploring marriage with was relinquished as a dialogue prospect as the notion of being married to him did not sit comfortably with the ability of her urban tribe to continue with business as usual. In fact further investigation revealed that her best friend did not regard him as a worthy suitor. What the example of the researcher shows is how much importance we assign to our urban tribe when assessing the suitability of a marriage prospect and often we can be swayed by our best friend to the point we decide not to pursue any further a particular prospect for marriage especially in the wake of our best friend or family of friends having declared the person in question to be an "unworthy candidate". Yet our friends as well intentioned as they may appear to be subconsciously become defensive when a member of their circle is in dialogue with a marriage prospect as they seek instinctively to defend and safeguard the membership of their urban tribe. Put simply the thought of losing a member of their urban tribe to marriage can impair their judgement when probed on the suitability or otherwise of someone that you, an existing member of that urban tribe, are exploring marriage with.

But should you be consulting your friends and gauging the suitability of a marriage prospect based on how that individual is perceived by them especially when the ones doing the perceiving are measuring his or her suitability based on a set of ideals that have inspired your social network as fellow singles integral to a coherent community consisting of singles? I have encountered many cases since founding Kamran A. Beg Events where an individual has indicated that they wish to discontinue a marriage-inspired dialogue as they are genuinely anxious that the person with whom they are exploring marriage will not fit in nicely with their urban tribe or that their best friend does not see eye to eye with the potential suitor. As I have expounded to the concerned Muslim professionals when exploring marriage what is being analysed is the extent to which the two individuals party to the marriage-inspired dialogue and their families overlap with a view to arriving on an informed position regarding the pivotal question: *"Will the person with whom I am exploring a marriage-based dialogue allow me to complete half of my faith?"* That is made abundantly clear by the 3-Dialogue Rule. The concern here is not to judge the dialogue prospect against the backdrop of your family of friends and whether he or she may fit in with the rituals that you as an urban tribe have become accustomed to. In any event once married you migrate away from leading the life of a single individual exercising many of their pastimes within the fold of your family of 'single' friends to an individual exercising a shared sense of responsibility construed within the sacred fold of marriage. That is not to say that you would not keep in touch with your friends once married, each of whom would also hopefully get married at some stage, but what you cannot expect is to lead the life of the unmarried individual devoid of your other half that you had experienced prior to securing the marriage tie that you had always yearned for.

Whatever your degree of affiliation to or reliance on your family of friends, however closely-knit this fraternity of 'singles' is, when exploring marriage with someone drawn from outside this circle if you are to give justice to that individual then only one question should show up on your decision-making radar: *"Will the person with whom I am exploring a marriage-based dialogue allow me to complete half of my faith?"* It is the emphatic insistence of the 3-

Dialogue Rule on making this question central to a marriage-inspired dialogue that allows the two Muslim professionals in dialogue not to be derailed from giving each other a fair chance and not to allow their urban tribe to adversely affect in any way their real take on each other's life partner potential! Given the seminal importance of marriage in Islam your view on the suitability of a marriage prospect should not be critically influenced by his or her approval ratings in the eyes of your family of friends – that person is not seeking approval to be co-opted as a member of your urban tribe and to partake in a shared set of activities that you enjoy as a single with your fellow singles. That is not to suggest that you and the person you ultimately marry will not have some shared interests and enjoy these interests together, once married. Note, however, the domain within which you articulate those interests once you are married will shift away from an environment where you had previously exercised them in the main within that coherent community of singles making up your family of friends to one where you will predominantly exercise them in partnership with your other half within the ambit of marriage and frequently also in the company of other couples so that you all form a vibrant family of couples!

The message is clear and could not be any more lucid: if you are engaged in exploring marriage with someone your endearing family of friends should take a step back and be sensitive to the process that this arduous journey inevitably necessitates. Emotional support provided by the urban tribe here should seek to reinforce your unmitigated wish to find a life partner and complete half of your faith. You are not choosing between your family of friends and the person who may ultimately prove to be your spouse. You are seeking to take a leap of faith that will allow you to embrace through the sacred institution of marriage half of your faith. That is a huge undertaking, which should not be inhibited by the need to gain the express approval of your best friend or the urban tribe that you belong to when it comes to deciding on whom you will tie the knot with. Such reinforcement is not necessary. Such pressure is uncalled for! What matters here is arriving on a clear position in terms of how much you and the person you have been introduced to feel that your personalities match, subject to the limits imposed by the 3-Dialogue Rule, and assuming that you both conclude that there is a significant degree of compatibility between your personalities having discharged the formalities of the 3-Dialogue Rule what matters then is to establish the degree to which there is an overlap between your respective family values, all in keeping with the overall aim of answering the pivotal question that should drive any marriage-inspired dialogue between two Muslims: *"Will the person with whom I am exploring a marriage-based dialogue allow me to complete half of my faith?"* It is only through observing an indomitable commitment to answering this question that you can overcome any apprehensions that you may feel from your best friend or your family of friends towards the person that you are engaged in the process of exploring marriage with. By keeping your mind trained on this overarching question the 3-Dialogue Rule inherently allows you to mitigate the effects of any indifference that may be expressed towards the marriage prospect by your best friend or your urban tribe. Otherwise the capacity for such indifference to disengage an individual from exploring marriage with a seemingly good prospect can be very telling. Some of the case studies that I have encountered since founding Kamran A. Beg Events clearly bear testimony to how this type of indifference can seriously disillusion an individual from further exploring marriage with someone when their best friend or family of friends has not given the dialogue prospect the affirmative.

In March 2006 I was contacted by a very seasoned 47 year-old Muslim female physician based in California. She had telephoned our offices to enquire about the various matrimonial services provided by Kamran A. Beg Events. The enquirer has never been married. During the course of our discussion she described an episode in her life, which helps to shed some light on just how far reaching the indifference shown by one's best friend towards someone you are exploring marriage with can prove to be. In 1990, when she had just turned 31, the physician had been introduced to an engineer based in the same state. They appeared to get on very well with each other and she felt "comfortable with his emotional wavelength". As she went on to say: "He was extremely urbane in his manner, very respectful and a very keen listener. I enjoyed conversing with him and he is probably the only man I have been introduced to in whose company I truly felt at ease. He was not in the least bit intimidating."

At the time the physician was part of a closely-knit community of friends. In keeping with the spirit of an urban tribe this family of 'singles' spent much of their spare time together, holidayed together and shared a whole plethora of pastimes, including sailing and hand-gliding, not to mention an inveterate disposition for a whole multitude of other outdoor activities. The engineer that she had been exploring marriage with apparently was not the "outdoor type" though he did confess to being a regular theatregoer and had an insatiable passion for chess. On one Saturday afternoon in July 1990 the physician invited her best friend to a lunch with the engineer. She had privately been hopeful that her best friend, also a member of the medical profession, would give the green light to the engineer she was engrossed in matrimonial dialogue with. During lunch it became apparent how little the engineer's interests converged with those shared by her urban tribe and celebrated by her best friend. As the physician went on to say: "My best friend and I spoke about the candidate a couple of days later. She felt that he was not exciting or dynamic enough for me and would hold me back. She felt his interests were sedentary compared to mine and not disposed to my personality and that pursuing marriage with him would suffocate my lively and colourful personality. She kept reminding me of the outgoing nature of our circle of friends and how that would not sit well with him. It was clear to me that he did not have her approval and by extension that of my other friends. Shortly after that feedback from my best friend I resolved it was better to call the whole thing off and I contacted the engineer and told him that whilst I had enjoyed speaking to him I felt that we were not suited as our interests were very different. After all how could my best friend misadvise me?"

The dialogue had therefore been brought to closure on account of her best friend's insistence whose counsel we incisively note was based on how different his and the physician's interests were and how she felt that he would not be accommodating of the interests that the physician shared with her very dynamic and adventurous urban tribe. The physician went on to confess in that discussion with me: "I now realise that had I not assigned so much importance to my best friend's opinion and gone instead with my own gut instincts things could have worked out with the engineer. I should not have gauged his marriage-worthiness in terms of whether he was acceptable to my best friend and my circle of friends. I have never felt as comfortable with any marriage prospect since meeting him and realise that if I had asked the right question at the right time that today I would be married. There is only one right question and that is what drives the 3-Dialogue Rule, which is whether the person you are exploring marriage with can help you to negotiate half of your faith. If I had asked that question and not looked for reinforcement from my best friend today I would be married. Instead almost sixteen years on I am still searching. I am now 47 and still unmarried!"

As the indelible and poignant experience of the physician illustrates benchmarking a marriage prospect against how they are viewed by your best friend and how they are likely to be perceived by your urban tribe can prove to have devastating consequences. She is still smarting from this chapter in her life. Her episode is not an isolated case. The irony is that while she to the present day remains unmarried her best friend tied the knot in 1995! It is not uncommon for an individual to discontinue dialogue reluctantly with an otherwise sound marriage candidate at the whim of their best friend adjudging that candidate to be unsuitable and that too based on a set of criteria specific to leading the life of a singleton. All too often when an individual is introduced to a marriage prospect there is a natural inclination to consult one's best friend or friends and elicit their advice and to keep them abreast of how things are developing. But what you must not fall prey to is to gauge the viability of the marriage prospect against the life of the single relatively carefree person that you have been acclimatised to within the precincts of your urban tribe. What is being scrutinised here is not the capacity of the person you are exploring marriage with to be initiated into your urban tribe. What is at stake here is your objectivity to assess the suitability of that individual for that covenant most sacred, namely marriage.

That is a life-changing analysis that you can only perform fairly provided when you discharge the 3-Dialogue Rule you remain unfalteringly loyal to fathoming where you stand when addressing the definitive question inspiring a marriage-inspired dialogue between two Muslims: *"Will the person with whom I am exploring a marriage-based dialogue allow me to complete half of my faith?"* Only then can you mitigate the impact of any aberration that could otherwise derail you from being able to see the wood for the trees. *'Best friend or urban tribe indifference'* towards the person you are exploring marriage with is a real risk that you need to legislate for and it is best mitigated by remaining tightly focused on this pivotal question! See chapter 3 for a list of ten questions, which are inspired by attempting to answer this overarching question and which you should factor into your deliberations as they keep you focused on answering this pivotal question. Notably the 3-Dialogue Rule through its constant stress on the need to address the definitive question above helps you to mitigate the very profound effects of urban tribalism!

Eliminating the Adverse Effects of Urban Tribalism: The Exemplary Contributions of Abid Hussain and Dr Waqaar Shah

At the very outset of this chapter we recounted the experiences of two outstanding Muslim couples who were introduced to each other through Kamran A. Beg Events, namely Umer Majid and Aisha Janjua and Dr Ashraful Mirza and Andleeb Anwar. Both couples are stellar exponents of the 3-Dialogue Rule! It is noteworthy at this point to take heed of the laudable role played by two Muslim professionals in particular in encouraging these two couples to progress to marriage and how their seminal role in relation to the dialogue incumbents expedited the healthy progress of those marriage-inspired dialogues without the individuals exploring marriage being exposed to the 'best friend or urban tribe indifference' intimated above.

Umer was actually introduced to Kamran A. Beg Events on account of "reliable" advice received from his good friend, Abid Hussain. Abid, a retail entrepreneur who hails from and resides in Manchester, is a very highly revered member of the Muslim community who has always inspired and guided his friends to excel to the zenith of their potential and to embrace accomplishment with humility. Ashraful was encouraged to pursue his life partner search with Kamran A. Beg Events on the "persuasive" recommendation of his exemplary friend, Dr Waqaar Shah, who lives in London and who like Ashraful is a doctor by profession. Waqaar is venerated for his prodigious altruism and has always served the Muslim Ummah indefatigably well. Abid and Waqaar who are both sterling ambassadors for the Muslim community are each essentially highly intelligent, very articulate and endowed with a very fine sense of humour and have both been blessed with a very formidable knowledge of Islam. They both discharge their faith with the utmost humility and conviction. Furthermore Abid and Waqaar are both in their own right two of the most highly regarded male attendees to have frequented the UK matrimonial events programme for Muslim professionals run by Kamran A. Beg Events. Their presence at the events has always lent very positively to the collaborative esprit de corps harboured by the attendees, which constitutes the very bedrock on which our global family of attendees is premised. Abid and Waqaar are both role models in terms of how friends in your urban tribe or family of friends should behave when you are engrossed in exploring the life-transforming question of marriage with a fellow Muslim.

When Umer and Aisha initiated their connubially inspired dialogue, subject to the 3-Dialogue Rule, Umer constantly reminded me in his regular feedback of how brilliantly sensitive Abid was to catalysing progress. At the very advent of the dialogue Abid had been quick to point out to Umer the special place marriage holds within the Muslim way of life and how important it was for Umer and Aisha to calibrate their compatibility vis-à-vis the one key question that should inspire any two Muslims when contemplating the sacred question of marriage: *"Will the person with whom I am exploring a marriage-based dialogue allow me to complete half of my faith?"* Abid would contact Umer every few days after Umer and Aisha had kick-started their deliberations to encourage Umer in his quest to complete half of his faith and to remind him how blessed he was to be exploring the possibility of marriage with Aisha. As Umer pointed out on the occasion of his marriage: "Abid was always a constant source of encouragement when Aisha and I got into dialogue. He played a crucial role when it mattered most. That is how all friends should discharge themselves when you are examining the question of marriage with someone."

Similarly Ashraful with great felicity celebrates the defining role played by Waqaar. As Ashraful vocalised shortly after his marriage to Andleeb: "When Andleeb and I were engaged in dialogue Waqaar never allowed me to forget the religious significance attributed to marriage insofar as completing half of one's faith is concerned. Whenever he asked about how things were progressing on the dialogue front his voice conveyed a vibrant sense of optimism. I knew Waqaar was rooting for Andleeb and me all the way and that made every difference. Knowing that my great friend was so happy to see me exploring marriage with Andleeb and so hopeful of a productive outcome almost catapulted Andleeb and me to the wedding altar!"

In both the above instructive scenarios we note the impeccably supportive role one of their very close friends played when Umer and Ashraful were respectfully embarked on their momentous journeys to the wedding altar. Both Umer and Ashraful had in that friend that much-need constructive pillar of support and enlightening wisdom that allowed them to see the wood for the trees by keeping their minds focused on the task at hand. Both Abid and Waqaar were quick to insist that Umer and Ashraful formulate a judgement on the basis of whether the marriage prospect (Aisha in Umer's case and Andleeb in Ashraful's case) they were exploring marriage with would allow them to address half of their faith. This is in direct contrast to the rueful experience of the female physician who had adjudged the engineer not to be marriage-worthy on the basis of her best friend's flawed intuition and who now realises that had she asked the key question when it really mattered - the very same question that Abid had encouraged Umer to remain alert to and Waqaar had stressed Ashraful to remain loyal to – she in all likelihood would have agreed to marrying the engineer.

Best friend or urban tribe indifference is eliminated as a potential risk when you are exploring marriage with someone and you have the likes of an Abid Hussain or a Dr Waqaar Shah to count on as a friend. But how many friends can readily show the vision, sensitivity, empathy, maturity and understanding that these two caring personalities exercised when their friend was embarked on the

matrimonial dialogue of a lifetime? Not many as our research highlights! Next time you are introduced to a marriage prospect put the part your best friend is playing into context by remembering the instrumental parts played by Abid and Waqaar in the marriages they helped to expedite and engineer. Perhaps then you will be able to objectively gauge the extent to which 'best friend or urban tribe indifference' is truly interfering with your judgement. In any case our counsel is clear. If you wish to ward off the adverse effects of 'best friend or urban tribe indifference' and not fall victim to it as the female physician sadly did much to her profound and well nigh unfathomable regret then remain true and unswervingly so to the one question that should always form the kernel of your decision-making when analysing a fellow Muslim's marriage potential: *"Will the person with whom I am exploring a marriage-based dialogue allow me to complete half of my faith?"* Total fidelity to this overarching question will always help your matrimonial cause no end!

The 3-Dialogue Rule Allows Individuals to Partake in Marriage-inspired Dialogue with Increasing Ease, Confidence and Comfort

One of the rejuvenating features particular to the beautiful countenance that is so emblematic of the 3-Dialogue Rule is the insatiable appetite that it conspicuously nurtures in the dialogue incumbent for a transparent and uninhibited marriage-inspired dialogue. Many Muslim professionals worldwide who have looked to Kamran A. Beg Events for advice on seeking a life partner have readily confessed in their initial deliberations with our enterprise that engaging in a marriage-led dialogue with another individual is not something that comes naturally to them. In the main it is not unknown for people to feel nervous, apprehensive, shy and defensive going into a dialogue. The prospect of engaging in a matrimonial dialogue with someone can initially prove quite daunting and understandably so.

Having said that though the same professionals have candidly acknowledged that having applied the 3-Dialogue Rule at least once allows them to develop an increasing appetite for negotiating future introductions with greater ease and if anything lends markedly to their confidence in being able to engage more comfortably with future dialogue prospects. What is especially noteworthy and decidedly heartening is how profoundly useful these professionals have found the definitive question at the very core of the 3-Dialogue Rule to be when encamped in the formalities of marriage-inspired dialogue: *"Will the person with whom I am exploring a marriage-based dialogue allow me to complete half of my faith?"* Furthermore these professionals have enthusiastically intimated that the ten questions we recommend in chapter 3 as an integral part of their discussions in deference to tackling the definitive question above allow them to see sooner rather than later, subject to the limits circumscribed by the 3-Dialogue Rule, whether there is enough overlap between them and the marriage prospect to get the families to engage directly thus affording their deliberations a much-needed impetus and sense of direction. These ten questions, inspired by the desire to answer the definitive question at the helm of any marriage-inspired dialogue, as their feedback abundantly suggests go a long, long way towards making them feel increasingly comfortable with the whole terrain of marriage-inspired dialogue. Such questions also give them a licence to raise other themes pertinent to their life partner search less apprehensively, more naturally and with palpably greater conviction enabling them to derive full value from applying the 3-Dialogue Rule as they navigate their way through the challenging topography of marriage-inspired dialogue.

The 3-Dialogue Rule indubitably invokes in the dialogue incumbent an appreciation for the art and science of marriage-inspired dialogue. There is inevitably a learning curve that needs to be mastered and as you progress from one marriage prospect to the next you develop an enhanced knack for addressing less apprehensively the precise themes that should inspire the dialogue with deference to the crucible question driving that dialogue: *"Will the person with whom I am exploring a marriage-based dialogue allow me to complete half of my faith?"* As you move from one dialogue scenario with one person to the next with a new introduction the ease with which you can broach themes germane to assessing the life partner potential of the other person against the backdrop of this overarching question improves tangibly so lending to your confidence to dialogue. Eventually you migrate to a steady state where the ability to engage in such transparent discourse with relatively consummate and ambidextrous ease becomes second nature to you. At that critical juncture in your veritable quest to master the art and science of marriage-inspired dialogue manifested by the 3-Dialogue Rule seminally as a Muslim dialogue incumbent you are comfortably ensconced at the dynamic interface between being able to interact effectively at a social level with a Muslim of the opposite gender and being able to engage effectively in a transparent matrimonial discourse with them. Both thresholds need to be satiated to allow a transparent marriage-inspired dialogue to take shape.

Without effective social interaction the Muslim male and Muslim female cannot reach a point in their discourse where they can have a truly transparent, upfront and unfettered matrimonial dialogue, which after all is the express intention underpinning their introduction. This is one of the reasons why Muslim professionals and Muslims generally find marriage-inspired dialogue such a challenging proposition. At most Muslim gatherings, such as, for example, at weddings and other community celebrations, the genders do not tend to mix and it would be true to say that most Muslims with the exception of their own family members have very limited exposure to Muslims of the opposite gender. When embarking on a marriage-inspired dialogue the first concern therefore for a dialogue incumbent is how to interact effectively in a social context with a Muslim of the opposite gender. Without attending to this concern migrating to a plane that then allows you to have a transparent discussion regarding marriage and exploring each other's life partner potential becomes very onerous, not to mention nerve-racking! The learning curve you experience, however, as an exponent of the 3-Dialogue Rule allows you to simultaneously master your brief to interact socially with a Muslim of the opposite gender on the one hand while at the same time allowing you to engage in an increasingly transparent marriage-inspired dialogue designed to establish each other's soulmate credentials on the basis of the potential of the other person to allow you to complete half of your faith. With the 3-Dialogue Rule you never lose sight of the marriage-inspired cornerstone that brings you into contact with the other party. That is the pillar on which the interaction is premised in the first place but you do have ample opportunity through the 3-Dialogue Rule to hone the social skills needed to allow such dialogue to surface in a less inhibited light.

A 26 year-old female social worker who attended a matrimonial event for Muslim professionals that I had the great pleasure of chairing in London on March 5, 2006, recently gave me some thought-provoking feedback in connection with her experiences. She indicated that until attending the event she had never previously experienced direct exposure to Muslim males in a social setting. Getting to grips then with the whole issue of marriage-inspired dialogue had required quite some effort on her part. As she wrote: "Until attending the matrimonial event in March I had never before visited a social gathering in which I would be expected to interact directly with a set of Muslim men. In my own profession I have not met many Muslims per se let alone Muslim men. Of course I have male colleagues belonging to other faiths and am accustomed to working with them. But the thought of going to an event where I would be amongst Muslim professionals and on top of that be expected to interact with Muslim men caused me a lot of worry. Throughout my childhood and schooling and certainly when I was at university and in my profession I have had very limited exposure to Muslims, with the exception of my family." It would be true to assert that the social worker's comments are actually indicative of many Muslim professionals living in the west. Her thoughts certainly strike a chord with the sentiments echoed by many Muslim professionals who access matrimonial services under the Kamran A. Beg Events umbrella.

The blueprint of social interaction on which the vast majority of Muslims have been raised does not expose them directly to Muslims of the opposite gender until the burning question of marriage inevitably surfaces on the tapestry of life. Any exposure up to that point is essentially family-based. Not having encountered many Muslims through the process of "schooling" or at "university" and in a professional setting, which invariably tends to be the norm in countries in which Muslims form a minority, effectively limits hugely any possibility of acceptable social interaction with Muslims of the opposite gender until the perennial question of marriage suddenly arrives on the scene. Yet no question is harder and more demanding to contend with than one that revolves around your choice of life partner and your desire therefore to cement half of your faith. Unless you are at ease when interacting socially with the person you are introduced to with a view to exploring marriage with your ability to engage in a meaningful marriage-inspired dialogue is considerably hampered. By analogy take your job, for instance: unless you have certain communication skills particular to your profession it is very difficult for you to excel to your true potential. The same applies to a transparent marriage-inspired dialogue: both the Muslim male and Muslim female need to be sufficiently confident in their ability to interact socially with a Muslim of the opposite gender so that they can migrate more immediately to a plane that allows them to tackle directly the themes germane to a marriage-inspired dialogue, such as for example, those manifested by the list of ten questions suggested in chapter 3 in deference to the definitive question central to the dialogue. The 3-Dialogue Rule inherently legislates for this. By constantly reminding the Muslim male and Muslim female in matrimonial dialogue that the religious stature assigned to marriage is such that it represents a completion of half of your faith the 3-Dialogue Rule automatically induces an urgency in them both to feel more at ease when interacting socially with the opposite gender, which in turn inspires both individuals to be more upfront and candid and less inhibited about discussing themes that are directly pertinent to exploring marriage in light of the pivotal sacred stature that it commands. The rate at which these social skills are mastered is speeded up by virtue of the fact that the 3-Dialogue Rule requires the Muslim male and Muslim female exploring the question of marriage to conclude by no later than their third dialogue and that too subject to a maximum time limit of 2 weeks whether they feel there is enough overlap certainly between their respective personalities to engage the families directly. The caps imposed by the 3-Dialogue Rule on the frequency of dialogue, that is the total number of permissible dialogues (three), and the maximum timescale (2 weeks) over which at maximum these three dialogues could occur when coupled with the pivotal question on which a marriage-inspired dialogue between two Muslims should be predicated propel the urgency with which the dialogue incumbents develop the necessary social skills needed to warrant a transparent marriage-inspired dialogue.

Remarking on a dialogue that she engaged in with a fellow male attendee shortly after attending the London event the social worker above intimated: "At the event I had enjoyed conversing with one male attendee in particular, a 34 year-old teacher. I knew the real test would come after the event when we initiated the 3-Dialogue Rule. I was so incredibly nervous. We had our first conversation by telephone and composing myself for that was not easy. We then agreed to meet and I took my sister with me. This is the first time I had met a Muslim man outside of my family socially. That was nerve-racking enough! But this meeting was about discussing marriage and my greatest fear was that not being equipped with the appropriate social toolkit to engage with a Muslim male in such circumstances I might become too inarticulate to say the things I really wanted to. I knew I would need to build up my confidence to get to a point where I could ask the questions that I really wanted to. By retaining in my mind the importance of marriage within Islam and how it allows you to master half of your religious duty I started to interact with the teacher with improved confidence and could feel the difference as the meeting continued. As I became more confident asking the right questions in order to assess how compatible he was with me became easier to ask. The ten questions stressed by Kamran A. Beg Events proved invaluable here putting a huge spring into my step! With the 3-Dialogue Rule you get the best of both worlds: you become more confident in your approach to conversing with a Muslim male and that in turn lends to your drive to be more determined to examine issues relevant to understanding his life partner potential without letting shyness get the better of you. You develop your confidence pretty quickly since you also know there is no time to beat about the bush – after all you only have three dialogues at your disposal spread over two weeks. Even though we brought our discussions to a close after that meeting I now feel more confident socially in terms of how to interact with a Muslim marriage prospect and how to dwell on topics that would allow me to assess his marriage potential without feeling embarrassed. The 3-Dialogue Rule has allowed me to develop in both regards and these are two massive pluses for me."

The social worker's endorsement of the 3-Dialogue Rule is supported by similar testimonials that Kamran A. Beg Events has received from many Muslim professionals worldwide who unanimously bear unfailing testimony to how the 3-Dialogue Rule has allowed them to partake in matrimonial dialogue with increasing ease, confidence and comfort. The deference of the 3-Dialogue Rule to equating marriage with completing half of one's faith instils in Muslim dialogue incumbents a constructive urgency that allows them to quickly hone their ability to interact more confidently with the other gender thereby permitting them to refine with greater tenacity the relevant social skills needed for such social interaction, which in turn feeds seamlessly into fostering an increasingly uninhibited penchant for discussing themes directly material to assessing the other person's life partner potential against the backdrop of the defining consideration: *"Will the person with whom I am exploring a marriage-based dialogue allow me to complete half of my faith?"* As we have noted the ten questions listed in chapter 3 represent such germane themes and provide an added impetus to raise other relevant themes more comfortably. This constructive urgency to groom the relevant social skills needed to interact with a Muslim of the opposite gender is further reinforced by the various limits imposed by the 3-Dialogue Rule: knowing that at most the Muslim male and Muslim female have three dialogues, subject to a 2-week time limit, to ascertain whether there is sufficient compatibility in terms of their personalities to warrant direct family engagement significantly catalyses the rate at which these social skills are developed and sharpened with a view to being able to partake in clinically transparent marriage-inspired dialogue. While the correspondence of marriage with completing half of one's faith instils in the minds of the Muslim male and Muslim female exploring marriage a resolute determination to interact more confidently and less apprehensively with each other the cap imposed by the 3-Dialogue Rule, however, on the frequency of dialogue and the time over which it is circumscribed helps to accelerate further the speed with which fostering this faculty for sound social interaction with a Muslim of the opposite gender is negotiated for that bridge of being at social ease with the dialogue prospect has to be crossed if both individuals are to be able to engage in a transparent, uninhibited and insightful marriage-inspired dialogue.

Muslim professionals worldwide employing the 3-Dialogue Rule have categorically hinted that their appetite for a marriage-inspired dialogue has increased markedly as they have moved from one dialogue prospect to the next and the relative ease with which they have been able to participate in effective marriage-inspired dialogue has improved significantly during that journey. This learning curve fathomed courtesy of invoking the 3-Dialogue Rule allows the Muslim dialogue incumbent in question to engage more readily in transparent, uninhibited and seamless marriage-inspired dialogue as they move from one matrimonial introduction to the next therefore enabling the life partner potential of the person that they are exploring the burning question of marriage with to be gauged sooner rather than later!

In the Final Analysis there is only One Matchmaker and He is The Lord Most High, Allah (SWT)

As you set sail in the ocean of discovery mapped out by the 3-Dialogue Rule being inspired and buoyed by your faith and being reminded of the equivalence of marriage to completing half of your faith constantly temper and enliven your tireless search for your life partner. As Muslims we believe that our choice of life partner is predestined subject to the will of Allah (SWT): "And among His signs is [the sign] that He created for you mates from among yourselves that you may dwell in peace and tranquillity with them and He put love and compassion between your hearts. Surely there are signs in this for those who reflect" (Quran 30:21).

For a more in-depth discussion see chapter 1. Predestination then serves to temper our life partner search. As the Prophet (PBUH) eloquently reminded us we should strive to fulfil a destiny that has already been preordained, subject to His will. Striving then serves to enliven our life partner search. With the choice of life partner already predestined subject to Allah's will in completing half of your faith through embracing the sacred institution of marriage as a Muslim you appreciate that in the final scheme of things you have no choice insofar as that special individual with whom your fate is intertwined in a matrimonial sense since that soulmate had already been preordained by Allah (SWT) as expressly revealed by the Quranic verse above. Should marriage visit you more than once during your mortal lifetime then those soulmates had been predestined in accordance with His will. By making completing your faith central to your life partner search since marriage is tantamount to negotiating half of your faith the 3-Dialogue Rule tempers expectations and allows them to be managed with greater sensitivity and understanding since the Muslim male and Muslim female exploring the question of marriage have already been reminded before embarking on that journey that the outcome of their dialogue had already been pre-determined subject to the will of Allah (SWT). The temporal journey, which has culminated in a conflux of their life partner search trajectories, will cultivate an outcome that had already been exercised subject to His will.

The pivotal question guiding your life partner search is: *"Will the person with whom I am exploring a marriage-based dialogue allow me to complete half of my faith?"* The answer to this life changing and transformative question is already known to Allah (SWT) as He had already preordained the outcome in accordance with His will. Since

319

the outcome had been decreed subject to a Divine will then as a Muslim seeking a life partner you should never surrender to becoming despondent or disheartened during your life partner search since the person with whom you ultimately tie the knot had already been preordained in accordance with His will. It is this appreciation for predestination that allows you to put your temporal journey, that arduous and seemingly never-ending search for your life partner, into perspective. You strive to greet a life partner destiny that had already been predestined subject to a Divine decree. By making the question of completing half of your faith absolutely central to your quest for a life partner the 3-Dialogue Rule sustains your enthusiasm, optimism and resolve to complete your faith and that you can only do once you have discovered your counterpart subject to His will. In sum there is only one matchmaker and He is Allah (SWT)!

A very significant proportion of the 100 Muslim professional couples who have been introduced through the medium of Kamran A. Beg Events so far have already averred through telling feedback that we have elicited from them after getting married their resolute belief in the central role that predestination, subject to a Divine will, has played in guiding them to their life partner choice and how predestination heralded a journey of discovery, which allowed them to navigate a route that ultimately culminated in finding that all-elusive and yet fated and much yearned for soulmate. Earlier in this chapter we mentioned two such wonderful couples arising through Kamran A. Beg Events, namely Umer Majid and Aisha Janjua who reside in Manchester and Dr Ashraful Mirza and Andleeb Anwar who are settled in London. As Umer so insightfully conveyed to me in a memorable telephone discussion shortly after returning from his joyous honeymoon with Aisha: "Aisha was that most important part of my life waiting to be discovered. I am so thankful to The Lord Most High for gifting me with such a sweet, majestic and impeccable wife, Alhamdulillah." Similarly after Ashraful and Andleeb returned from their momentous honeymoon Ashraful kindly contacted me and proceeded to elaborate: "Andleeb and I sailed to the wedding altar so effortlessly. Allah (SWT) made this journey possible. He wanted this matrimonial union to happen and how blessed I am that he has endowed me with the perfect wife."

Both these testimonials show the role that predestination has played in rendering "two marriages made in heaven" to emerge. Both these submissions show how it is only through the will of Allah (SWT) that marriage can materialise. As Muslims we are duty-bound by virtue of our beautiful faith to keep the faith in the verdict of Allah (SWT) and to strive to achieve and accomplish that which He in accordance with His will had preordained for each of us: "And you cannot will unless [it be] that Allah wills, the Lord of Creation" (Quran 81:29). Thus it is that our beloved Prophet (PBUH) clarified: "Strive for each individual will be directed to do that for which he was created" (Muslim). See chapter 1 for more detail.

In our odyssey then to find our other half we must therefore never despair or become demoralised: "Verily in the remembrance of Allah do hearts find rest!" (Quran 13:28). Strive we must as it is only through such engagement that we can work our way towards destiny's outcome and since that outcome had already been willed subject to His omnipotent will then surely we should take heart from the fact that spiritually the answer is already known to the one Being that is all-knowing, Allah (SWT). Temporally we continue to persevere, to engage, to struggle in a bid to discover our other half until we encounter our other half so allowing us to complete half of our faith. A journey that permits us subject to His will to complete our faith is surely a journey worth undertaking, a journey that we must keep alive and kicking and a journey we should sincerely endeavour to complete. The 3-Dialogue Rule reinforces that indomitable conviction for seeking half of our faith. As you are riding a wave of discourse with a Muslim on the back of a marriage-inspired dialogue you are simultaneously exposed to the spiritual undercurrent that has already fated the outcome of that introduction. In embracing Allah's preordained will regarding your choice of spouse for the choice you exercise will be that which He had already preordained the 3-Dialogue Rule rejuvenates your growing resolve to find your other half as you disengage from one introduction and move to the next. The 3-Dialogue Rule insists that you do not despair if a particular introduction does not bear nuptial fruit since predestination had already fated the outcome. The 3-Dialogue Rule stresses that you keep your life partner search vibrant, ongoing and buoyant, that you do not succumb to the malaise of despondency and allow your yearning for marriage to capitulate under the shadow of despair The 3 Dialogue Rule warrants that your longing for that special person grows in the light of hope, a hope that is inspired by your faith, a faith that is driven by your unfailing conviction in the supreme will of Allah (SWT), a will which you know as a God-fearing Muslim had already decreed your choice of spouse, a choice that you wait to encounter during life's remarkable journey, a choice that one day, subject to His will, you will make and so enter that most sacred covenant of marriage with and thereby negotiate half of your faith and therefore totalise your faith and so in the process complete your faith.

Marriage-inspired dialogues propelled by the 3-Dialogue Rule oblige the Muslim male and Muslim female in search of their life partner to embrace the outcome of a particular introduction, whatever the conclusion, wholeheartedly and not dishearteningly in total deference to the decree that had already been exercised by Allah (SWT) and to remain constantly alert and enlivened to sustaining their search until that life partner is discovered, subject to the Divine will. Your zest to complete half of your faith should not be dented on account of having previously explored marriage with someone with whom you felt a connection but who could not reciprocate your sentiments so that you and the individual in question had parted company, much to your reluctance. You should not regard that as "rejection" and so allow your insatiable appetite to find your soulmate to languish on the back of such an outcome. On the contrary such a happening should replenish your appetite for finding your other half. You should take heart from the fact that you were and still are engaged in the soul-searching process of identifying your soulmate.

If as we have seen the will of Allah (SWT) has dictated your choice of life partner can we not see that whatever choices come our way in this world of mortals in relation to potential suitors the choice that we ultimately exercise in terms of marriage had already been spiritually-legislated for courtesy of The Lord Most High. "Rejection" is a word then that notably should not enter into our vernacular. No human being is in a position to reject or accept you in the true sense since it was always God's truth that would determine the outcome of your marriage-inspired deliberations with that person in the first place. No one is in a position to make you feel rejected nor has anyone been empowered by Allah (SWT) to make you feel rejected. Anyone under that illusion is living in delusion and is arrogating to themselves a faculty that belongs only to the Creator. Only He has the right to accept or reject. As His creation we are merely subservient to His will and accept His will we must unconditionally. Whatever the outcome of your interaction with a marriage prospect as a Muslim you should embrace unconditionally the eventuality that Allah (SWT) had willed for He knows best and only He knows best, Alhamdulillah. This unmitigated faith in God's truth should therefore strengthen and deepen your resolve to remain in constant pursuit of that special person – your life partner - knowing intuitively as a God-fearing Muslim that in the spiritual realm that person's unique predisposition to you in the connubial sense was inspired and made possible only by Allah's will. Whatever the degree of individual compatibility between the Muslim male and Muslim female encamped in marriage-inspired dialogue, whatever the degree of overlap between their respective family values, however likely the likelihood of marriage between those two individuals, unless the will of Allah (SWT) had viewed that marriage as tenable there can be no marriage and where there is marriage ultimately it was made possible subject to His supreme will being amenable to and sanctioning that sacred union.

With the 3-Dialogue Rule you know sooner rather than later whether there is enough mileage between you and the other person to engage the families directly. The limits imposed by the 3-Dialogue Rule safeguard your emotional territory. These carefully defined limits ensure that as a God-fearing Muslim seeking their much-yearned for other half you do not fall prey to the lure of dating or partake in a pre-marital relationship and therefore do not victimise and compromise your own sense of faith. If the families engage only then can you calibrate the actual extent of the compatibility that the 3-

Dialogue Rule allowed you to initially detect. But compatibility can only cultivate a marriage tie if the will of Allah (SWT) had sanctioned that marriage to happen, a will that has been scribed as part of His blueprint for you in Al-Lauh al-Mahfooz (the Preserved Tablet or the Book of Decrees), which we discussed at length in chapter 1: "Verily, we have created all things with Qadar [Divine Preordainments of all things before their creation as written in the Book of Decrees – Al-Lauh al-Mahfooz]" (Quran 54:49). Surely if as Muslims we abide by the correspondence of marriage with securing half of our faith this particular verse (Quran 54:49) and the verse (Quran 30:21) we cited earlier should make it abundantly conspicuous that without Allah's will marriage cannot happen and only with His will can it happen. As Allah (SWT) reminds us in His Majesty: "Say: 'Nothing will befall us except what Allah has decreed for us; He is our Protector.' Let the believers, then, put all their trust in Allah" (Quran 9:51). And so it is that Allah's will always reigns supreme, Alhamdulillah!

By making the quest for completing half of your faith central to your life partner search the 3-Dialogue Rule allows you to put all marriage introductions into perspective recognising that as you strive to embrace your matrimonial destiny you are embarked on a voyage of discovery that will ultimately navigate you into the path of the choice preordained by Allah (SWT). On your part as part of His creation and subservient to His will you must nonetheless strive and continue to strive relentlessly and tirelessly with a view to unveiling and greeting that choice at a point in space and time already legislated for in accordance with the Divine will. The 3-Dialogue Rule does not allow you to surrender to the feeling of resignation that can come to pass if you do not make the question of faith central to your life partner search. The 3-

Dialogue Rule allows you to sustain your desire to complete half of your faith without your optimism being enfeebled by the dark forces of despair and without your person being enfolded by the scourge of despondency. As you move from one marriage prospect to the next the 3-Dialogue Rule spurs you on as your longing to complete half of your faith increases and multiplies, a longing that is subservient to a Divine will that had earmarked your life partner choice as preordained in Al-Lauh al-Mahfooz. Your soulful appetite for being with your soulmate increases your seemingly insatiable longing for that soulmate, which in turn lends to your increasing determination to find that soulmate. The 3-Dialogue Rule encourages you to keep a constant foothold in the vast continuum of marriage-inspired dialogue and as you progress from one marriage prospect to the next you do so with the knowledge and faith that predestination willed by Providence will finally allow you to unlock the life partner potential of that one special person who Allah (SWT) had willed you to marry in accordance with His nuptial prescription for you as scribed in Al-Lauh al-Mahfooz. There can only be one certainty and that is the life partner destiny you avail is that which He had willed for you for Allah (SWT) knows best and only He knows best, Alhamdulillah!

And so it is through perseverance and patience, through resolve and determination, through optimism and vigour, through fortitude and commitment, and above all through an unfailing, unmitigated and unshakeable faith in Allah (SWT) you eventually embrace the sacred covenant of marriage, subject to His will, with the life partner He had willed and by completing half of your faith you totalise your faith. Your momentous journey to the wedding altar constantly tests your faith as a Muslim in Allah (SWT). Such an enlightening odyssey could only but reinforce your faith in Allah (SWT).

In the final analysis there is only one matchmaker and He is The Lord Most High, Allah (SWT)!

Bibliography

Maudoodi, Abul A'ala, *Towards Understanding The Qur'an*, Leicester: The Islamic Foundation, 2006.

al-Ashqar, Umar S., *Divine will and predestination in the light of the Qur'an and Sunnah,* Islamic Creed Series: Vol.6, Riyadh: International Islamic Publishing House, 2003.

Maudoodi, Abul A'ala, *The Laws of Marriage and Divorce in Islam*, Third Edition, Safat: Islamic Book Publishers, 2000.

Al-Omar, Nasir, *The Ingredients for a Happy Marriage*, Second Edition, London: Ta-Ha Publishers Ltd., 1999.

Rauf, Feisal Abdul, *What's Right With Islam: A New Vision for Muslims and the West*, New York: HarperCollins Publishers Inc., 2004.